TWO
AGAINST
HITLER

TWO AGAINST HITLER

Stealing the Nazis' Best-Kept Secrets

JOHN V. H. DIPPEL

New York
Westport, Connecticut
London

Library of Congress Cataloging-in-Publication Data

Dippel, John Van Houten, 1946–
    Two against Hitler : stealing the Nazis' best-kept secrets / John
V.H. Dippel.
       p.   cm.
    Includes bibliographical references and index.
    ISBN 0-275-93745-3 (alk. paper)
    1. Woods, Sam, d. 1953. 2. Respondek, Erwin, 1894–1971. 3. World
War, 1939–1945—Secret service—United States. 4. Spies—United
States—Biography. 5. Spies—Germany—Biography. I. Title.
D810.S8W664   1992
940.54′8673—dc20   91-25248

British Library Cataloguing in Publication Data is available.

Library of Congress Catalog Card Number: 91-25248
ISBN: 0-275-93745-3

First published in 1992

Praeger Publishers, One Madison Avenue, New York, NY 10010
An imprint of Greenwood Publishing Group, Inc.

Printed in the United States of America

The paper used in this book complies with the
Permanent Paper Standard issued by the National
Information Standards Organization (Z39.48–1984).

10 9 8 7 6 5 4 3 2 1

To My Mother
And in Memory of My Father

CONTENTS

PREFACE

Some time ago, while reading a book about Allied knowledge of the Holocaust, I happened upon a cryptic reference to the "legendary" Sam Woods and his role in tipping off Washington about Hitler's plan to invade the Soviet Union.[1] Now nothing is more intriguing to a student of history than a legend of which he is ignorant. Sam Woods was certainly news to me. Who was he? How had he managed to find out about one of Nazi Germany's biggest secrets? Intrigued, I got in touch with the author of this particular book, Walter Laqueur. He revealed more fascinating details: Woods, commercial attaché at the prewar U.S. embassy in Berlin, then consul general in Zurich, not only had passed along the first accurate intelligence about Operation Barbarossa but had also learned, from a Berlin contact, about German atomic experiments. Laqueur also gave me the titles of several books that described Woods's espionage activities and suggested that I consult them.

These tantalizingly brief paragraphs offered an overview of Woods's life: a poor boy from backwoods Texas, he had ended his days in a fairytale Bavarian *Schloss*, a millionaire many times over. But these books divulged little about how Woods, a rank amateur in the wartime cloak-and-dagger business, could have pulled off such astonishing intelligence coups. What information there was about Sam Woods, spy, was muddled, exaggerated, or contradictory, making it clear how he had come to be a "legend." (Some sources claimed Woods had a direct, personal link to President Roosevelt. At least one wartime colleague believed he was the real-life model for Commander Victor "Pug" Henry, the main character in Herman Wouk's *Winds of War*.[2])

To get to the bottom of this story, I needed to pursue another course.

Sam Woods himself would be of no help. Before he died, in 1953, he had never bothered to put down on paper the story of his extraordinary career. Nor did any collection of his letters exist. There was a daughter somewhere in the South, but that trail was 30 years old and of dubious value. The only feasible approach was to track down persons who might have known Woods in prewar Berlin or wartime Switzerland and find out what they could remember of him. Books like William Shirer's *Berlin Diary* and William Russell's *Berlin Embassy* yielded the names of many Germany-based diplomats and foreign correspondents, many of whom (Shirer, Howard K. Smith, George Kennan, Richard Helms, and Richard C. Hottelet) had later gone on to distinguished careers.

Unfortunately, their recollections of Sam Woods proved fuzzy. To most he was simply a "good ol' boy" from the South, a man who loved good food and told amusing stories at Berlin dinner parties, and who otherwise sat at his embassy desk compiling humdrum statistics on German crop production. Woods a spy? "As they say in Missouri, you'll have to show me," wrote back one old Associated Press and Central Intelligence Agency (CIA) hand. "The last person you'd suspect of anything like that," replied another correspondent who had been interned in Germany with Woods. George Kennan, the number-two man at the U.S. embassy before Pearl Harbor, knew nothing about Woods's spying. A few members of the American community in Nazi Berlin did recall rumors about some clandestine activities, but these were vague and half-forgotten.

My first real breakthrough came when an archivist at the Library of Congress, in answering a query of mine, unearthed a 24-page report, written by Woods after the war, among the papers of Roosevelt's secretary of state, Cordell Hull. Here Woods traced his dealings with a German professor of economics and financial consultant, whom he called by his codename "Ralph." He described how "Ralph" had obtained—from sources in the German general staff, industrial circles, the Nazi Party's "old guard," and scientists at the internationally renowned Kaiser Wilhelm Society—a vast array of military, political, and economic secrets. Several accompanying letters even revealed "Ralph" 's real name—Dr. Erwin Respondek. But who Respondek was—what had motivated him, and how he had managed to pilfer Hitler's most closely guarded secrets and pass them along to a U.S. diplomat right under the noses of the Gestapo—this remained a mystery.

If Sam Woods was a colorful if enigmatic figure, Erwin Respondek was a nearly vanished one. No book on the German resistance devoted a single line to him or his "small Catholic organization." All I could discover was that he had advised leading German firms, belonged to the Catholic Center Party, served briefly in the Reichstag, and lived in Berlin.

As to what had happened to him after the war, I had no idea. Respondek had covered his tracks well, all too well.

It was not much to go on. For want of a better alternative, I checked the current West Berlin telephone directory. There was an Erwin Respondek! Alas, in response to my hastily dashed-off letter, he declared himself to be an unrelated namesake. However, this Berliner directed me elsewhere, and finally, after a long string of letters, I heard from one of Respondek's surviving children. She turned out to have been born out of a second marriage of his, eleven years after the war ended, and was very surprised to hear about all the remarkable deeds her father was supposed to have accomplished. She did know about a half-sister living outside Baltimore.

Not long afterward I visited Valeska (Respondek) Hoffmann at her home. The oldest of Respondek's four children, she vividly remembered the comings and goings of prominent Berlin personalities at her parents' dinner parties nearly half a century ago. She also remembered Sam Woods and another U.S. diplomat who had already been quite helpful to me—Jacob Beam, a third secretary in the prewar embassy, subsequently U.S. ambassador to Warsaw and Moscow. It was he who had apparently introduced Woods to Respondek and thus initiated their partnership in espionage. Mrs. Hoffmann was able to tell me a great deal about her father and mother and about close friends of theirs who had gotten mixed up in their dangerous cat-and-mouse game with the Gestapo.

Meanwhile, other pieces of the Woods–Respondek story were slowly falling into place, thanks to the labors of archivists sifting through files in East and West Germany, Switzerland, France, Sweden, England, and the United States. (I was also helped by newspaper notices: one I placed in the Berlin *Tagesspiegel* miraculously caught the eye of the former secretary of a State Department official who had known Respondek after the war and who still had a sizable cache of his letters.) In a small town in southern Vermont I found some wrinkled reports and letters of Respondek's, buried among the papers of Heinrich Brüning—Germany's last democratically-minded chancellor before the Nazi deluge and a mentor of "Ralph" 's. In Berlin I was fortunate to meet with two extraordinary women in their eighties, Agnes Dreimann and Herta Chojnacki, who had known the Respondek family and their good friend Hermann Muckermann since the 1920s. And, after a year and a half of persistent searching and coaxing, I succeeded in convincing Woods's elusive and hesitant Czech widow, Milada, to meet with me in a Westchester restaurant and describe details about events in her husband's life and career that no one else could have known.

With his top-level ties to German industry, the Wehrmacht High Command, the Catholic Church, and scientific circles in Berlin, Respondek was unquestionably the most widely connected and one of the most important informants the United States had during the Second World War. As Secretary of State Hull acknowledged, his information on Barbarossa was one of the most valuable reports received by his office in the early years of the war.[3] Yet the history books were silent about Erwin Respondek. Why?

Obviously this was a tribute to his skill at subterfuge. Operating at the very heart of Hitler's Third Reich, under the ever-watchful eyes of the secret police, Respondek escaped detection and death by virtue of his wits. Inside Nazi Germany he shunned contact with other resistance circles—circles mercilessly annihilated after the failed attempt on Hitler's life on July 20, 1944. In Washington, Respondek's name was known to only a half dozen State Department officials, and only one of these, Cordell Hull, ever wrote about "Ralph"'s contribution to the Allied war effort. And even here, in Hull's memoirs, Respondek was not credited by name, for obvious, compelling reasons. As a German who had actively worked for the defeat of a Nazi regime he detested, Respondek was also liable to the postwar charge of *Hochverrat*—high treason.

Technically, this had some validity: Respondek had betrayed wartime secrets to an enemy power. While many persons outside Germany, as well as other anti-Nazi Germans, might regard his actions as expressing a higher form of patriotism, Respondek had good reason to fear that most of his countrymen would condemn him as a traitor. As Willy Brandt and others of his generation were to discover, resistance fighters and Allied "informants" would not be hailed as German heroes. (Throughout this book Respondek will be referred to occasionally as a "spy" and his work as "espionage." Although these words cannot escape moral reverberations, they are intended as neutral descriptions of Respondek's role: knowingly and willfully to gather information surreptiously for the purpose of conveying it to a hostile power. In this sense there are neither "good" spies nor "bad" spies, only successful and unsuccessful ones. By using these terms I mean to skirt the inevitable debate about the "rightness" of Respondek's deeds: one man's "patriot" is another's "traitor.")

Even though Respondek was loathe to disclose what he had done (destroying all his remaining papers and admonishing those who knew of his espionage not to write about it), he also suffered from this long neglect and complained about it bitterly. When Erwin Respondek died, in 1971, he was a broken and sorely disappointed man. He deserved better. As Sam Woods put it in his report to Hull:

Today, when I look back on the dark days of the summer of 1941, I am deeply grateful to Ralph, who stood bravely on our side in the mortal struggle we fought, risking all for our cause.... [I]t is a bitter humiliation to me ... that his services to our country have never been recognized or even acknowledged.[4]

It is largely to repay that debt that this book has been written.

History is not so much a record of the past as a record of the records of the past—an interpretation of what was once known and written down and passed on. A story such as the Woods–Respondek espionage collaboration thus poses a troubling historical challenge. Documentary evidence is spotty, often unsubstantiated. Key players remain hidden in the shadows, their names and activities largely obliterated. Surviving relatives of Woods's and Respondek's often have little to add. Those few individuals who did know about Respondek's resistance group and his ties to Sam Woods have to rely on fading memories of those now-distant years. Even with the best of intentions, names are forgotten, dates confused, events distorted. And, finally, there are persons who prefer this story not be told—a reminder that even today the exploits of this little-known professor of economics and his convivial American confidant remain highly controversial.

Because of these limitations, the historian must proceed with extreme caution. Missing or unconfirmed facts are lacunae that ought not to be glossed over or filled in with speculative fictions. The temptation to tell a dramatic tale urges this, but it cheats the main characters in this true-life tale. Having struggled so much in the cause of freedom and truth, Erwin Respondek and Sam Woods deserve to have their exploits recounted as accurately as possible.

In these pages I have attempted to do this, presenting the facts that an exhaustive probing has disinterred, along with the questions it has not fully answered. Thus, the remarkable story of the espionage collaboration between a daring German professor and an obscure Texas-born diplomat is here told not finally, but for the first time. With luck, others will pick up the dangling threads and tie them together, and then we will know the whole story.

ACKNOWLEDGMENTS

This book is a mosaic of historical documentation and personal reminiscence, pieced together from literally hundreds of sources. In this brief space I cannot express my gratitude to all the persons who contributed to this enterprise by answering my relentless questions about Sam Woods and Erwin Respondek, digging up old papers and photographs, and pointing me further in the right direction. But without their help this story could not have been told. For special acknowledgment I would like to single out the following individuals: Valeska (Respondek) Hoffmann, for several lengthy interviews detailing her family's life and activities in Berlin; Milada Woods, for conversations and correspondence that filled in many holes in the written record of her husband's career; Jacob D. Beam, for colorful accounts of his association with Woods and Respondek; the late Agnes Dreimann, for clarifying many personal and professional aspects of Respondek's life; the late Thomas B. Stauffer, for generously sharing with me his files on Respondek and for a lively exchange of letters about their postwar friendship; and Henriette Respondek and her mother, Elsbeth (Respondek) Schukat, for their poignant recollections of Respondek's later years.

In addition, these persons are owed a debt of gratitude: H. Grady Miller, Jr., for making available correspondence between Sam and Milada Woods and Senator and Mrs. Joseph T. Robinson; C. Brooks Peters, for invaluable talks about life in prewar Berlin; Mary Bancroft, for her impressions of Woods and Allen Dulles in wartime Switzerland; and Herta Chojnacki, for anecdotes about Hermann Muckermann and Respondek's resistance circle. I would also like to thank Professor Richard Breitman, Professor Charles Burdick, Forrest S. Clark, Alex Dreier,

Ernest G. Fischer, Lt. Gen. Cord Hobe, Ret., Dr. Diether Koch, Cpt. Richard G. Koloian, USAF, Arnold Kramish, Robert A. Long, Professor Rudolf Morsey, Professor William L. Patch, Sr. Irma Rech, OP, Amelie Riddleberger, Leonard L. Slade, Sr., Thomas Powers, and Professor Henry A. Turner, Jr., for their kind assistance.

I gratefully acknowledge permission to make use of the following unpublished materials: correspondence and unpublished memoir of Jacob D. Beam (Jacob D. Beam); papers of Heinrich Brüning (Claire Nix and Harvard University); papers of H. Walter Dällenbach (Marguerite Dällenbach and the Max Planck Gesellschaft); correspondence of Friedrich Dessauer (Kommission für Zeitgeschichte); diary of Ernest G. Fischer (Ernest G. Fischer); papers of George F. Kennan (Princeton University Libraries); correspondence of Mrs. Hardin McClendon (Mrs. Hardin McClendon); files of Friedrich and Hermann Muckermann (Nordrhein-Westfälisches Hauptstaatsarchiv); compensation claim (Elsbeth Schukat), report (Max Planck Gesellschaft), and family papers (Valeska R. Hoffman) of Erwin Respondek; correspondence of Sen. Joseph T. Robinson (H. Grady Miller, Jr.); correspondence of Thomas B. Stauffer (Lucia Stauffer-Savage and Penny Schwyn); correspondence of Karl Stefan (Karl F. Stefan, M.D.); papers of Alvin Steinkopf (Irene Steinkopf); papers of Thomas J. Watson Sr. (International Business Machines); and correspondence of Helene Wessel (Friedrich Ebert Stiftung).

Of the numerous archivists and librarians who labored tirelessly on my behalf while I was researching this book, I would like to pay tribute to the following:

In the United States: the staff of the Niels Bohr Library, Center for History of Physics, New York; Dr. Richard J. Sommers, U.S. Army Military History Institute, Carlisle Barracks, Pa.; Raymond Teichmann and his colleagues at the Franklin D. Roosevelt Library, Hyde Park, N.Y.; Evelyn Ehrlich, Leo Baeck Institute, New York; Kathy Reynolds-Frisch, Hoover Institution on War, Revolution and Peace, Stanford, Calif.; the staff of the Manuscript Division, Library of Congress; Dwight Harris, Department of Archives and History, State of Mississippi; Richard Boylan, George C. Chalou, Marjorie H. Ciarlante, J. Dane Hartgrove, Sally M. Marks, Edward J. Reese, and John E. Taylor of the National Archives in Washington; Janice L. O'Connell, Mass Communications History Center, State Historical Society of Wisconsin; and Terry S., Latour, McCain Library and Archives, University of Southern Mississippi, Hattiesburg.

In Germany: Daniel P. Simon, Berlin Document Center; staff of the Landesverwaltungsamt, Berlin; Marianne Loenartz and her colleagues at the Bundesarchiv in Koblenz; Hermann Weiss, Institut für Zeitgeschichte, in Munich; Fr. Erwin Bücken, SJ, of the North German Province Archives, Cologne; Dr. Ulrich von Hehl, Kommission für Zeitgeschichte, Bonn; Silva Sandow, of the Library and Archives of the Max Planck Gesellschaft, Berlin; and Dr. Georg Meyer and Dr. Gerd Überschar of the Militärisches Forschungsmat, Freiburg.

In Switzerland: Dr. Klaus Urner and Dr. Beat Glaus of the Eidgenössische Technische Hochschule, Zurich.

In the United Kingdom: Angela M. Wootton, Imperial War Museum, London; and W. R. Chorley, researcher at the Public Record Office, Kew, Richmond.

For badly needed encouragement and advice on turning my manuscript into a finished book I would like to thank Thomas C. Wallace. Brian Ross assisted with the formatting and printing of what I had stored on my computer disks. At Praeger I have been fortunate to have Dan Eades as my editor. To my wife, Cecilia, goes a final bow for her unfailing interest and support as this project slowly unfolded over the years.

TWO
AGAINST
HITLER

1

THE MAKING OF A SPY

Two days before Christmas 1971 a frail, white-haired, seventy-seven-year-old man was quietly laid to rest in a wintry West Berlin cemetery, beside the graves of two of his children. Although he had served high-ranking German politicians as far back as the Weimar days, no flowers from the West German government adorned his coffin. Although he had advised industrial giants like Carl Bosch and Carl Friedrich von Siemens, no representatives of the German business community stood respectfully at the graveside. Although he had helped dozens of Jews to flee Hitler's Third Reich and saved the fortunes of many more, no note of his passing was made in Israel or by Jewish organizations elsewhere. Although he had pulled off some of the most daring and important espionage feats for the United States during the Second World War, not a single American newspaper recorded his death and no official from the U.S. government sent condolences.

Indeed, only a few relatives and close friends gathered in the Parkfriedhof on this cold December day to pay their last respects to this man, who had died in his bed of a heart attack a few days before, virtually penniless and intestate. The simple dignity of the Roman Catholic service reflected both the wishes and the circumstances of his family. But it was also an ironic farewell for a man who had struggled stubbornly, heroically, and against great odds to free his country from the Nazis, who had seen his efforts ultimately prevail, but who then, in the hour of his triumph, had faded into obscurity.

In the end, history simply forgot him and marched on. The United States—the country he had helped so much, at such great personal risk—did not know the debt it owed him. In Germany, most of his fellow countrymen did not care to hear of wartime deeds motivated by a "higher patriotism" than loyalty to the Fatherland. Such exploits were better left untold.

Erwin Respondek would have appreciated these rich ironies. A lone wolf for most of his life, with few friends and fewer confidants, he must have realized years before that his life would end like this. He would die as he had lived—at the center of great events, but invisible in them: a maker of history, but not a figure upon its stage. In life his great skill at deftly concealing his tracks would serve him well, but in death it would be his undoing.

Although he lived in Berlin for almost all his life, Respondek was born some 300 miles to the east, in the industrial city of Königshütte, on the fringes of Silesia. This happenstance of geography was important for several reasons. First, it fixed his identity as an outsider who would grow familiar but never wholly comfortable with the personalities and ways of the cosmopolitan German capital. Second, born in a part of Germany wedded historically and by continuing Slavic influence to Roman Catholicism, Respondek would grow up a member of that faith. Third, Silesia was a bastion of German democracy. This tradition, too, would serve as a lodestone for Respondek's actions under the Third Reich.

Respondek was born on October 26, 1894, into a middle-class family of local officials and small businessmen. His ancestors were French Huguenots, seafarers from the port city of Cherbourg who went by the name of de Répond. During the First Silesian War, around 1740, the family responded to Frederick the Great's tolerant attitude toward Protestants by resettling in the recently conquered Silesian cities of Glatz and Neisse.[1] There they eventually converted to Catholicism, and the name was changed in church records to Respondek. Erwin's father, Wilhelm, owned a shop in Königshütte, and his mother, born Valeska Fabisch, was a typical German housewife.[2] There were three other brothers— Georg, Max, and Wilhelm—all of whom went on to careers in business or education.[3] Otherwise, very little is known about the family's circumstances.

As a bright, promising boy of fourteen, Erwin Respondek left Königshütte in 1908 and followed his eldest brother to Berlin to attend gymnasium. In school he developed a fascination and a keen ability with numbers. Later in life, one of his fondest youthful memories would be of accompanying his brother Georg, 18 years his senior, to a lecture given by the great French mathematician Jules Henri Poincaré at the University of Berlin.[4] At that point, in 1911, Erwin had already been a student at the Goetheschule, in the Berlin suburb of Deutsch-Wilmersdorf, for three years.[5] After graduating in 1914, he worked briefly as an apprentice in a Berlin bank and then, seeking to build a career, earned a diploma from the High School of Commerce. Whatever business prospects loomed on the horizon for this intent, highly intelligent, ambitious young man from the Silesian province were abruptly put on hold by the outbreak of war. Along with hundreds of thousands of his contemporaries, Respondek was recruited for service in the Kaiser's army. As a patriotic young German he went gladly.

Assigned to a signal unit in 1915, the twenty-one-year-old Respondek quickly grew to dislike military life. After recovering from pleurisy and pneumonia contracted on the front,[6] he was happily transferred, in 1915, first to Darmstadt and then to the War Ministry in Berlin to apply his knowledge of economics in the war raw materials department, formed the year before by Walther Rathenau.[7] In this post Respondek became deeply involved in the strategic planning and sustaining of modern conflict. War he came to analyze and understand in economic terms. With machines far more important than manpower, a nation of Germany's limited resources could not possibly hope to prevail. War, Respondek realized, was a futile way for Germany to gain its national ends. This was a lesson he would not forget.

While working in the War Ministry, Respondek found time to take graduate courses in economics at the University of Berlin. Toward the end of the war he was given the task of writing a letter of condolence to the family of a slain army comrade. Impressed by his letter, the Neumanns—a prosperous Protestant family in the farming region of Lower Silesia—invited Respondek to visit their home outside Posen and tell them more about their son's experiences in the war.[8] Paying this visit, in 1918, Respondek met and fell in love with the Neumanns' nineteen-year-old daughter, Charlotte, who had served as a nurse during the war.[9] August Neumann, her father, was a landowner who also operated an inn and the local post office in the village of Uchorow.[10] He and his wife Olga did not think too highly of this impetuous Catholic suitor of modest means, but the couple was headstrong, and they had made up their minds to marry. With Polish troops massed along the border, there was unrest in Silesia at that time, and seeking both greater security and a new life, Charlotte vowed to follow Erwin Respondek back to Berlin.

There the young economist was making a name for himself. His analytical skill with figures and finances had gained him, in July 1916, a post in the Ministry of Finance, where he was kept busy with budget and tax legislation. Meanwhile Respondek had earned his doctoral degree at the University of Frankfurt, writing a thesis on France's tax and borrowing policies during the war,[11] and publishing an article based on this research.[12] By 1919 he was teaching economics courses at the University of Berlin. His first-hand knowledge of war-related finances was making Respondek a respected authority on the growing controversy of

German war reparations. Early in 1919 he attracted considerable attention with a pamphlet titled "War Reparations: The Claims of Our Enemies."[13] Here the twenty-five-year-old economist vented his nationalistic feelings by lambasting the French and British for their superficial and naive negotiating positions on war payments, accusing them of trying to break the back of the German economy with excessive, long-term demands.[14] Writing in the wake of Versailles, Respondek was voicing a bitterness felt by Germans of many political stripes, including the ultranationalists who banded together in Munich that same year to found the German Workers Party—forerunner of the Nazi movement.

Talent and hard work brought Respondek a good income in the German capital, and after living for a while in cramped quarters at a Catholic home for itinerants, the couple moved into a more spacious residence in the quiet, countrylike suburb of Lichterfelde, favored by academics, writers, and industrialists.[15] Their first child—Olga Valeska—was born on June 24, 1920, and six months later Charlotte Neumann (recently a convert) and Erwin Respondek were married in a small Catholic service. Within a few years the couple had a three-story, brick and wood-frame house with a large garden built for them, just down the road, at Mariannestrasse 3.[16]

In the years after the war, life for the uprooted young family from Silesia was close to idyllic. Having left the Finance Ministry in March 1921, once the Reichsmark had been stabilized, Respondek was now sequestered in the foreign office, over on the Wilhelmstrasse, occupied with reparations issues, preparing the first League of Nations conference on finances, drafting commercial treaties, and tackling questions of political economy.[17] For his achievements he was given the honorary title of "consul" at the end of 1923—a title he would proudly and ostentatiously use throughout his life. In elite business circles Respondek was highly valued for his intellect and financial expertise. One industrialist, Hermann Bücher, got to know Respondek through collaboration on various government and business matters.[18] When Bücher assumed a top post at the Reichsverband der Deutschen Industrie (National Industrial Association), Respondek served him informally as an assistant.[19] Through his affiliation with this leading business organization, and, specifically, through his ties to Clemens Lammers, a member of the Reichsverband's governing body, Respondek came into contact with such individuals as Carl Duisberg, the inventor of ersatz clothing and food and one of the founders of the IG Farben chemical conglomerate; sparkplug manufacturer Robert Bosch; his nephew (and cofounder of IG Farben) Geheimrat Carl Bosch; Dr. Wilhelm Kalle, owner of a Farben subsidiary in Wiesbaden; and the new board chairman of the Siemens electrical company, Carl Friedrich von Siemens.[20]

In conversations with these liberal-minded Weimar businessmen, Respondek learned of their mounting fears about the collapse of Germany's fragile democracy. During visits to Duisberg's home in Leverkusen and to Carl Bosch's estate in Heidelberg, and in meetings with like-minded industrialists in Berlin, Respondek's own long-held democratic beliefs were confirmed and strengthened.

During the Weimar era German business leaders sought to influence the course of political events not only by contributing to various parties but by holding office themselves. Kalle, a chemical engineer by training, held a seat in the Reichstag, representing the bourgeoise- and industry-backed German People's Party (Deutsche Volkspartei), founded by Gustav Stresemann. Clemens Lammers, who served with Respondek on the German delegation to the 1927 Geneva economic conference of the League of Nations,[21] represented the Catholic Center Party in the German parliament. Urged by Lammers and by his Reichstag colleague Heinrich Brüning,[22] Respondek became more actively involved in this party during the turbulent 1920s, following the example of his father and grandfather before him.[23]

Formed during Bismarck's Kulturkampf to protect the Church against restrictions on its religious freedom, the Center Party was a venerable and formidable body in the fragmented, topsy-turvy world of German party politics. Staunchly anti-Marxist and supported almost entirely by moderate Catholics, the Center Party appealed to voters of all social classes.[24] Although its popularity was greatest in predominantly Catholic areas, it was a strong national political force. In the Reichstag elections held between 1919 and 1932 it won an average of 67 seats, making it second in voter allegiance only to the Social Democrats.

During Weimar's years of revolving-door governments, the Center Party produced a series of chancellors—Konstantin Fehrenbach, Joseph Wirth, Wilhelm Marx, and Heinrich Brüning—and helped stabilize a shaky parliamentary system. In its struggle to preserve the political middle ground, the Center Party naively believed that Weimar Germany's basic political and moral values were inviolable. That a person by the name of Adolf Hitler was bent on destroying this young tradition was a rude reality Center Party supporters were slow to grasp and even slower to oppose.

A pivotal figure in the final act of Weimar democracy would be Heinrich Brüning. First elected to the Reichstag in 1924, and head of its parliamentary faction since 1928, Brüning was an intellectually forceful leader, admired by many for his "upright and impartial character."[25] Yet constitutionally he was incapable of fathoming or thwarting an opponent as ruthless as Hitler. A conservative champion of parliamentary democracy, Brüning would end up presiding over the demise of that system.

Around 1928 Brüning became acquainted with Erwin Respondek. The two men had much in common. Both were Catholics from the province. (Brüning hailed from Münster, in Westfalia.) Both were well educated, clear thinking, and practical minded, with an expertise in financial matters and a strong interest in the subject of German reparations. Both had strong ties to the Center Party. Both were cerebral, somewhat socially ill-at-ease. Even physically the two men were similar—prominent foreheads, narrowly set eyes, and bespectacled, scholarly mien. Not surprisingly, they came to respect each other's opinions and to develop a mutual trust and openness that was unusual for both.[26]

Meanwhile, Respondek was building other important ties. At international conferences on reparations he came to know individuals such as the finance minister (and later chancellor) Hans Luther and the Jewish state secretary in the Finance Ministry, Hans Schäffer. Through his work with the Reichsbank on currency matters, Respondek became acquainted with many of its top officers, including Vice-President Friedrich W. Dreyse. He also came into contact with the dominant figure in German economic affairs—Hjalmar Schacht. (Other personal ties were formed with two persons who would figure prominently in the wartime opposition to Hitler: the Prussian finance minister Johannes Popitz and the industrialist Paul Lejeune-Jung.[27])

Within the Center Party, Respondek was on cordial terms with its chairman, Ludwig Kaas, justice minister Johannes Bell, the Munich attorney Josef Müller, Heinrich Lübke, and Konrad Adenauer.[28] He was also a close friend of the Berlin attorney Joseph Wirmer:[29] both had belonged to the politically engaged Catholic student organization Semnonia.[30]

Respondek's chief link to the Church hierarchy was Professor Hermann Muckermann. The oldest of nine children in a devout Westfalian Catholic family, Muckermann had decided to become a Jesuit upon graduating from gymnasium in 1896. After studying in Germany he attended the College of the Sacred Heart, in Wisconsin, writing a doctoral thesis in 1902 on the "essential difference between the human and animal soul proved from their specific activities." Returning to Europe Muckermann studied theology at a Jesuit college in Holland, but his real intellectual passion was biology and anthropology. Following his ordination in 1909, Muckermann did research on the cell at the University of Loewen, in Belgium, and then began writing scientific articles.[31]

Service as a chaplain on the Russian front briefly interrupted this work, but Muckermann soon returned to his scholarly interests, becoming widely known as a leading "Christian anthropologist." In such works as *Kind und Volk* and *Eugenik und Katholizismus*, he strove to reconcile modern scientific insight with Christian ethics.[32] Muckermann was a worldly priest, a devotee of fine food and wines, a stylish dresser, vain about his appearance. (He was tall, dark haired, and handsome, with piercing black eyes.) Over time his taste for the "good life" and unorthodox scientific views clashed with his priestly duties, and in 1927 Muckermann submitted his resignation from the Jesuit order. This was ostensibly so that he could carry on his studies in the field of eugenics unhampered. (There was, however, a whiff of scandal surrounding Muckermann's departure from the Jesuits. Rumors about an improperly close relationship with his sister, Gertrud, may have led Church officials in Munich to expel him from the order.[33])

At this point in his career the articulate Muckermann had acquired a considerable following among well-to-do and well-educated German Catholics for his views on the family, children, race, and the emerging science of eugenics. In numerous lectures before packed houses in churches and public halls, and in his scholarly articles, the former Jesuit sought to define a middle course between the Nazis' theories of racial superiority and traditional Church positions on evolution, heredity, and genetics.

Urged by the Kaiser Wilhelm Society, which was alarmed by how race issues were being crudely politicized, Muckermann raised a million marks for a new, Berlin-based institute of anthropology, human heredity, and eugenics—the first of its kind in the world.[34] Headed by the noted anthropologist Eugen Fischer, this institute opened its doors in 1927. From the outset it resisted mounting Nazi pressures to espouse any notion of the "master race."[35] After 1933, however, the continuing popularity of Muckermann's lectures made him a focus of Gestapo attention, and in 1936 he was banned from speaking. Until he ran afoul of the regime[36] Muckermann lived comfortably in an opulently furnished villa in the fashionable Schlachtensee section of western Berlin. There, dressed elegantly in tails, he entertained his guests with the finest wines and classical music from his expensive, modern radio.[37]

The Respondeks became friends of Muckermann's through his brother, Friedrich, who was also a Jesuit. The younger Muckermann was a student of contemporary literature and culture and active in Center Party circles as well. He was also particularly interested in Polish affairs, and it was apparently this common concern that brought him and Charlotte Respondek together.[38] Soon his older brother was a regular visitor at the Respondek's newly built home on the Mariannestrasse, arriving evenings in his shiny new Fiat and formal attire to escort the music-loving Charlotte to the opera, accompany Erwin downtown for coffee at the Hotel Adlon, or stay for dinner. When the couple's son, Franz Peter, was born in April 1930, Hermann Muckermann was his godfather.[39]

Muckermann moved easily through the upper echelons of German Catholic society. During his tenure as papal nuncio to Berlin, Eugenio

Pacelli enjoyed Muckermann's company over dinner as well as his intellect.[40] Pius XI was also impressed by the independent-minded, strong-willed priest from Westfalia. After delivering an address on "racial hygiene" in Rome, Muckermann was granted a private audience with the pope and given a rosary for his mother.[41] He had at least one other Rome meeting with Pius XI before the latter's death in 1939.[42] Even after Muckermann left the Jesuit order, he maintained friendships with high Church officials and priests. Under the Nazis these ties would bring him into contact with the opposition to Hitler. They would also be of great service to his close friend Erwin Respondek.

In 1926 Respondek retired from government service and set up his own, more lucrative consulting firm, doing commissioned studies of economic and financial matters for banks, industrial firms, and trade unions.[43] (He also took the post of Privatdozent in economics at the University of Frankfurt and published numerous articles and books in his field.[44]) This made it even more important for him to cultivate friendships with leaders of the financial and business communities. During these years the Respondek home in the quiet suburb of Lichterfelde became the setting for numerous formal dinner parties and Herrenabende. These elaborate soirees were presided over by Charlotte Respondek, who charmed her female guests with her Silesian cooking and her amusing anecdotes. In the adjoining room, her more earnest and intent husband, pipe in hand and planted near the piano, engaged the men in long discussions of business and politics. With drinks flowing freely from an ample wine cellar, these parties often ran to the early hours of the morning.[45]

Important foreigners visited the Respondek home as well. Japanese diplomats, whom Respondek had met during League of Nations conferences, came for dinner, as did a number of Americans. Some were involved in administration of the Dawes Plan governing German reparations.[46] Another occasional American guest was Douglas P. Miller, the stocky, balding assistant commercial attaché at the U.S. embassy.[47] A former Rhodes scholar from the University of Denver, married to a German and fluent in the language, Miller was a well-connected and astute observer of German affairs. He was regarded by William Shirer and other Americans as one of the best-informed members of the embassy staff.[48] Miller was drawn to Respondek by the latter's network of business associates and knowledge of the German economic and financial situation. For Respondek, Miller provided an invaluable entree to his superiors at the embassy, notably Roosevelt's ambassador, William E. Dodd.[49] In the years leading up to the Second World War, this channel to the U.S. embassy would provide Respondek access to the secretary of state and the president of the United States.

A workaholic who made heavy demands on himself and others, Respondek put in long hours for his industrial and banking clients, working out of a centrally located, four-room office on the Pariser Platz,[50] near the Brandenburger Tor and just one door away from the U.S. embassy. He was a methodical, well-organized man, (who even kept files on his children), accomplished at synthesizing and analyzing economic statistics. Demand for his financial consulting grew, and in Weimar's last, turbulent years, Respondek prospered. Tastefully selected Oriental rugs, expensive paintings, antique furniture, and Renaissance sculptures now decorated the outwardly unpretentious house on the Mariannenstrasse. The Respondeks could afford two live-in housekeepers, a tutor for their two small daughters, Valeska and Dorothea, and extended vacations to the Bavarian Allgäu.[51]

But ominous changes were afoot. The German nationalist right was in ascendancy, and rumors popped up in the Berlin press about a possible army coup to restore the Hohenzollerns to the vacated imperial throne.[52] Unbeknownst to the civilian German cabinet, over on the Bendlerstrasse the general staff was busy plotting a massive arms build-up in clear violation of the Versailles Treaty.[53] Word of these military projects reached Respondek and his democratically minded business colleagues, who were worried by this news but failed to grasp its full implications.[54]

A deeply moral person, Respondek was more upset by the Nazis. Enflamed by Joseph Goebbels's speeches, storm troopers were beating up their Communist opponents on the streets of Berlin and declaring, on billboards plastered all over the city, that the days of German democracy were numbered.[55] At the polls the National Socialist German Workers' Party (NSDAP) was rapidly gaining strength. Its 12 seats in the 1928 Reichstag mushroomed to 107 by 1930. Instinctively Respondek detested all that the Nazis represented—their demagoguery, their brutality, their disdain for bourgeois democratic values, their utter ruthlessness. Unlike Carl Bosch, who at first welcomed Adolf Hitler as a "man of peace,"[56] Respondek had no illusions whatsoever about the Nazis' objectives. His indignation aroused, this stern-tempered professor of economics resolved to do all that he could to stop them.

In his hatred for Nazism Respondek stood side by side with Heinrich Brüning. After the collapse of the left-center coalition government in March 1930, the forty-four-year-old Brüning was called upon by Reichspräsident Paul von Hindenburg to become chancellor and put Germany's chaotic, debt-ridden finances in order.[57] Hampered by a stiff personal manner—he was described by one Weimar observer as "half Prussian officer, half Roman cardinal"—the former Center Party leader was forced to rule without a parliamentary majority.[58] Brüning was not particularly sanguine about the prospects for German democracy: "I am assuming a task that is already nine-tenths lost," he declared. Matters quickly went from bad to worse. Deflationary policies designed to stabilize the mark proved disastrous and, coupled with Brüning's decision to dissolve the Reichstag and rule by decree, led to the Nazis' huge success in the elections that September. Abroad, Brüning tried to strike a bargain on reparations with the Allies. In October he announced a plan to sell foreign loans as a way of balancing the budget[59] and restoring integrity to the German economy. Reluctant to have this initiative blow up in his face, Brüning dispatched several Center Party colleagues on a secret mission to Paris the next spring to sound out the French on the chances of obtaining a loan. A prominent figure in this delegation was Erwin Respondek,[60] who was well acquainted with French fiscal experts from earlier economic conferences he had attended. Unfortunately, the mission did not succeed. The French, Respondek reported back to Berlin, were not prepared to pull their old enemy Germany out of the fire.

If Brüning was going to relieve Germany's crippling reparations burden, he also needed to solidify support for his fiscal policies at home. In the Reichstag his own Center Party delegation was woefully ignorant of financial matters, now that Brüning himself had left its ranks. The chancellor and the party chairman, Kaas, realized the Center needed a knowledgeable expert on reparations, budgeting, and price-controlling legislation to fill this void. Early in 1932, Erwin Respondek suggested he meet this need by running for parliament on the Center list.

Well-connected and respected in business circles, Respondek was an excellent choice to provide the party with economic and financial know-how.[61] With Kaas and Brüning's blessing, he sought the party's nomination for a seat in the Oppeln electoral district of his native Silesia.[62] To bankroll his campaign, Respondek turned to his business friends. Herman Bücher, now head of the Allgemeine Elektricitäts-Gesellschaft (AEG), gladly agreed to back his former assistant's campaign, as did Carl Duisberg, Wilhelm Kalle, Carl Bosch of IG Farben, the influential Center Party member and manufacturer Friedrich Dessauer, and the Reichsbank vice-president, Friedrich Dreyse.[63] In July the nomination was secured, and in the general election later that month, after campaigning hard against the Nazis,[64] Respondek was handily elected. At thirty-seven, he was one of the youngest men ever to hold a Center seat in the German parliament.

In the July 1932 elections the Center picked up 74 other seats in the Reichstag, but this was small consolation in light of the Nazis' tremendous gains (with 230 seats the NSDAP was now the strongest parliamentary bloc) and the near collapse of the other moderate parties. Smelling victory, Hitler now demanded the chancellorship, while stepping up his efforts to bully the demoralized and disoriented opposition into submission.[65] By the time Erwin Respondek took his seat, the rickety German parliamentary system was

ded remaining Jews and Jewish-owned companies against Nazi
pression and confiscation.[94] In one of the more bizarre ironies of the
hird Reich, the Nazis bestowed upon Respondek the title of "Bearer
the Knight Cross for Judaism"—for his "brilliant" services to the race
ey were trying to eliminate.[95]

already in its death throes. In the November 1932 balloting the Nazis suffered a setback, but less than three months later Adolf Hitler was named
chancellor. Germany was now in Nazi hands.

These rapidly unfolding events angered and frustrated Respondek.
It was now clear the Center was fighting for its very survival. During
the Reichstag campaign in March 1933, Hitler unleashed a wave of terror
against his old enemies. Center Party speeches were banned, newspapers
suspended, meetings prohibited. Trumped-up charges were brought
against the party's old chancellor, Marx, and several other officials, including Respondek's close associate Clemens Lammers and his ailing
patron, Friedrich Dessauer.[66]

Meanwhile, Hitler moved to weaken the Center's hold over German
Catholics by negotiating a concordat with the Vatican. His strategy
worked. After the concordat was signed in Rome, Catholics began deserting the Center in droves, switching over to the Nazis. All of this was
deeply depressing to Respondek, who toured his Silesian electoral district
in March and found voters dismayed by the "panickiness and lack of
direction" exhibited by the party's leadership.[67]

The situation deteriorated with introduction of the Enabling Act, a
law that would give Hitler free rein to rule by requiring the other political
parties to vote themselves out of existence. Put before the Reichstag on
the day after the March 5th election (in which the Center had held its
ground, and Respondek his seat), the Enabling Act precipitated a crisis
of conscience within the Center Party. After a heated, rancorous debate,
its parliamentary representatives finally agreed to vote in favor. Erwin
Respondek joined with them, hoping to give the Nazis enough rope to
hang themselves. Hitler's "national experiment," he reasoned, would
soon "run itself into the ground," paving the way for a "policy based on
reason."[68] Like so many Germans, Respondek made a grave miscalculation. The Nazi experiment would end disastrously, but it would take
all of Germany down with it.

With passage of the Enabling Act the fate of German democracy was
sealed. On July 5, 1933, broken and adrift, the Center voted to dissolve
itself. As a member of an opposition party, Respondek lost his political
base and was barred from holding any public office, publishing any new
works, or teaching at the university.[69] But unlike Kaas or Friedrich Dessauer, who had to flee abroad, or other Center members (such as the
future president of West Germany Heinrich Lübke) who were imprisoned, Respondek escaped persecution. His relatively insignificant
status[70] shielded him from closer scrutiny by the Gestapo. (Indeed, at
least for a while, Respondek either naively or opportunistically tried to
accommodate himself to Hitler's process of "national renewal." In October he wrote the Nazi interior minister Wilhelm Frick, offering to run

as a "unity" candidate in the upcoming election. Respondek pledged his support for Hitler's goal of restoring Germany's "moral equilibrium" and declared his willingness to serve the new regime "honestly and loyally."[71] His offer, like those of other former opponents of the Nazis, was ignored.[72]) Despite his ties to Brüning and other Center leaders, Respondek was allowed to remain in Berlin throughout the duration of the Third Reich. This was an oversight that would cost the Nazis dearly.

Heinrich Brüning was not so lucky. In 1934 he was living in seclusion at a Catholic hospital, fearful, yet reluctant to flee. Friends and Center Party associates, including Respondek and Hermann Muckermann, urged him to leave Germany, but Brüning hesitated,[73] even after bullets were fired at his windows.[74] Finally a plan was worked out for him to travel secretly south in the late spring to a spot near Füssen, where the Respondeks had rented a cottage, and from there to slip across the border into Austria.[75]

But Brüning did not have that much time left. In May he was warned by an old war comrade that an attempt was going to be made on his life at Muckermann's villa. Convinced of the Nazis' intentions, the former Jesuit decided to take matters into his own hands. At dawn on Palm Sunday, after dining and listening to a recording of Beethoven's Ninth Symphony the night before, Brüning and his host climbed inside Muckermann's Fiat and set out for the Dutch frontier.[76] There, leaving his suitcase, money, and passport behind, the former chancellor of Germany escaped without incident past a lackadaisical border guard into exile.[77]

Before leaving, Brüning had arranged for Respondek to keep him apprised of economic and financial developments inside the Reich. Drawing on statistics and other confidential information garnered from the Reichsbank and the finance and economics ministries, Respondek was in the habit of preparing biannual reports for his industrial clients,[78] and he agreed to share these data with his former mentor. While Brüning was staying in the Dutch town of Heerlen, Respondek personally delivered copies of his reports to him there.[79] These memorandums—which Brüning later praised as having proven "100% correct"[80]—would serve as Respondek's apprenticeship in espionage.

The now largely unemployed Respondek also offered his services to a foreign power. He passed on his economic analyses to the U.S. commercial attaché, Douglas Miller,[81] who incorporated much of this material in his own annual economic reports to Washington.[82]

Respondek was also in contact with the scholarly U.S. ambassador, William E. Dodd, dispatched to Berlin to hold aloft the candle of liberal democracy in the gathering German darkness.[83] On several occasions Respondek discussed the general direction of Hitler's policies with this intensely anti-Nazi, courtly mannered historian and supplied him with important details about the Nazis' intentions.[84] This information con-

firmed the outspoken Dodd's fears about where Germ[...] fears he confided to the president of the United Stat[...]

Once, in 1936, Respondek was nearly exposed. One [...] dums was carelessly left lying around and fell into the ha[...] minister Schacht and Goebbels. (Part of the wide-rangin[...] ysis was even published in a Swiss newspaper.[85]) Goeb[...] pressed with this document that he declared its anonymou[...] to be appointed economics minister to carry out the N[...] plan. Schacht, not so eager to admit any rivals, suspected [...] dum was some kind of American plot, concocted by th[...] negotiators Owen D. Young and Charles G. Dawes. He[...] German government lodge a formal protest with Washingto[...] secretly sent these experts to Germany to ferret out such [...] mation.[86] The two Nazi ministers feverishly sought to track[...] author of this memorandum. In a state of agitation, Miller[...] spondek to a secluded spot outside Berlin and told him what [...] spired. To conceal Respondek's identity, Miller printed up a [...] extra copies of the report and spread them around offices in th[...] The stratagem worked. The document was never traced bac[...] spondek.

While he was conveying his privileged information to the Ame[...] Respondek was also helping his Jewish business clients smuggle [...] and other belongings safely out of Germany as the Nazi noose [...] ened.[87] During the mid-1930s Jews in Berlin and from other Ge[...] cities, knowing that Respondek could handle their affairs, came ca[...] at the house on the Mariannenstrasse bearing briefcases filled with [...] and other valuables.[88] By dint of his business connections abroad [...] spondek was able to arrange for these assets to be transferred safely [...] of Germany. As German Jews faced growing personal danger in the la[...] 1930s, several turned to the Respondeks for help in fleeing the countr[...] An Oriental-rug dealer named Rosenblatt was brought safely to Hol[...] land.[89] A son, daughter-in-law, and grandchild of the Munich antique[...] dealer Otto Bernheimer were also aided in escaping the Third Reich.[90] After Kristallnacht the plight of German Jews dramatically worsened—[...] just as Respondek had foreseen.[91] In spite of growing restrictions on the [...] Jews' activities, and the greater personal dangers involved, he continued [...] to do what he could for his clients. Now they came to his door surrep[...] tiously, cradling their small suitcases to conceal the telltale Star of [...] David.[92] Thanks to Respondek's wife, Charlotte, numerous Jewish doc[...] tors, university professors, antique dealers, and businessmen were given [...] food, money, and a place to live until their time to leave arrived. Her [...] husband found them the necessary exit papers.[93] Many Jews whom Re[...] spondek helped to get out of Germany entrusted their property to him, [...] and from 1936 to 1944 the otherwise unemployed financial expert de[...]

2

THE FLOWERING OF
A CONSPIRACY

At some point the casual anti-Nazi sentiments voiced at dinner parties at Mariannenstrasse 3 coalesced into tightly knit and well-organized resistance activities. The history of this opposition circle is veiled, its deeds well concealed, its membership only partially known. Still, led by Erwin Respondek, this small band of Berliners played an important wartime role in protecting persecuted Germans and supplying the United States with some of Hitler's most carefully hidden secrets. Respondek's circle was predominantly Catholic but motivated more by political than religious convictions. (Respondek attended mass only occasionally, whereas his wife, a convert, practiced her faith more devoutly.) Like Respondek, most of its members were professional men and women, well informed, sophisticated, level-headed, pragmatic. They detested Nazism in their hearts but fought it with their heads. Their involvement in the resistance stemmed from a common conviction that the National Socialists were bent on destroying Germany and somehow had to be stopped before that happened.

A pivotal figure in this group was Hermann Muckermann. Stripped of his duties at the Kaiser Wilhelm Institute in 1937 for upholding views on race and the family that were anathema to the regime,[1] the former Jesuit stayed in touch with Church officials unenamored of Adolf Hitler. He also kept abreast of scientific research at the Kaiser Wilhem Society. Although forced to sell his Zehlendorf villa and move to a modest home in the northern suburb of Frohnau, and periodically interrogated by the Gestapo about alleged ties to the Vatican,[2] Muckermann managed—thanks to friends in the Interior Ministry—to avoid arrest for his resistance activities throughout the war years.

His younger brother Friedrich was a more obvious target. By brazenly assailing the Nazis' "new heathenism"[3] in Catholic journals, he had attracted their wrath and, in 1934, had to flee across the border into Holland, just hours ahead of a Gestapo raid on his home in Münster. He was stripped of his citizenship and, because he persisted in his polemics from abroad, branded Nazi Germany's "Enemy Number One" at one point in 1938.[4] But this did not deter the stubborn Westfalian priest from fighting against the regime, in part by serving as a conduit for his brother to the Vatican.

Another member of Respondek's inner circle was an attorney named Herbert Müller. A native of Berlin, Müller had studied law there and then, in the year of the Nazi takeover, landed a research post at the Institute for Foreign and International Civil Law, in Dahlem. Shortly thereafter he became a legal advisor to the Kaiser Wilhelm Society's administration. Privy to what was going on inside the society's scientific laboratories, Müller would help keep Respondek informed about German atomic research and seek to undermine work leading toward the building of a bomb.

Several Catholic politicians also belonged to Respondek's group. These included Josef Müller, later liaison for the German military opposition in its peace feeler to the British, and the Center Party leader, Ludwig Kaas. Heinrich Lübke and his wife were good friends of the Respondeks, as were the Wirmer brothers, Joseph and Otto, and Heinrich Krone, a Center Party politician and a postwar founder of the Christian Democratic Union. Other Respondek intimates included the manager of the Elizabeth Arden salon on the Kurfürstendamm, Lili von Hartmann; Dr. Johannes Schornstein, a lawyer and government official; a pediatrician named von Schopf; an aspiring young businessman, Franz Curt Fetzer; and a family named Haacke.[5]

Although mainly engaged in gathering information, the small Catholic group in Lichterfelde also came to the aid of German Jews. Muckermann once hid a businessman named Salomon in his Frohnau house. To spirit him out of the country, Muckermann and his housekeeper somehow procured an army private's uniform and drilled the would-be refugee in marching until he was able to pass as one of Hitler's soldiers. Then, with the housekeeper posing as his tearful fiancée, Salomon strode smartly down to the Potsdam station and boarded a train bound for the Netherlands. Later, during the war, other Berlin Jews awaiting deportation to the camps were slipped food, soap, and other necessities.[6] Although Respondek's nameless circle[7] met openly in Lichterfelde, under Gestapo surveillance,[8] to plan these and other anti-Nazi activities, its work was never revealed.

Preoccupied with averting disaster for the desperate Jews who knocked on his door, Respondek could not avert tragedy in his own life. In late

May 1936 the couple's youngest child, Peter, barely six years old, contracted a serious ear infection and grew gravely ill. The Jewish physician summoned to his bedside tried valiantly but could not save him, and Peter died on June 5th.

Throughout these darkening, depressing years Respondek regularly kept in touch with his political mentor, Heinrich Brüning. Now teaching at Harvard, the exiled politician received Respondek's economic reports via a variety of couriers—Douglas Miller, a Brussels-based engineer by the name of Heinemann, Paul Legers, employed by a Berlin electrical firm, and the sister of a U.S. diplomat based in the German capital.[9] Each summer Brüning returned to Europe for vacations in Switzerland, Holland, and England, where he conferred with Churchill and other British leaders. At least once he met with the former mayor of Leipzig, Carl Goerdeler, who was then emerging as the leader of the conservative civilian opposition to Hitler.[10] In the fall of 1938 Brüning traveled to England for what would prove to be his last meeting with Churchill.

This conversation took place on September 11th, just a few weeks before Prime Minister Neville Chamberlain made his fateful flight to Munich. During their tête-à-tête the former chancellor warned the future prime minister of the growing danger of a European war and flatly stated that he saw little prospect of England's winning it, given Germany's clear superiority in armaments and other war materiel.[11] Brüning argued there could be no real chance of peace unless the British first came up with a "constructive" solution to the Sudetenland problem.

Information compiled by Respondek may have buttressed Brüning's warnings to the British leader. Respondek spoke with the exiled chancellor in London around this date, as fear of war held the continent in its grip.[12] It is not known what the two men discussed, but it is unlikely Respondek would have gone to the risk and trouble of traveling to England unless he had important news to bring with him.[13]

What is known is that Respondek's well-placed sources within the Reich ministries were now unwittingly furnishing him with more than sheets of economic statistics. With war approaching, they began telling him about German strategic intentions in the east and Britain and France's lack of resolve to defend a threatened Czechoslovakia.

In 1933 the Germans had established a clandestine office to monitor wireless transmissions in and out of the Reich. Later on, this counter-intelligence unit tapped the telephones of foreign diplomats and correspondents in Berlin.[14] Bearing the innocuous title of Forschungsamt (Research Office), this organization contributed significantly to Germany's prewar diplomatic successes. During the Munich crisis, for example, the Forschungsamt listened in on a telephone conversation between the Czech president Eduard Beneš and his minister in London, Jan Masaryk. From this Hitler learned details of the forthcoming Czech response to his demands.[15] At the same time, an outfit in the Foreign Ministry, working out of a girls' school in Dahlem,[16] was trying to crack the diplomatic codes used by the French, Italians, and British.

On top of this, while Hitler was browbeating Chamberlain and the French premier, Edouard Daladier, to accept his terms on Czechoslovakia, the Germans had in their hands decoded transcripts of top-secret telegrams sent between the French and British capitals. According to what Respondek was able to piece together and pass on to Brüning, Hitler thus knew that neither France nor England was prepared to go to war to save the Czech nation from annexation. The German dictator was free to press ahead with his demands for "peace in our time."[17]

Respondek also gave Brüning details of German plans regarding Poland. In a July 1939 letter he asserted that Hitler was bent on circulating rumors of an imminent German attack in order to "frighten" and "tire out" public opinion in France and England and to divert attention from his hidden timetable: the attack on Poland was not due to commence until August 28th.[18] From his informants Respondek also learned that the Führer had scheduled a speech around this time before a massive Nazi rally at Tannenberg—the site of Hindenburg's historic victory over the Russians. In this address the German leader was going to present himself as a man of peace, eager to settle his differences with Poland without bloodshed so long as Danzig was returned to the Reich. By this ploy Hitler hoped to pressure Chamberlain and Daladier into sacrificing Danzig as the price of staving off war.

Respondek's prediction turned out to be quite accurate. Hitler did schedule a speech at Tannenberg on August 27th[19] but had to cancel it at the last minute because Germany was too close to war. The original German military plan for Operation White called for the first Panzer units to breach the Polish frontier on August 25th.[20] (The order to attack was actually given on that date but then rescinded when Hitler learned Britain was going to ratify a defensive pact with Poland that same evening.[21])

Whatever the source of Respondek's warnings, they came too late to help the Poles. And it is highly unlikely that they ever reached the desks of top Allied officials. For Brüning did not think very highly of Western intelligence services[22] and apparently elected not to share any of Respondek's reports with the U.S. government. Furthermore, there is no evidence of Respondek's ever having personally handed this crucial piece of military intelligence to anyone at the U.S. embassy.

Kristallnacht had brought turmoil to Berlin. In Lichterfelde, Respondek had followed the smashing of windows, looting of Jewish shops, and burning of synagogues with great trepidation. He and his wife were convinced the Nazis would turn on the Catholics once they had finished with the Jews, and that day now appeared close at hand.[23] It had occurred already in its death throes. In the November 1932 balloting the Nazis suffered a setback, but less than three months later Adolf Hitler was named chancellor. Germany was now in Nazi hands.

These rapidly unfolding events angered and frustrated Respondek. It was now clear the Center was fighting for its very survival. During the Reichstag campaign in March 1933, Hitler unleashed a wave of terror against his old enemies. Center Party speeches were banned, newspapers suspended, meetings prohibited. Trumped-up charges were brought against the party's old chancellor, Marx, and several other officials, including Respondek's close associate Clemens Lammers and his ailing patron, Friedrich Dessauer.[66]

Meanwhile, Hitler moved to weaken the Center's hold over German Catholics by negotiating a concordat with the Vatican. His strategy worked. After the concordat was signed in Rome, Catholics began deserting the Center in droves, switching over to the Nazis. All of this was deeply depressing to Respondek, who toured his Silesian electoral district in March and found voters dismayed by the "panickiness and lack of direction" exhibited by the party's leadership.[67]

The situation deteriorated with introduction of the Enabling Act, a law that would give Hitler free rein to rule by requiring the other political parties to vote themselves out of existence. Put before the Reichstag on the day after the March 5th election (in which the Center had held its ground, and Respondek his seat), the Enabling Act precipitated a crisis of conscience within the Center Party. After a heated, rancorous debate, its parliamentary representatives finally agreed to vote in favor. Erwin Respondek joined with them, hoping to give the Nazis enough rope to hang themselves. Hitler's "national experiment," he reasoned, would soon "run itself into the ground," paving the way for a "policy based on reason."[68] Like so many Germans, Respondek made a grave miscalculation. The Nazi experiment would end disastrously, but it would take all of Germany down with it.

With passage of the Enabling Act the fate of German democracy was sealed. On July 5, 1933, broken and adrift, the Center voted to dissolve itself. As a member of an opposition party, Respondek lost his political base and was barred from holding any public office, publishing any new works, or teaching at the university.[69] But unlike Kaas or Friedrich Dessauer, who had to flee abroad, or other Center members (such as the future president of West Germany Heinrich Lübke) who were imprisoned, Respondek escaped persecution. His relatively insignificant status[70] shielded him from closer scrutiny by the Gestapo. (Indeed, at least for a while, Respondek either naively or opportunistically tried to accommodate himself to Hitler's process of "national renewal." In October he wrote the Nazi interior minister Wilhelm Frick, offering to run as a "unity" candidate in the upcoming election. Respondek pledged his support for Hitler's goal of restoring Germany's "moral equilibrium" and declared his willingness to serve the new regime "honestly and loyally."[71] His offer, like those of other former opponents of the Nazis, was ignored.[72]) Despite his ties to Brüning and other Center leaders, Respondek was allowed to remain in Berlin throughout the duration of the Third Reich. This was an oversight that would cost the Nazis dearly.

Heinrich Brüning was not so lucky. In 1934 he was living in seclusion at a Catholic hospital, fearful, yet reluctant to flee. Friends and Center Party associates, including Respondek and Hermann Muckermann, urged him to leave Germany, but Brüning hesitated,[73] even after bullets were fired at his windows.[74] Finally a plan was worked out for him to travel secretly south in the late spring to a spot near Füssen, where the Respondeks had rented a cottage, and from there to slip across the border into Austria.[75]

But Brüning did not have that much time left. In May he was warned by an old war comrade that an attempt was going to be made on his life at Muckermann's villa. Convinced of the Nazis' intentions, the former Jesuit decided to take matters into his own hands. At dawn on Palm Sunday, after dining and listening to a recording of Beethoven's Ninth Symphony the night before, Brüning and his host climbed inside Muckermann's Fiat and set out for the Dutch frontier.[76] There, leaving his suitcase, money, and passport behind, the former chancellor of Germany escaped without incident past a lackadaisical border guard into exile.[77]

Before leaving, Brüning had arranged for Respondek to keep him apprised of economic and financial developments inside the Reich. Drawing on statistics and other confidential information garnered from the Reichsbank and the finance and economics ministries, Respondek was in the habit of preparing biannual reports for his industrial clients,[78] and he agreed to share these data with his former mentor. While Brüning was staying in the Dutch town of Heerlen, Respondek personally delivered copies of his reports to him there.[79] These memorandums—which Brüning later praised as having proven "100% correct"[80]—would serve as Respondek's apprenticeship in espionage.

The now largely unemployed Respondek also offered his services to a foreign power. He passed on his economic analyses to the U.S. commercial attaché, Douglas Miller,[81] who incorporated much of this material in his own annual economic reports to Washington.[82]

Respondek was also in contact with the scholarly U.S. ambassador, William E. Dodd, dispatched to Berlin to hold aloft the candle of liberal democracy in the gathering German darkness.[83] On several occasions Respondek discussed the general direction of Hitler's policies with this intensely anti-Nazi, courtly mannered historian and supplied him with important details about the Nazis' intentions.[84] This information confirmed the outspoken Dodd's fears about where Germany was headed—fears he confided to the president of the United States.

Once, in 1936, Respondek was nearly exposed. One of his memorandums was carelessly left lying around and fell into the hands of economics minister Schacht and Goebbels. (Part of the wide-ranging economic analysis was even published in a Swiss newspaper.[85]) Goebbels was so impressed with this document that he declared its anonymous author ought to be appointed economics minister to carry out the Nazis' four-year plan. Schacht, not so eager to admit any rivals, suspected the memorandum was some kind of American plot, concocted by the reparations negotiators Owen D. Young and Charles G. Dawes. He insisted the German government lodge a formal protest with Washington for having secretly sent these experts to Germany to ferret out such vital information.[86] The two Nazi ministers feverishly sought to track down the author of this memorandum. In a state of agitation, Miller drove Respondek to a secluded spot outside Berlin and told him what had transpired. To conceal Respondek's identity, Miller printed up a hundred extra copies of the report and spread them around offices in the capital. The stratagem worked. The document was never traced back to Respondek.

While he was conveying his privileged information to the Americans, Respondek was also helping his Jewish business clients smuggle money and other belongings safely out of Germany as the Nazi noose tightened.[87] During the mid-1930s Jews in Berlin and from other German cities, knowing that Respondek could handle their affairs, came calling at the house on the Mariannenstrasse bearing briefcases filled with cash and other valuables.[88] By dint of his business connections abroad Respondek was able to arrange for these assets to be transferred safely out of Germany. As German Jews faced growing personal danger in the late 1930s, several turned to the Respondeks for help in fleeing the country. An Oriental-rug dealer named Rosenblatt was brought safely to Holland.[89] A son, daughter-in-law, and grandchild of the Munich antique dealer Otto Bernheimer were also aided in escaping the Third Reich.[90] After Kristallnacht the plight of German Jews dramatically worsened—just as Respondek had foreseen.[91] In spite of growing restrictions on the Jews' activities, and the greater personal dangers involved, he continued to do what he could for his clients. Now they came to his door surreptitiously, cradling their small suitcases to conceal the telltale Star of David.[92] Thanks to Respondek's wife, Charlotte, numerous Jewish doctors, university professors, antique dealers, and businessmen were given food, money, and a place to live until their time to leave arrived. Her husband found them the necessary exit papers.[93] Many Jews whom Respondek helped to get out of Germany entrusted their property to him, and from 1936 to 1944 the otherwise unemployed financial expert defended remaining Jews and Jewish-owned companies against Nazi repression and confiscation.[94] In one of the more bizarre ironies of the Third Reich, the Nazis bestowed upon Respondek the title of "Bearer of the Knight Cross for Judaism"—for his "brilliant" services to the race they were trying to eliminate.[95]

2

THE FLOWERING OF
A CONSPIRACY

At some point the casual anti-Nazi sentiments voiced at dinner parties at Mariannenstrasse 3 coalesced into tightly knit and well-organized resistance activities. The history of this opposition circle is veiled, its deeds well concealed, its membership only partially known. Still, led by Erwin Respondek, this small band of Berliners played an important wartime role in protecting persecuted Germans and supplying the United States with some of Hitler's most carefully hidden secrets. Respondek's circle was predominantly Catholic but motivated more by political than religious convictions. (Respondek attended mass only occasionally, whereas his wife, a convert, practiced her faith more devoutly.) Like Respondek, most of its members were professional men and women, well informed, sophisticated, level-headed, pragmatic. They detested Nazism in their hearts but fought it with their heads. Their involvement in the resistance stemmed from a common conviction that the National Socialists were bent on destroying Germany and somehow had to be stopped before that happened.

A pivotal figure in this group was Hermann Muckermann. Stripped of his duties at the Kaiser Wilhelm Institute in 1937 for upholding views on race and the family that were anathema to the regime,[1] the former Jesuit stayed in touch with Church officials unenamored of Adolf Hitler. He also kept abreast of scientific research at the Kaiser Wilhem Society. Although forced to sell his Zehlendorf villa and move to a modest home in the northern suburb of Frohnau, and periodically interrogated by the Gestapo about alleged ties to the Vatican,[2] Muckermann managed—thanks to friends in the Interior Ministry—to avoid arrest for his resistance activities throughout the war years.

His younger brother Friedrich was a more obvious target. By brazenly assailing the Nazis' "new heathenism"[3] in Catholic journals, he had attracted their wrath and, in 1934, had to flee across the border into Holland, just hours ahead of a Gestapo raid on his home in Münster. He was stripped of his citizenship and, because he persisted in his polemics from abroad, branded Nazi Germany's "Enemy Number One" at one point in 1938.[4] But this did not deter the stubborn Westfalian priest from fighting against the regime, in part by serving as a conduit for his brother to the Vatican.

Another member of Respondek's inner circle was an attorney named Herbert Müller. A native of Berlin, Müller had studied law there and then, in the year of the Nazi takeover, landed a research post at the Institute for Foreign and International Civil Law, in Dahlem. Shortly thereafter he became a legal advisor to the Kaiser Wilhelm Society's administration. Privy to what was going on inside the society's scientific laboratories, Müller would help keep Respondek informed about German atomic research and seek to undermine work leading toward the building of a bomb.

Several Catholic politicians also belonged to Respondek's group. These included Josef Müller, later liaison for the German military opposition in its peace feeler to the British, and the Center Party leader, Ludwig Kaas. Heinrich Lübke and his wife were good friends of the Respondeks, as were the Wirmer brothers, Joseph and Otto, and Heinrich Krone, a Center Party politician and a postwar founder of the Christian Democratic Union. Other Respondek intimates included the manager of the Elizabeth Arden salon on the Kurfürstendamm, Lili von Hartmann; Dr. Johannes Schornstein, a lawyer and government official; a pediatrician named von Schopf; an aspiring young businessman, Franz Curt Fetzer; and a family named Haacke.[5]

Although mainly engaged in gathering information, the small Catholic group in Lichterfelde also came to the aid of German Jews. Muckermann once hid a businessman named Salomon in his Frohnau house. To spirit him out of the country, Muckermann and his housekeeper somehow procured an army private's uniform and drilled the would-be refugee in marching until he was able to pass as one of Hitler's soldiers. Then, with the housekeeper posing as his tearful fiancée, Salomon strode smartly down to the Potsdam station and boarded a train bound for the Netherlands. Later, during the war, other Berlin Jews awaiting deportation to the camps were slipped food, soap, and other necessities.[6] Although Respondek's nameless circle[7] met openly in Lichterfelde, under Gestapo surveillance,[8] to plan these and other anti-Nazi activities, its work was never revealed.

Preoccupied with averting disaster for the desperate Jews who knocked on his door, Respondek could not avert tragedy in his own life. In late

May 1936 the couple's youngest child, Peter, barely six years old, contracted a serious ear infection and grew gravely ill. The Jewish physician summoned to his bedside tried valiantly but could not save him, and Peter died on June 5th.

Throughout these darkening, depressing years Respondek regularly kept in touch with his political mentor, Heinrich Brüning. Now teaching at Harvard, the exiled politician received Respondek's economic reports via a variety of couriers—Douglas Miller, a Brussels-based engineer by the name of Heinemann, Paul Legers, employed by a Berlin electrical firm, and the sister of a U.S. diplomat based in the German capital.[9] Each summer Brüning returned to Europe for vacations in Switzerland, Holland, and England, where he conferred with Churchill and other British leaders. At least once he met with the former mayor of Leipzig, Carl Goerdeler, who was then emerging as the leader of the conservative civilian opposition to Hitler.[10] In the fall of 1938 Brüning traveled to England for what would prove to be his last meeting with Churchill.

This conversation took place on September 11th, just a few weeks before Prime Minister Neville Chamberlain made his fateful flight to Munich. During their tête-à-tête the former chancellor warned the future prime minister of the growing danger of a European war and flatly stated that he saw little prospect of England's winning it, given Germany's clear superiority in armaments and other war materiel.[11] Brüning argued there could be no real chance of peace unless the British first came up with a "constructive" solution to the Sudetenland problem.

Information compiled by Respondek may have buttressed Brüning's warnings to the British leader. Respondek spoke with the exiled chancellor in London around this date, as fear of war held the continent in its grip.[12] It is not known what the two men discussed, but it is unlikely Respondek would have gone to the risk and trouble of traveling to England unless he had important news to bring with him.[13]

What is known is that Respondek's well-placed sources within the Reich ministries were now unwittingly furnishing him with more than sheets of economic statistics. With war approaching, they began telling him about German strategic intentions in the east and Britain and France's lack of resolve to defend a threatened Czechoslovakia.

In 1933 the Germans had established a clandestine office to monitor wireless transmissions in and out of the Reich. Later on, this counterintelligence unit tapped the telephones of foreign diplomats and correspondents in Berlin.[14] Bearing the innocuous title of Forschungsamt (Research Office), this organization contributed significantly to Germany's prewar diplomatic successes. During the Munich crisis, for example, the Forschungsamt listened in on a telephone conversation between the Czech president Eduard Beneš and his minister in London, Jan Masaryk. From this Hitler learned details of the forthcoming Czech response to his demands.[15] At the same time, an outfit in the Foreign Ministry, working out of a girls' school in Dahlem,[16] was trying to crack the diplomatic codes used by the French, Italians, and British.

On top of this, while Hitler was browbeating Chamberlain and the French premier, Edouard Daladier, to accept his terms on Czechoslovakia, the Germans had in their hands decoded transcripts of top-secret telegrams sent between the French and British capitals. According to what Respondek was able to piece together and pass on to Brüning, Hitler thus knew that neither France nor England was prepared to go to war to save the Czech nation from annexation. The German dictator was free to press ahead with his demands for "peace in our time."[17]

Respondek also gave Brüning details of German plans regarding Poland. In a July 1939 letter he asserted that Hitler was bent on circulating rumors of an imminent German attack in order to "frighten" and "tire out" public opinion in France and England and to divert attention from his hidden timetable: the attack on Poland was not due to commence until August 28th.[18] From his informants Respondek also learned that the Führer had scheduled a speech around this time before a massive Nazi rally at Tannenberg—the site of Hindenburg's historic victory over the Russians. In this address the German leader was going to present himself as a man of peace, eager to settle his differences with Poland without bloodshed so long as Danzig was returned to the Reich. By this ploy Hitler hoped to pressure Chamberlain and Daladier into sacrificing Danzig as the price of staving off war.

Respondek's prediction turned out to be quite accurate. Hitler did schedule a speech at Tannenberg on August 27th[19] but had to cancel it at the last minute because Germany was too close to war. The original German military plan for Operation White called for the first Panzer units to breach the Polish frontier on August 25th.[20] (The order to attack was actually given on that date but then rescinded when Hitler learned Britain was going to ratify a defensive pact with Poland that same evening.[21])

Whatever the source of Respondek's warnings, they came too late to help the Poles. And it is highly unlikely that they ever reached the desks of top Allied officials. For Brüning did not think very highly of Western intelligence services[22] and apparently elected not to share any of Respondek's reports with the U.S. government. Furthermore, there is no evidence of Respondek's ever having personally handed this crucial piece of military intelligence to anyone at the U.S. embassy.

Kristallnacht had brought turmoil to Berlin. In Lichterfelde, Respondek had followed the smashing of windows, looting of Jewish shops, and burning of synagogues with great trepidation. He and his wife were convinced the Nazis would turn on the Catholics once they had finished with the Jews, and that day now appeared close at hand.[23] It had occurred to Respondek that the time had come for him to leave the country, before it was too late. One day he broached this idea with friends at the adjacent U.S. embassy. But he was advised to stay where he was: it would not be prudent for Respondek to travel abroad at a time when the situation in Europe was in such flux.

To show his displeasure at the Nazis' anti-Semitic outrages, President Roosevelt ordered home his last prewar ambassador, Hugh Wilson. Washington also recalled the old Berlin hand, Miller, upset by revelations he was mixed up in black-market currency dealings.[24] (Ironically, Miller would later publish a book entitled *You Can't Do Business with Hitler*.) Before he left the German capital early in 1939, Miller made a point of entrusting his prized German contact to a younger colleague on the embassy staff.[25]

This was Jacob D. Beam, a lanky, thirty-year-old bachelor who was then holding the post of third secretary. Son of a Princeton professor, Beam had studied at the same university and then gone on to Cambridge to pursue an interest in languages before entering the Foreign Service as a clerk in Geneva. Toward the end of 1934 he had been assigned to Berlin to be put in charge of monitoring German internal affairs.[26] Later Beam was given the task of looking after Jewish interests. Unattached, a good listener, and adept at picking up information unobtrusively, Beam proceeded to cultivate a number of important anti-Nazi ties. Through a Dutch journalist working for a British newspaper he was introduced to members of the German aristocracy and officer corps.[27] (His later contacts included the son of former chancellor Papen; Werner and Hans Bernd von Haeften, both later executed for their participation in the 1944 attempt on Hitler's life; and Hans Herwarth von Bittenfeld, another wartime conspirator.) The gregarious Beam also became friendly with leaders of the church opposition to Hitler.

By the summer of 1938 Beam was a regular dinner guest at the Respondeks' home in Lichterfelde. To his host he appeared a kindred spirit—a closemouthed intellectual with a dry sense of humor who liked to read the Bible in Greek, Hebrew, and English and who could sit for hours in the green easy chair in the Respondeks' living room, polishing off one cocktail after another without missing a single word.[28]

In mid-September Beam happened to hear some startling news. At one of the Respondeks' men-only evening gatherings he found himself in the company of Hermann Muckermann and a man who was introduced as a colonel in the Luftwaffe and deputy commander of the Richthofen squadron.[29] After Charlotte Respondek had served dinner and excused herself, Respondek curtly announced: "Now let's get down to business and talk about what we came here to discuss."[30] They were there to plan a military conspiracy that involved several high-ranking German officers, including the colonel who was present, and that was centered around the German army's newly appointed chief of staff, General Franz Halder. Respondek had a role in this as well. The group was agreed that if Hitler went to war over the Sudetenland, they would then take swift action: the Führer would be assassinated.

Around midnight an agitated Muckermann pulled Beam aside in the hallway and whispered in his ear, "Let's get out of here fast." In silence the two men then drove back to the center of Berlin, with Beam pondering what to do with this incredible story.

After mulling it over, Beam drafted a memorandum for Ambassador Wilson. Before submitting it, he showed the document to Colonel Truman Smith, the highly respected U.S. military attaché. An imposing figure at six foot four, Smith was the son of a career army officer. As a young man he had set his sights on a career as a historian but after being called up for active duty in the First World War had stayed on in the army, serving in occupation posts in the Rhineland.[31] At that time Smith had befriended numerous young German officers—officers who were now assigned to the general staff. These friendships, coupled with a thorough knowledge of German history, culture, and language, made Smith a formidable intelligence officer.[32]

However, the colonel's reports of an alarming build-up of the Luftwaffe had not sat well with his military superiors in Washington, who concluded he was either a naive dupe of Nazi propaganda or a German sympathizer. Instead of being praised for his information, Smith had been told to "keep his feet on the ground."[33]

Perhaps stung by these rebuffs, more likely too much a soldier of the old school to believe German officers could ever contemplate a coup d'état, Smith laughed off Beam's story.[34]

Although the United States would thus remain ignorant of it, a military conspiracy against Hitler *did* exist. Angered by the Führer's dismissal of General Werner von Fritsch, chief of the Army High Command, on a trumped-up charge of homosexuality, and worried about his dragging Germany into an unwanted war, a small nucleus of officers, led by the former army chief of staff General Ludwig Beck and his successor Halder, was preparing to mount a coup if Hitler should move against Czechoslovakia. Beam's information was right on target.

The identity of Respondek's associates among these anti-Nazi army officers remains unclear. In his earlier government service he had come to know General Georg Thomas, chief of economic military planning and a critic of Hitler's war plans. During the first years of the war Thomas was peripherally involved in the military conspiracy.[35] But after 1945 Respondek attacked him sharply for having organized the Nazis' gigantic military machine, so Thomas is not a likely candidate.[36] The closest Respondek ever came to revealing the names of his confidants among the rebellious officers was when he confided to Secretary of State Hull that he had once been asked by a "general field marshal" to join the plot to assassinate Hitler.[37] The only person of that rank who was committed to a coup in 1938 was Erwin von Witzleben, commander of the Berlin military district. Since he was also a native of Silesia, it is possible that he met Respondek through mutual friends during Witzleben's tour of duty in the German capital.

Vital for Respondek's survival under the Nazis was the looseness of his ties to opposition figures. Strongly opinionated, fiercely independent, and distrustful of the motives of many latter-day enemies of the regime, he shrewdly kept his distance. (As he wrote to Brüning: "Here it is becoming increasingly lonely for those few who stand their ground. Soon there will only be two or three of us left."[38]) To the Kreisau Circle of idealistic-minded Christian socialist professionals, army officers, and academics he had no direct link.[39] Nor was he connected to leaders of the Catholic resistance, such as the labor organizer Bernhard Letterhaus.[40] In Carl Goerdeler's group Respondek had some acquaintances, but he resisted being drawn into their activities.

Instead, Respondek worked quietly, alone, putting together his economic analyses for Heinrich Brüning, picking up information from former colleagues in the finance and economic ministries and in the Reichsbank. As Germany edged closer to war, Respondek hastened to enlarge the scope of his intelligence gathering to encompass military secrets as well—secrets that might hasten Hitler's defeat. To collect these secrets, he would exploit friendships inside the Nazi Party's "old guard" and in the Army High Command. To convey them to Washington, he would use his conduit of the U.S. embassy. There he would link up with an unlikely collaborator. His name was Sam Edison Woods.

3

ENTER THE MAN
FROM MISSISSIPPI

A more improbable partner in espionage is difficult to imagine. But Sam Woods led an improbable life, rising in a few decades from poverty and obscurity to fabulous wealth and influence—a true-life Horatio Alger. Through sheer force of personality, this onetime sawmill worker and country schoolteacher from rural Mississippi forged an enviable career as a diplomat and won the friendship and respect of many powerful figures in Washington. Along the way he scored some of the greatest intelligence coups of the Second World War. He became something of a legend.

Woods was born on May 15, 1892, near the village of Starrville, amid the gently rolling, thickly forested hills of eastern Texas. There, about a hundred miles east of Dallas, in countryside where Cherokees had once fought encroaching white settlers, his peripatetic parents had set-tled briefly, hoping to better their luck and raise a family. Woods's father, Roderick Samuel, a Kentuckian, found work at one of the sawmills then thriving outside Starrville, while his mother, Annie Lee, looked after the children. Sam Edison,[1] second-born and the oldest son, spent his earliest years playing under a relentless Texas sun, beside the banks of the meandering Sabine River. When he was five his family piled its few belongings in a wagon and headed east, to bayou country along the Mississippi.[2] Allegedly related to General George A. Custer,[3] they had been ceded some Louisiana plantation acres as a token of the govern-ment's appreciation for the martyr of Little Big Horn. This land the Woods family tilled until they were required to pay taxes on it, and then they packed up and moved on again, across the broad, majestic Missis-sippi to Natchez. There young Sam and his brother Clarence labored for a while beside their parents in the fields until the family decided to settle down in the town of Purvis, Mississippi, just south of Hattiesburg.

Annie Lee Woods happened to have relatives there, and the sawmills sorely needed men who knew how to cut and handle timber. After returning for a while to Natchez,[4] the Woodses finally stayed put in Purvis, buying a plot of land on the edge of town in May 1906 and building a home on it.[5]

But stability and good fortune would not last for long. Tragedy first struck the family one autumn day in 1907, when fifteen-year-old Sam and the local boy his sister, Julia, had just married, Willie A. Ewell, were out in the woods, hunting for squirrels. In the dense undergrowth, Sam saw something move and fired.[6] The single rifle shot killed Willie Ewell on the spot. For Sam Woods this horrific accident would spell the end of his youth and innocence: he would now shoulder the responsibility of caring for both his seventeen-year-old sister and her soon-to-be-born daughter.[7] The shooting would also fundamentally alter the course of his life. From that day on Woods would bear a scar of guilt that only acts of generosity and kindness, repeated over and over in a kind of desperate penance, could ever hope to obliterate.[8]

A second calamity hit Purvis barely six months later. A killer tornado roared through the prosperous little milling town on the afternoon of April 24, 1908, splintering homes and killing 83 persons, including one of Sam Woods's young cousins. The Woodses' home on Mitchell Avenue was leveled to the ground, and Sam himself was reporting missing. Fearing the worst, his family frantically searched the wrecked buildings, but it was only when his sister, Julia, checked the dead bodies laid out on the ground that he was finally found, unconscious, badly shaken, but all right.[9]

Adversity only stiffened his resolve to better his lot. Young Woods stood out in the local schools, especially for his skill at mathematics, and after graduating from high school in Purvis in 1909, he took a job teaching local sixth-grade pupils not much younger than himself. At the age of seventeen Woods was discovering he had a knack with people— a Southerner's easy, affable charm combined with a genuine liking and concern for others. He also enjoyed working with lumber and his hands—he was as good with a saw as any boy his age—and thought about a career teaching the manual arts. To save money for his education Woods took a job at a local sawmill, which paid him a dollar an hour for an 11-hour day[10] and taught him the meaning of hard work.

In the spring of 1912 Woods enrolled in a manual training program at Valparaiso University, in faraway Indiana. There he excelled in mathematics, woodwork, debate, and mechanical drawing and managed to earn his bachelor's degree within two years.[11] Afterward he went back to Mississippi and taught briefly at the Pearl River Agricultural High

School in Poplarville. He became friendly with a pretty, young home economics teacher from Tennessee named Katie Rose Anderson and proposed to her. The couple was married on August 2, 1917, and settled in Hattiesburg, where Woods was put in charge of setting up a manual arts department at Mississippi Normal College. He had barely taken up these duties when he was summoned off to war. Volunteering for the Marine Aviation Corps, Woods was ordered first down to Miami[12] and then up north to the Massachusetts Institute of Technology for courses in military aeronautics.

Arriving in Cambridge unkempt, unshaven, and in a rumpled uniform with missing buttons, the twenty-five-year-old recruit was ushered into a classroom where he found several men sitting around a table. "What the hell are you doing in here?" they roared at him. Losing his temper, Woods shouted back. The men looked at each other and smiled. Congratulations, they said: he had passed the test. He would make a fine officer.[13]

Shipped across the Atlantic, Woods reached France just as the war was coming to an end. He made the long, anticlimactic journey back home to Mississippi to be met by more tragic news: the devastating influenza epidemic had claimed his wife, Katie Rose, just ten days after she had given birth to a daughter.[14] This shock came on the heels of another: two days before, on September 12, 1918, after having failed once to kill herself with a rifle, Woods's mother had come down to the breakfast table and calmly announced that she had just swallowed poison. Within a few minutes she was dead.[15]

An emotionally devastated Woods entrusted his infant daughter, Katie Rose, to relatives in Nashville and immersed himself in his teaching duties in Hattiesburg, working toward another degree and writing articles on education. He might not ever have left the South again if he had not happened to hear about a civil service position that was being offered in Atlanta. Looking for the government agency, Woods got off the elevator on the wrong floor and strolled into another office that was recruiting teachers for assignments with U.S. occupation forces in Europe. Turning on all his charm, Woods convinced the interviewer he was the right man for the job, and soon he was bidding farewell to his daughter and relatives in Mississippi and boarding another ship bound for France,[16] this time wearing the uniform of an Army Education Corps officer.

After a short stint as head of vocational education work in Germany and France, Woods was reassigned to Czechoslovakia to help the Education Ministry build badly needed playground equipment.[17] Because of a housing shortage in Prague the young Mississippian was given quarters in the spacious home of a well-to-do banker and businessman named

Vondracekova. He soon fell in love with the Vondracekovas' only child, Milada, a petite, somewhat spoiled, and cosmopolitan girl of seventeen. After Woods returned to Mississippi, the couple corresponded for three years, until December 1923, when he came back to Prague to marry her.

Woods brought his Czech bride back to the state capital of Jackson, where he was now overseeing a nationally innovative rehabilitation program for crippled children and adults. Part of his time was spent criss-crossing the state inside a Ford truck,[18] spreading the word about how to eradicate hookworm.[19] Woods also set up a clinic for cripples in Memphis, dabbled in rural development, and rode around the country on a special train, promoting tourism in Mississippi.[20] When his good friend Dennis Murphree, a former lieutenant governor, decided to run for governor in 1929, Woods boosted his campaign war chest by designing a mosquito-net-covered crib on wheels, which he promoted with the slogan "Not A Bug on Baby."[21]

Living in Jackson gave Woods a chance to meet Mississippi's political leaders. But the hot, humid Southern climate did not agree with Milada, and Woods started looking for a job that would take them back to Europe. In July 1929, with some strings being pulled by Senator Pat Harrison, he was appointed assistant U.S. trade commissioner in Prague.[22] This was the start of a sojourn in Czechoslovakia that would last eight years, as Woods moved up the Department of Commerce career ladder, first to assistant commercial attaché, and then commercial attaché at the U.S. embassy. These were halcyon days for the fledgling Czech democracy and, for the Woodses, a peaceful interlude before they were to be catapulted into the Nazi maelstrom. Sam and Milada made friends with well-to-do Czechs and U.S. diplomats, as well as with occasional visitors from the United States.

One of these was Joseph T. Robinson, the Senate majority leader from Arkansas, then spearheading passage of Roosevelt's New Deal legislation. During a 1934 stay in Prague, Robinson and his wife accepted the Woodses' invitation to drive with them to see the Passion Play at Oberammergau.[23] During this extended holiday the two easygoing, down-to-earth Southerners also joined a hunting party hosted by Bernard Baruch at Slovensky Meder in eastern Czechoslovakia. One of the other guests was the U.S. ambassador to Italy, Breckenridge Long.[24] Descended from two distinguished Southern families, the wealthy, Princeton-educated Long would later help open doors for Woods in the wartime State Department.

Eager to advance his career, Woods frequently appealed to his many friends in Washington for help.[25] Senator Robinson tried to have him named minister to Prague.[26] Although this did not work out, the powerful Arkansas politician did manage, in August 1937, to have Woods appointed inspector of all U.S. commercial attachés on the European continent, England, and Egypt.[27] His homebase was to be Berlin, center stage in an increasingly tense and foreboding international drama.

Woods arrived in the German capital early in September, finding the bustling, modern city with its cosmopolitan atmosphere to his liking. Soon Milada and her mother joined him in the spacious, sunny apartment he had located on the Sigismundstrasse, just off the Tiergarten.[28] With frequent trips to commercial outposts in Turkey, Egypt, Jerusalem, Italy, France, Belgium, and Switzerland, and back to Washington for consultations, Woods had little time to partake of Berlin's social life or to assess the events rapidly unfolding around him. In Berlin he and Milada did become friendly with diplomats at various Eastern European missions, who kept them well informed.[29] Woods was also on cordial terms with at least one senior Nazi official—Count Wolf Heinrich von Helldorf, chief of the city's police.[30]

But few Americans in Berlin got to know the easy-going, likable commercial attaché from Mississippi. Those who did run into the portly, solicitous Woods at embassy cocktail parties found him amusing and captivating, but superficial. (The minister at the American church, Stewart Herman, recalls Woods as someone who could "charm the birds out of the trees."[31]) Few found him a person of depth or substance. That impression did not change in August 1939, when Woods was named commercial attaché at the Berlin embassy. As a replacement for the highly knowledgeable Douglas Miller, he hardly seemed up to par. At his second-floor office on the Pariser Platz Woods quietly carried out the routine duties of his office, scanning the German press and extracting facts and figures of interest to American commerce. He compiled regular reports on the German economy, nurtured useful contacts, and followed the rivalries and intrigues in the various government ministries.[32] He and his translator, Patrick Nieburg, made a small contribution to the English language by coining the term "whole wheat" to describe a German bread then unknown on the other side of the Atlantic.[33]

When the Wehrmacht invaded Poland, Woods's official duties changed very little. He filed statistics on such mundane topics as the German army's consumption of Coca Cola.[34] But, outside the office, another side of his complex character was emerging. When the wives and children of U.S. diplomats based in Germany were evacuated to Denmark that fall, it was Sam Woods who stepped forward to lend a comforting and calming hand at the Berlin railway station.[35] (Milada and a few other embassy wives elected to stay behind.[36]) Discreetly he arranged for food supplies to be sent on to these dependents.[37] On his own he performed countless small acts of kindness, even for Germans. William Russell, a young consular official from Mississippi, once came across Woods in a Berlin grocery store. When the woman in line ahead of him was refused milk because she lacked the right ration cards, an exasperated Woods stepped forward, displayed his diplomatic cards, and blurted out in his inimitable, heavily accented German, "Here, give this woman all the milk she wants."[38]

The new commercial attaché also helped out German Jews by converting currency and arranging to have rents on their expropriated properties paid in more profitable U.S. dollars.[39] He came to the aid of at least one Jewish family in Berlin, securing passage to the United States when prospects of obtaining visas were dim.[40]

Beneath his kindly, good-ol'-boy demeanor, Woods was also a coolly calculating careerist who rarely missed an opportunity to ingratiate himself back in Washington. He kept up a steady correspondence with his benefactors in Congress, particularly with key members of the appropriations committees, to ensure that his name would not be overlooked when it came to authorizing more funds for officials serving overseas.[41] Woods's manipulation of personal connections on the Hill led to his being promoted to Foreign Service Officer, Class I, when the Bureau of Foreign Commerce was transferred to the State Department in 1939.[42]

When Carl Norden, son of the inventor of the famed Norden bombsight, was traveling across the Atlantic to take up his first Foreign Service post in August 1938, he shared a steamer cabin with Sam Woods and another junior consular official. A seasoned hand after nearly a decade of European service, Woods took the two neophytes under his wing and gave them pointers about how to stay out of trouble while still making as much money as possible.[43] Norden judged Woods a "shrewd cookie" who "knew all the angles."

But neither Woods's shrewd financial dealings nor his backwoods Mississippi manner impressed his colleagues in striped pants on the Pariser Platz. In those days the U.S. Foreign Service was still the domain of a well-heeled Ivy League clique whose members considered diplomacy their birthright and who looked askance at anyone who intruded upon their territory. With mounds of suitcases and servants to carry them, they moved elegantly from post to post as if on an extended holiday. In their eyes, Woods was a parvenu from Mississippi who owed all his professional advancement to his friends on the Hill. They thought of him as a person who never cracked a book and who fell asleep at the opera.[44] Career diplomats like George Kennan[45] and Hugh Wilson, who succeeded Dodd as U.S. ambassador, had little regard for him. Behind Woods's back, Alexander C. Kirk, the eccentric U.S. chargé d'affaires, educated at the Sorbonne and Harvard Law School and heir to a family soap fortune, dubbed him disparagingly "childe Samuel."[46] Woods, of course, liked to fool people with his Southern version of the innocent abroad. If others underestimated his abilities, that was all right with him: the role of amiable buffoon made a fine disguise.[47]

That Sam Woods ended up acquiring more valuable military intelligence during the Second World War than practically any other U.S. diplomat speaks volumes about how disdainfully the State Department regarded the craft of espionage. Ever since Hoover's secretary of state, Henry L. Stimson, had decreed that "gentlemen did not open other people's mail," officers of the U.S. Foreign Service had looked upon spying as a dirty business—a necessary business, perhaps, but certainly not *their* business. According to the prevailing diplomatic mores, officials were only supposed to pick up useful information from their counterparts within the international community, local officials, and other well-placed contacts and then incorporate this material into their dispatches to Washington. Invariably this was "soft" intelligence—rumors and second-hand gossip that circulate freely in foreign capitals—not concrete facts about military forces and operations. Diplomats were official representatives of their governments, entitled to certain privileges and protection, but bound by internationally recognized rules. Anyone who bent these rules was like a cheat at the card table and was treated accordingly.

America's emissaries in prewar Berlin showed no great inclination to cheat. Roosevelt had dispatched Dodd to the Nazi capital to show U.S. contempt for the Hitler regime. The civilized, *bürgerlich* Germany beloved by this distinguished historian in his student days[48] no longer existed, and Dodd, an "honest and subtle, gentle and slightly nervous scholar"[49] lacked both the inquisitiveness and the desire to come to grips with the "new order" that had destroyed it. Instead, depressed by what he saw happening in Nazi Germany,[50] Dodd held himself aloof from his day-to-day ambassadorial duties, preoccupied with writing a book on the Old South. Only rarely did he bother to read the reports prepared by his staff—which he considered pro-Nazi[51]—or attempt to find out for himself what was actually going on inside Germany. As a result, the U.S. ambassador was poorly informed. (The wife of the U.S. military attaché, Colonel Smith, relates how shortly after her arrival in Berlin in August 1935 Dodd greeted her by exclaiming, "You've come just in time!" When she asked what he meant by this, the ambassador confided, "The Germans are going to kick Hitler out in three weeks."[52])

The man who succeeded Dodd,[53] Hugh Wilson, was an experienced and capable career diplomat who had previously served in Weimar Germany.[54] A more adroit negotiator than Dodd (and more willing to seek a *modus vivendi* with the Nazi regime), the short, mustachioed Wilson relied on his genial personality and supple mind to strike a bargain with Hermann Goering allowing Jews to take some of their wealth out of the country with them.[55] Wilson was also persuaded by Colonel Smith in August 1938 to pool intelligence—the first such arrangement worked out between an ambassador and his military attaché.[56] But Wilson's tenure in Berlin was short-lived, ended abruptly by the violence of Kristallnacht. Roosevelt then downgraded the Berlin post to the level of chargé d'affaires and awarded it to his old friend Kirk.

Coolly aristocratic, always immaculately dressed, with dark, arching eyebrows and languid, owlish eyes, Kirk was a character lifted straight out of Proust. He descended upon Berlin in April 1939 accompanied by an urn containing the ashes of his late mother (as well as one for his own remains[57]) and escorted by a gaggle of giggling Italian servants,[58] including a chauffeur rumored to be his lover.[59] In short order Kirk established himself in grand style, leasing a mansion in fashionable Grunewald, taking a suite in the Hotel Adlon, and fixing up a pied à terre next to his embassy office, decorated in his preferred funereal black.[60] Generous to a fault, "Buffie" Kirk hosted elaborate "spaghetti parties" during the Sitzkrieg for several hundred guests, flying in oysters and other delicacies from Denmark, and showered the embassy staff with Christmas gifts.

Toward the Nazis the chargé d'affaires did not attempt to conceal his disdain. He once greeted a delegation of formally attired German officials in a "collarless checked tweed jacket, gray flannel trousers, clerical black waistcoat, heavy gold chain almost to his waist, and purple suede shoes with inch-thick crepe rubber soles"—the sartorial equivalent of a slap in the face.[61]

For all his personal eccentricities Kirk was an intuitively astute, intelligent, hard-working, and fearless diplomat. The Nazis grudgingly came to respect him, even if they avoided him.[62] Kirk did extend some feelers to opposition circles, chiefly to the young Count Helmuth von Moltke. When Kirk left Berlin in October 1940, he passed on Moltke to his administrative officer, George Kennan. But in general Kirk minimized the value of dealings with Hitler's opponents and did not encourage his staff to develop such associations.[63]

In this diplomatic climate it is even more surprising that Sam Woods could become engaged in passing along Nazi secrets. The commercial attaché was extremely fortunate in that Jacob Beam turned over Respondek to him just when the well-connected former professor was about to unearth some extraordinary, war-related intelligence. But Woods was not just lucky. He had created the perfect cover: he was the one American in Berlin the Nazis would never suspect of dabbling in espionage.

This was a quality of Woods's that was not lost on Respondek. After his close call in 1936, when someone at the U.S. embassy had left a report of his lying around, Respondek had grown uneasy with his American friends, whom he considered "leaky sieves."[64] He was in need of a reliable, tight-lipped confidant. By chance Charlotte Respondek appears to have run across Sam Woods. She may have met him, on a trip to Rome, as early as 1936.[65] An accomplished cook, Frau Respondek discovered a common culinary passion in the ruddy-cheeked, Texas-born gourmand. From the start she also realized Woods was more than the jocose, extraverted country boy he pretended to be: here was someone shrewd enough to be trusted with her husband's secrets.

In Berlin, Erwin Respondek took his wife's advice and began inviting Woods and his wife Milada over for dinner not long after the newcomers settled in the city.[66] Justifying Charlotte Respondek's confidence in him, Woods kept this friendship to himself: when Beam mentioned Respondek's name before heading back to the States in August 1940, the commercial attaché did not confess that he had already been a regular guest on the Mariannenstrasse for several years.[67] Lured by exquisite meals prepared by Charlotte, who called him her "sweet little piglet,"[68] Woods would show up about once a month at the Respondeks' home to savor the food and talk politics.

There was a great deal of bad news to discuss. Europe was teetering on a precipice, and Germany was plunging into madness. As a discouraged Respondek wrote to Heinrich Brüning, "There is no escaping the atrocities since 1933, neither by turning inward nor by fighting back."[69] As he had predicted, war broke out in September 1939. Around noon on the 3rd, news of England's declaration of war was broadcast by loudspeaker to a silent and uncomprehending throng of Berliners gathered in the Wilhelmplatz. After over a year of futile negotiations, the illusion of a lasting peace was finally shattered. If war brought death and destruction, it also brought opportunities: for Sam Woods and Erwin Respondek it was the chance to play the most important roles of their lives.

It was a chance gladly seized by both men. Aware of Respondek's sources inside the Nazi regime, Woods

encouraged him to increase his contacts, particularly with those people who worked for the OKW (Oberkommando der Wehrmacht, the German general staff), in the hope of securing detailed information regarding the supply and reserves of materials to be used in the conduct of the war, the methods of war economy and finance, the transfer of war industries from congested areas to less exposed situations in the country, and the efforts and attainments of scientific research groups in Germany.[70]

Spurred on by Woods, Respondek threw himself wholeheartedly into the task of gathering this sort of information by exploiting his existing contacts and adding to them so that he built a pipeline leading into the very heart of Hitler's vast military machine.[71] The fruits of his endeavors after 1940 would be rather remarkable. They would include a warning about the greatest military operation of all time.

4

THE GREATEST MILITARY OPERATION IN HISTORY

Adolf Hitler never bothered to hide his hatred for Bolshevik Russia. It was clearly spelled out in his *Mein Kampf* for all the world to read.[1] Short-term territorial ambitions in Poland prevailed over ideology in August 1939, when the Nazis signed a stunning nonaggression pact with Stalin. But the goal of crushing Soviet Russia was never really abandoned, only postponed. It was Hitler's most grandiose, fatal obsession, destined to doom him and the Third Reich.

This preoccupation with an annihilating strike against the Soviet Union resurfaced only two months after Ribbentrop flew to Moscow pledging peace. Poland, the Führer informed his generals in mid-October, was to serve as an "assembly area for future German operations."[2] His dreams of a major offensive eastward took another fateful step toward realization as German troops were subduing the last pockets of resistance in France. "The moment our military position makes it at all possible," he confided to his obsequious chief of the operations staff, General Alfred Jodl, the Wehrmacht would attack the Soviet Union.[3] By this condition Hitler meant an end to the fighting in the west. Just as much as his generals, the ex-corporal feared the prospect of a two-front war.[4]

Hitler held an initial planning session with his commanders in Berchtesgaden on July 31, 1940, just two days after Chief of Staff Halder had ordered his counterpart in the XVIII Army, Major General Erich Marcks, to prepare a "theoretical groundwork for an eastern campaign."[5] With the goals of diverting attention from a preliminary build-up of forces in the east and of applying pressure on the recalcitrant British to sue for peace, Hitler almost simultaneously conferred with several of his top generals at his Black Forest field headquarters to lay plans for an invasion of England.[6] Word of this combined amphibious and airborne assault across the English Channel, codenamed "Sea Lion," would confuse Germany's adversaries about Hitler's intentions.

Based on "Ultra" intercepts and other sources, British intelligence, for instance, became convinced that the Germans were going to attack Channel beachheads in September. On the 7th of that month an Invasion Alert No. 1 was issued to all defense forces, warning that an invasion could be expected within 12 hours.[7] Already frightened by rumors of German paratroopers[8] and saboteurs in their midst,[9] and badly demoralized by the debacle at Dunkirk, the British peered nervously into the Channel mists that fall, not knowing that Hitler had already decided to scrap further preparations for Sea Lion in favor of a strike eastward.[10]

Maintaining a strict secrecy about his actual plans was as crucial to Hitler's military strategy as creating false impressions. Thus, preparations for what was then called Aufbau Ost were revealed to only a few officers within the Army High Command, including generals Brauchitsch and Halder and field marshals Keitel and von Rundstedt.[11] Goering was not informed of the proposed operation against the Soviet Union until August 9; Himmler first learned on January 1, 1941; and Ribbentrop on March 27, 1941—less than three months before the invasion was to start.[12] In spite of all this tight security, word of what came to be known as Operation Barbarossa would leak out and reach the Soviets from many sources, only to be disparaged and ignored by Stalin. The first authoritative tip-off about this massive military undertaking, emanating from the highest German military circles, would come from the U.S. government, based on what Erwin Respondek told Sam Woods.

The story of that warning is even today not fully known. Factual inconsistencies, conflicting dates, and varying interpretations of what Woods actually passed on to Washington cloud the historical record. What follows is a reconstruction of the events surrounding the Barbarossa warning as they can be pieced together from the evidence that is available and deemed generally reliable.[13] Respondek, it appears, learned of Hitler's plans practically from the moment they were formulated. As early as August 1940 he arranged for Woods to meet him clandestinely in Berlin and, in an excited voice, told him he had heard of war preparations against the Soviet Union being discussed atop the Obersalzberg.[14] These talks had taken place only a few weeks before and had involved the military leaders Halder, Admiral Raeder, Keitel, Jodl, Lt. Colonel Adolf Heusinger, Major General Marcks, Colonel Walther Warlimont, Lt. Colonel Bernhard von Lossberg, Captain Wolfgang Junge, Major Baron Sigismund von Falkenstein, and Commander Karl Jesko von Puttkammer.[15]

Respondek did not specify the source for this information, either then or later. Keitel, Jodl, and Warlimont were all loyal Nazis, and the lower-ranking officers present during these conferences were equally committed to the German war effort and unlikely to talk about such a top-secret operation. Colonel Lossberg (who was given the assignment of preparing an operations study for the Soviet invasion, then codenamed "Fritz,") did confide in at least one other person—his cousin and fellow officer Hans Herwarth von Bittenfeld.[16] Because of this fact, and because of Herwarth's friendly ties to several U.S. diplomats stationed in Berlin (George Kennan, Jacob Beam, Alexander Kirk, and Sam Woods[17]), some historians have surmised that Herwarth was the chief German source for the Barbarossa warning.[18] But though Herwarth did inform the anti-Nazi German ambassador in Moscow about the Soviet invasion plans in September 1940,[19] he did not tell any of his American associates. As he summed up, somewhat erroneously, in his memoirs:

Sammy Woods showed great friendliness towards me and we had a number of far-ranging conversations. Unknown to me, Woods was apparently on the American intelligence staff and filed reports about our meetings which later gave rise to certain legends regarding my own supposed links with American intelligence. Granted that . . . my reports to Woods may have been useful, I cannot flatter myself that I played the cloak-and-dagger role assigned to me after the event.[20]

Seeking to identify Respondek's informant raises several intriguing questions. Were other senior German officers involved in a plot against Hitler in 1940? Did Respondek find out about the invasion plans from General Halder (with whom, at least indirectly, he had conspired two years before)? That the same general entrusted with organizing Germany's onslaught on the Soviet Union would have divulged this top-secret operation to a person hostile to the regime, in regular touch with U.S. diplomats, seems, on the surface, most implausible. But there is strong evidence that the army chief of staff did, at a later point, reveal details of Barbarossa, that these reached Respondek, and that he subsequently conveyed them to Sam Woods. So the possibility that Halder was Respondek's original source cannot be lightly discounted.

In any event, an initially skeptical Respondek[21] could scarcely conceal his delight at this news. For the first time since the Nazis had come to power, he was genuinely happy.[22] He foresaw that by hurling German troops across the vast Soviet steppe, Hitler was committing a grievous military blunder that would lead to his defeat.

But how could he warn the Soviets in time? Respondek had no entree to the Soviet embassy in Berlin, only to the Americans. And, without proof, they might not believe him. In light of Hitler's recent pact with Stalin and Germany's military involvement in the west, an eastern offensive did seem incredible. To convince his American friends, Respondek would need corroborating information.

During the summer of 1940, when triumphant Axis armies stretched from Norway to North Africa, the unemployed professor of economics set out to confirm Hitler's intentions, first by quietly sounding out his usually well-informed Berlin contacts.[23] But this proved fruitless: no one knew anything about an invasion of the U.S.S.R. Next Respondek traveled by train to Salzburg, Bad Reichenhall, and Berchtesgaden to observe the comings and goings of Hitler's visitors to see what this might reveal. Failing to note anything of significance, he took another train to Munich.

In the Bavarian capital Respondek happened to be acquainted with two individuals who belonged to the Nazi Party's "old guard." Their names are not known.[24] Respondek carefully concealed their identities, only revealing that both men were founding members of the NSDAP, lived in Munich, attended the annual *alte Kämpfer* (old guard) reunion in the Bürger Bräu, and died early in the war.[25] To have learned so soon about this secret operation they must also have enjoyed Hitler's trust and confidence as few party members did.

Anton Drexler, the near-sighted toolmaker who founded the German Workers' Party, did live in Munich, and died there in 1942, but he had long since quit the Nazi movement and was not privy to Hitler's wartime secrets. As a fellow economist and advocate of closer cooperation with the Center Party,[26] Gottfried Feder is a more plausible friend of Respondek's. (He died in 1942.) However, Feder also fell out of favor in the party, for opposing Hitler's scheme to manufacture synthetic petroleum,[27] and dropped out of political life completely after 1934. Other prominent members of the "old guard" either quit the movement before the war, assumed high-level party posts in Berlin, or died after 1945.

The only other clue Respondek gives about the identities of his unwitting party informants is that he gained their confidence before 1933.[28] It is, therefore, quite possible that his two Nazi sources were former business associates. Support for this hypothesis can be found in a July 8, 1939, report to Heinrich Brüning in which Respondek cites a member of economics minister Funk's entourage as the person who told him about Hitler's hopes of bringing England to its knees without having to go to war.[29] Elsewhere Respondek revealed that he enjoyed "correct personal relations" with members of Nazi economic organizations, including the Deutsche Arbeitsfront (German Labor Front), headed by the erratic and alcoholic Robert Ley.[30] Ley was a close friend of Hitler's and stayed on intimate terms with him throughout the war years. But it is virtually certain Hitler kept his invasion plan a secret from Ley until almost the last minute.[31] Furthermore, it strains credulity to imagine a friendship between this loutish, ardent Nazi and the cultivated Berlin professor of economics.[32] So the mystery remains.

After visiting these unsuspecting party friends in Munich several times,

Respondek succeeded in coaxing them into admitting what he had hoped to hear: the Führer was bent on annihilating the Soviet Union, with the goal of having his soldiers subjugate all territory "from Vladivostock to Gibraltar."[33] According to what Respondek stated after the war, his informants conceded that Hitler's preparations for a landing on the English coast were merely a blind for a contemplated "sudden and devastating attack on Soviet Russia."[34]

Filled with nervous excitement at these revelations, Respondek immediately caught an express train back to Berlin. Having confirmed his initial warning, he was now determined to gather as many facts about the planned attack as possible, to give to Sam Woods. To do so, he first approached former colleagues in various Reich ministries, who disclosed that "special hidden offices" had been set up preliminary to administering a conquered Soviet Union.[35] Behind locked doors, unbeknownst to civil servants who were working in the very same buildings, details of the occupation were being worked out with typical German thoroughness, including the printing of millions of "occupation rubles." A chart was also being prepared, dividing up Wehrmacht authority into 21 governmental units within the Soviet Union.[36]

As he gathered more of these details, Respondek would pass them on to Woods. Aware they were now under Gestapo surveillance,[37] the two men devised rendezvous that might have been borrowed from second-rate spy novels. On a rare, urgent occasion Respondek might brazenly walk into the U.S. embassy building and ask to see the commercial attaché, but usually he and Woods met in deserted, out-of-the-way spots around Berlin. Often they spoke on empty railway platforms at outlying stations. Now and then Woods received messages through an intermediary cryptically known as the "elephant man" because he liked to frequent the Berlin zoo.[38] Once or twice Respondek was so daring he climbed inside the commercial attaché's large black Buick, as it stood idling in one of the city's busiest squares, and conveyed to Woods his latest information as the car with diplomatic plates sped off through the congested Berlin streets.

The U.S. diplomat approached his extracurricular espionage playfully. Richard C. Hottelet, then a cub reporter for United Press, remembers Woods once telling him how one day

when he left the embassy and saw that he was being tailed, he headed down the Ost-West Achse to the Grosser Stern (a large traffic circle with the Siegessäule in the center). There he picked up speed, driving round and round, leaving the tail farther and farther behind until he was gaining on them, at which point he turned off and was gone before they could make it around the circle again.[39]

Another Berlin-based journalist, Alex Dreier, remembers how Woods once shook another Gestapo "shadow" that had been doggedly following his Buick for days. Before driving off to the embassy one day, he slid out of his car, walked over to the parked sedan belonging to the secret police agents, and casually invited them up to his apartment for a drink. Upstairs in his living room Woods handed the abashed Gestapo agents tumblers of Scotch and a sheet of paper: here was his itinerary for the next three days, Woods said. Did the gentlemen not want to save themselves a lot of trouble and just take this along with them? Grateful for the liquor, and finding Woods's advice preferable to sitting in a car all day, the agents went blithely on their way, grinning and a little tipsy, leaving the commercial attaché free to keep one of his more important appointments with Respondek.[40]

Most often the two met inside darkened theaters and opera houses. A member of Respondek's circle owned a ticket service in Berlin. When Respondek wanted to contact Woods, he would drop by his friend's office and order tickets for himself and his wife, while reserving the two adjacent seats for Sam and Milada Woods. The girl who operated the ticket office would then call Woods at the embassy and notify him that two tickets were being held for him. The commercial attaché would have one of his assistants stop by and pick up the tickets. When the two couples arrived, separately, at the theater, the men would take seats next to each other without acknowledging each other or saying a word. During a moment of loud singing or commotion on the stage, Respondek would reach inside his coat, remove some papers, and hand them to Woods.[41] Through these various means valuable information on German military plans was exchanged throughout the second half of 1940, as British defensive forces braced for an expected German amphibious assault across the Channel.[42]

This was a time of growing uneasiness in the German capital. Hopes for a quick, easy German victory were now fading. Small formations of Royal Air Force (RAF) bombers appeared high in the Berlin sky on warm August and September nights, dropping their whistling bombs and making a bitter mockery of Goering's boast that no enemy plane would ever attack the Reichshauptstadt.[43] Night after night incessant air raid alarms sent cynical Berliners scurrying into their basements. Standing in long lines to buy rationed eggs, meat, and butter was straining their fabled sense of humor.

At night the camouflaged capital of Nazi Germany resembled "an immense cage of parrots which had been covered for the night."[44] Under the stars the city lay listless and depressed, its streets pitchblack and empty save for the ghostly, pale blue lights of an otherwise darkened bus crawling down the Kurfürstendamm. For the remaining U.S. diplomats, deprived of their debonair British and French colleagues and coping with gasoline shortages, blackouts, and curfews, the lighthearted prewar social whirl was only a faint memory,[45] replaced by a claustrophobic tedium.

Except when a British bomb exploded close by,[46] the Americans experienced little of the war firsthand. Even the attendant inconveniences were assuaged by diplomatic privilege: circumventing the ration system, the embassy managed to procure food otherwise in short supply from nearby Denmark.[47] (The food-loving Sam Woods had planned for these shortages, importing hundreds of canned staples from the United States and filling the extra guest room on the Sigismundstrasse with these provisions.[48]) In the early war years the Woodses continued to live well enough that Sam contracted gout—apparently the only known case in undernourished Berlin at that time—and thus attracted the interest of a professor of medicine and his curious interns.[49]

Concerts and operas were performed according to schedule, the top hotels kept serving guests, and so, on the whole, the war proved only a minor nuisance to the remaining U.S. diplomats and their families, who lingered in the eye of the storm. As Milada Woods wrote to a friend that fall, life in drab, wartime Berlin was strangely quiet and normal, despite the nightmare that was gripping the rest of Europe.[50]

The Respondeks, too, succeeded in avoiding most hardships, even though they were living without a regular income. The family kept two servants and had plenty to eat, thanks in part to a backyard bunker they had crammed with enough foodstuffs to last a month.[51]

All this while, Respondek was amassing further details about the forthcoming invasion of the Soviet Union. From friends in government ministries he learned that the Russophobe Alfred Rosenberg was prominently involved in its planning.[52] As irrefutable proof of what was in the offing, Respondek got his hands on a 1,000-ruble note destined for use in German-occupied Russia. This large bill he folded and stuffed into Sam Woods's pocket during one of their theater encounters. Woods brought this to his superiors at the U.S. embassy, but they were not impressed. As Woods recalled:

I took this 1,000 ruble note to Kirk, who was then serving as Chargé d'Affaires, and was told by him to give it to the Russian expert at the Embassy, who examined it and returned it to me without making any report to Washington. Therefore, in an effort to create doubt and possibly a conflict between Russia and her "loyal ally," Germany, I decided to get the note into the hands of the Russian Ambassador in Berlin. As I had no direct contacts with the Russians, I depended on Dr. Flasenbergas, Press Attaché of the Lithuanian Legation in Berlin, for information from the Russian Embassy. Dr. Flasenbergas, to whom I gave the note, passed it on to his friends in the Russian Embassy, who agreed to see that it was brought to the attention of the ambassador. As a result, when the Russians took over the Lithuanian Legation in Berlin (after June 1940) Dr. Flasenbergas was the only member of the staff retained by them. He was ordered to Moscow almost immediately thereafter, and a few weeks later his wife and daughter were rendered every assistance by the Counselor of the Russian Embassy in getting off to Moscow. He has not been heard of since![53]

The "Russian expert" was most probably George Kennan.[54] Although busy primarily with administrative matters, Kennan had a thorough knowledge of Nazi politics and policies.[55] He was also fluent in Russian, contemplating a career as a translator, and well versed in Soviet and Eastern European affairs from his earlier postings to Prague and Moscow. But like most of his colleagues in Berlin, Kennan was skeptical of recurrent rumors about German military operations in the east. He was particularly dubious of any information emanating from Sam Woods, whom he considered a lightweight. So, it may well be that Respondek's "invasion ruble" never found its way to Washington.[56]

For ultimate confirmation of this mammoth Nazi military operation Respondek now decided to turn to the one person in Germany who, next to Adolf Hitler, had to know everything about it: Colonel General Franz Halder, the army's chief of staff.

Halder is one of the Third Reich's more complex and enigmatic figures. Descended from a Bavarian Protestant family with a 300-year-old tradition of soldiering, Halder was torn between a rigid code of military obedience and his own moral sense of right and wrong in the face of Hitler's actions. Earlier in his career, after serving on the general staff during the First World War, he had held several command and staff positions before being named to replace General Ludwig Beck as chief of staff in August 1938. As Jacob Beam had discovered, Halder was prepared at that time to help carry out a coup, should Hitler go to war over Czechoslovakia.[57] But the crew-cut Halder, once likened to a "colorless, bespectacled schoolmaster,"[58] was at heart a cautious man. Once the ink on the Munich pact had dried, he dissociated himself from anti-Nazi officers like Hans Oster and Beck,[59] believing Hitler now sat too firmly in the saddle to be dislodged.

By the beginning of 1939 the army chief of staff was no longer willing to give any encouragement to the military conspirators.[60] By then he was also preoccupied with working out plans for the Blitzkrieg strike against Poland. Only slowly did Halder again come around to believing the war was a grave mistake. Vaguely he hoped a German setback on the battlefield would increase popular support for a coup.[61]

While an emotional Halder wrestled with his conscience, he angered and frustrated those officers who felt his participation in a military coup was crucial.[62] Steeling himself to take matters into his own hands, Halder carried a loaded pistol to all of his meetings at the Reichs-chancellery starting in the fall of 1939[63] but as a "human being and a Christian"[64] could never bring himself to draw his weapon and fire. As the war spread across the continent, Halder longed to see Hitler stopped, but he could not accept that it was largely up to him—and General Brauchitsch, the army's commander in chief—to make this happen.

As chief military planner, Halder was well informed about Operation Barbarossa from the start. As early as July 2, 1940, he had heard his fellow generals talk of attacking the Soviet Union.[65] From that point until he was dismissed as chief of staff in September 1942, the Bavarian general was the architect of German military operations against the Soviet Union. All his distaste for Hitler and his war, all his doubts about the wisdom of attacking Russia,[66] and all his disagreements with the Führer's tactical objectives did not deter Halder from carrying out these duties to the best of his ability.[67] To have aided the forces arrayed against Hitler by revealing anything about Barbarossa would, he argued after the war, have been treasonous, costing "the blood of German soldiers."[68] Yet these protestations notwithstanding, Halder did disclose this military secret. The only question is whether or not he did so deliberately.

As was noted earlier, the army chief of staff was linked to Respondek in the organizing of the 1938 coup.[69] But the two men apparently did not know each other personally; so in order to gain confirmation from Halder about the invasion plans, Respondek had to rely on a carefully constructed chain of intermediaries.

The first of these was Hermann Muckermann. After being ousted from his research post at the Kaiser Wilhelm Society,[70] Muckermann had lived in semiseclusion, continuing to publish scientific articles under the pseudonymn "Braun."[71] Respondek now asked him to take a more active part in his anti-Nazi activities: would Muckermann be willing to speak to former crown prince Georg of Saxony, now a Jesuit priest, about contacting General Halder?[72]

Father Georg was the oldest son of the last reigning monarch of Saxony, Friedrich August, who had abdicated at the end of the First World War. Though raised to succeed his father on the throne, the modest and introspective[73] Georg had never acquired any princely airs. As head of a Catholic ruling family in an overwhelmingly Protestant part of Germany, his father had taught him to live and help his people humbly.[74] During the Great War, the large, powerfully built Georg served as an ordnance officer on the western front, where he came to know and admire a captain who was then charged with planning the withdrawal of German forces from France—Franz Halder.[75]

Already a friend of Georg's father,[76] Halder took a liking to the egalitarian-minded young prince, and a firm friendship developed between them. A devout believer, the twenty-five-year-old prince first entered the Franciscan order in 1918, after his father renounced the throne,[77] but then he applied for admission to the Jesuits, whom he found aesthetically and philosophically more appealing.

Through his Jesuit duties, first in Bavaria and later in Berlin, Georg came into periodic contact with his fellow priest Muckermann, possibly having been introduced by the latter's brother, Friedrich.[78] Outwardly he was Muckermann's antithesis. Clad in a threadbare loden coat and wearing the shoes of a Bavarian farmer, the self-effacing Georg served Berlin's poorest Catholics as a simple pastor, riding the tram across the city each day to reach them. In this austere way of life,he was sustained by two great moral imperatives. One was to bring together Catholics and Protestants by means of an ecumenical movement known as *Una sancta*.[79] The other was to defeat Nazism. To opponents and victims of Hitler alike, Georg was a steadily shining beacon of hope:

He had there (in Berlin) a large sphere of activity and considerable influence. Many people in dire straits came to him. Christians and Jews. He had contact with high-ranking generals, top government officials, influential personalities, and politically persecuted persons in all professions. He strengthened their resistance to the new heathenism of Hitler.[80]

One of the high-ranking persons he saw socially was Halder, who frequently came to stay for short spells at a Grunewald villa on the Kronberger Strasse.[81] There the two continued to meet, even after Georg's hostility toward the Nazis had brought him under Gestapo scrutiny.[82] Exactly what the Protestant general and the Catholic priest talked about is not known. To protect both himself and his long-time friend, Halder was circumspect about mentioning their conversations in his diary.[83]

At some point in late November 1940—according to Respondek and his State Department confidants[84]—Hitler's chief of staff divulged the entire strategic outline of Barbarossa to Pater Georg, noting that the German armies intended to drive three wedges deep into Soviet territory.[85] Some time later Halder also allegedly gave the timeframe for the attack: the spring of 1941.[86] Subsequently, Georg shared this news with Muckermann, who immediately told Respondek. Coming as it did directly from Halder's lips, this had to be extremely accurate information. Indeed, the plan drawn up by Major General Marcks at Halder's request and presented at an August 4th briefing did call for a three-pronged offensive, with separate German spearheads aimed at Leningrad in the north, Moscow directly to the east, and Kiev in the south.[87] This troop deployment was not favored by Halder,[88] and it was not wholly identical to the plan of attack finally approved by Halder and adopted by Hitler in February 1941.[89] But it did represent the interim consensus of the German general staff at that time.

Why would Halder have divulged these vital secrets to a known enemy of the regime? After the war both Woods and Respondek took pains to point out that both Halder and Father Georg had aided the Allied cause unwittingly.[90] But there are other indications the normally closemouthed Halder may have spoken with the hope that his news might eventually reach Hitler's opponents.

For one thing, the general was worried about Germany's becoming embroiled in a two-front war.[91] He did not understand why an attack on the Soviet Union was being launched.[92] Furthermore, Halder had already played the part of informant in April 1939, tipping off Donald Heath, first secretary of the U.S. embassy, about Germany's coming attack on Poland.[93] After being dismissed by Hitler, Halder renewed his ties to such anti-Nazi figures as Count von Stauffenberg.[94] These associations prompted the Gestapo to arrest him after the 1944 Attentat and keep him under arrest for the remainder of the war.

Halder's postwar comments about his role in the resistance are characteristically guarded and ambiguous. In 1948 he acknowledged having received the famous "X" report proposing peace terms with the British. (At the time, Halder had branded such contact with the enemy "treason."[95]) But not until shortly before his death, in 1972, did the ex-general hint of having played a greater role in the wartime conspiracy. In a paper presented at an air force symposium in Colorado, Halder made this reference to his little-documented acts of resistance:

The other circle of the military resistance against Hitler, which had its focal point in my own person, avoided any written records. Only in such singular and urgent instances, as for example during the winter of 1939–40 when it became necessary to have written records for the implementation of practical actions, . . . did I allow these to be made. For this reason, there is much less actual source material available for this circle of resistance; most of it consists more of "rumors" and assumptions.[96]

On top of this evidence comes Halder's confessions to his postwar American interrogators that he had violated his oath as an officer.[97] And in at least one of his wartime reports to the State Department Woods explicitly names Halder as one of Respondek's "friends" supplying information about the eastern front.[98] Finally there are parallels between what Halder knew about Hitler's strategic intentions and what Respondek told his American confidant. Both felt, as late as February 1941, that Sea Lion was still a viable military option.[99] And both men appear to have learned of Hitler's original Barbarossa target date of May at roughly the same time.[100]

Did Gestapo agents know of Halder's contact with the ex-crown prince of Saxony—or of his role in revealing military secrets to Respondek? The records that might settle these questions have all been destroyed.

There is, however, the curious circumstance of Father Georg's death. On May 14, 1943, the fifty-year-old, healthy, physically fit priest left his home on the Neue Kantstrasse to go swimming and work on a sermon at a lake west of Berlin. He did not return from that excursion. The next day his clothes were found, together with his watch, an open breviary, and his notes for the sermon, ending with the haunting Latin phrase *Vado ad patrem* ("I go to Thee, Father"). Several weeks later his body was found. An autopsy determined the cause of the priest's death was a heart attack.[101]

Toward the end of 1940 Respondek presented a detailed summary of his findings about the proposed German invasion plan to Sam Woods.[102] The genial Mississippian now held in his hands Hitler's greatest military secret. Somehow he had to find a way to safeguard this vital information until he could convey it back to Washington. There were perils of all kinds, and Woods had to watch every step he made: the secretary in his embassy office was a Nazi who had turned in a Czech friend of Milada's for underground activities. The concierge in their apartment building was also a zealous party member assumed to be notifying the authorities about the American's comings and goings. The telephone in the Woodses' apartment was almost certainly tapped. Milada had wisely hired a cook and butler who spoke only Czech, but the possibility of someone eavesdropping still existed. One loose word at a cocktail party could spell disaster. Mindful of her husband's garrulous manner, Milada concocted a warning system: if she overheard him saying too much at a reception or dinner party, she would utter the Czech word *kure*—"chicken"—in a loud voice, and Woods would stop talking.[103] They also made a point of not leaving any incriminating papers lying around: Milada was so afraid the Germans might find Respondek's report describing Barbarossa that she stuck it in her purse and carried it with her one evening to the opera.[104]

Woods did not have to keep this secret to himself for long.[105] Almost as soon as he found a chance he handed Respondek's report to the new chargé d'affaires, Leland Morris.[106] Morris was a more restrained, less flamboyant career diplomat than his predecessor, Kirk. A stickler for rules, he was more noted for his talent on the tennis court than for his professional nerve and aplomb. When the commercial attaché ventured his opinion that the embassy ought to forward this highly important document immediately to Washington, Morris tartly reminded Woods that U.S. diplomats were not supposed to go sneaking around Berlin, ferreting out secrets and acting like spies.[107] Becoming just as testy, Woods retorted that the time for such conventional niceties had passed. By agreeing in August to swap some 50 U.S. destroyers for British bases, President Roosevelt had already abandoned his policy of strict neutrality toward the Germans. Woods then offered to carry Respondek's report personally to Lisbon, where it could be safely placed inside a sealed pouch for the trip across the Atlantic. Backing off somewhat, Morris said this would not be necessary. If Woods had a friend in the State Department, he could send the document directly to him from Berlin, marked "personal."

That was no problem: Woods had plenty of friends in Washington. Avra Warren, chief of the department's visa section, was one of them, and so the commercial attaché went back to his office and penned a brief note, expressing his confidence in the enclosed German-language report and suggesting that Warren have someone get in touch with Heinrich Brüning to verify its authenticity.[108] Woods then handed over Respondek's original document to Lloyd Yates, second secretary at the embassy, who was on his way back to the States and due to pass through Washington.[109] This arrangement satisfied Morris's sense of propriety, and so early in the new year of 1941[110]—that fateful, bloody year that would see first the Soviet Union and then the United States engulfed by war—the tall, easygoing Yates boarded a Reichsbahn train for the first leg of his trip overseas. In his diplomatic pouch he carried news that would spur the highest circles of the U.S. government to extraordinary action.

5

A WARNING UNHEEDED

It was not until late in February that Lloyd Yates finally delivered Respondek's revelations to the State Department.[1] On the 21st of that month, a chilly, clear Friday, a messenger entered Secretary of State Cordell Hull's wood-panelled, second-floor office in the south wing of the State, War, and Navy Building clutching a sealed envelope.

It was not a happy time for the sixty-nine-year-old, white-haired Hull. The year before, after faithfully serving the Democratic Party for so long, this onetime Tennessee judge had contemplated making a run for the White House. At first the president had even hinted at endorsing him. By then Franklin Delano Roosevelt had confounded political tradition by seeking, and easily winning, election to a historic third term. In the nominating process the deferential Hull had missed out on the vice-presidential nomination as well.[2] In January the secretary of state had sat silently, muffled in his gray topcoat, on the steps of the Capitol and listened to the reelected president solemnly deliver his third inaugural address. Another four years under Franklin Roosevelt did not bode well for him. With the European conflict spreading, the charismatic, dynamic leader whom Hull had been first helped to elect back in 1932 was meddling more and more in State Department affairs, undercutting Hull's authority by consorting with his rival, Sumner Welles.[3] The secretary was a tired man, unhappy in his job, yet loathe to leave it at a time of such world crisis.

The envelope he was handed had come over from the visa section. It contained a cover letter from the commercial attaché in Berlin and a small sheaf of papers, all typed in German.[4] The name Sam Woods did not mean much to him, and he did not read German, so Hull summoned

Assistant Secretary of State Breckenridge Long from across the hall to attend to the documents.

Long was another longtime Roosevelt backer. After retiring briefly from public life, he had jumped at an offer to return to Washington to handle emergency war matters within the State Department.[5] Long had previously held the coveted ambassadorship to Italy, but he ended up causing some embarrassment to himself and his president by sending back ecstatic dispatches about Mussolini.[6] Now he was back on more familiar ground. He had walked these same ornate marble halls and held the same post of assistant secretary back in Woodrow Wilson's day. Long and Hull had known each other for many years (having vied for the Democratic Party chairmanship in 1921) and, despite their different backgrounds (Hull was born in a log cabin in the Cumberland Mountains), got along well.

During recent months Long had come under heavy attack for his restrictive immigration policies aimed at keeping out "undesirable" refugees—that is, Jews fleeing a Nazi-dominated Europe.[7] This was wearing him down, and the packet of papers now entrusted to him by Hull may have provided a welcome diversion.[8]

He remembered Sam Woods, of course, from their hunting expedition in Czechoslovakia. As he read how the Berlin-based commercial attaché had come by his information, Long thus had good reason to take it seriously.[9] This initial impression was reinforced when he scanned a translated summary of the report, hastily prepared by one of his aides. Long was startled by what he read: in concluding a thorough analysis of Germany's financial and economic situation, the anonymous author flatly asserted, as Long recorded in his diary, that Hitler's "war decision lies in England and immediately thereafter in Soviet Russia."[10]

Nothing could be further from official wisdom in Washington. The Soviets were, after all, an ally of the Nazis. The two totalitarian states had signed a nonaggression pact and agreed to carve up the vast chunks of (mostly Polish) territory lying between them. Just 11 days before, Long had made note of Germany's continuing build-up in the Balkans, preparatory, he presumed, to an occupation of Turkey and the strategic straits that controlled the Black Sea. In the face of this offensive, he believed the Soviet Union would remain "quiescent."[11] Like the British, the U.S. government was so mesmerized by the likelihood of an imminent German strike across the Channel that it could scarcely imagine Hitler sending his forces eastward.[12] Nonetheless, Long did not hesitate to pronounce the report forwarded by Sam Woods "authentic" and "probably the most important document that has arrived in the Department of State, certainly since the war began."[13]

Hoping to goad the Soviets into launching a preemptive strike against Germany, the assistant secretary of state asked two of his aides to give up their Washington's Birthday holiday weekend to prepare a full English version of the critical economic section for the president to read when he returned on Monday from Hyde Park.[14]

Respondek had come by his economic statistics, detailing German shortages of labor, rubber, iron, and other heavy metals,[15] by chance. In preparing for Operation Barbarossa, Goering, as coordinator for economic administration, had requested all Reich organizations that dealt with strategical resources to compile figures on available stocks, as well as estimates of the amounts that would be needed for an all-out attack on the Soviet Union.[16] (This was to be presented to Hitler and his top military advisors during a January war council at Berchtesgaden.[17]) The private secretary of Goering's asked to collate these figures happened to be a young Catholic whose first position in the government had been secured by Respondek. When he stopped by this secretary's office in December, Respondek was innocently told about the economic report. When the official was momentarily called away from his desk, Respondek seized pen and paper and jotted down the most important statistics.[18] These indicated an economic rationale for Barbarossa: by mid-1941 shortages in heavy metals alone, unless offset by new supplies (from a source such as the Soviet Union), would hamper Germany's war effort.[19]

In Washington, Long and Hull moved swiftly to make use of this extraordinary intelligence. Long first had handed to the president a translation of the critical economic assessment, stating that Germany's goal was to "make war on Russia as soon as a war against England can be finished."[20]

Long also gained Roosevelt's approval to notify the British,[21] both to advise them about Germany's war plans and to encourage more RAF raids on the Nazis' vulnerable and largely undamaged oil and gas refineries, in light of the report's economic findings.[22] Finally transmitted by the British embassy to London on March 21,[23] the State Department's warning about Barbarossa received a mixed response. Churchill had already made up his mind back in October that the Nazis' need for oil would force them to attack the Soviet Union.[24] So, if he read the cable, he would have felt confirmed in his thinking.[25] British intelligence officers were more dubious, preferring to base their professional judgments on hard military evidence, and what was available to them did not clearly point to an impending eastern offensive.[26] The contents of the cable from Washington were regarded as ambiguous and, therefore, of little value.[27]

Long also made sure that intelligence staff officers at the War Department received copies of the Berlin documents, which they deemed "very important."[28] Meanwhile, at Secretary Hull's request, he took steps to check out the unnamed source for this intelligence. Taking Woods's advice, he arranged for Heinrich Brüning to be invited down to Washington on March 6th, ostensibly to deliver a speech at the Brookings Institution.[29] At a dinner beforehand Long took the former German chancellor aside and asked if he would stop by the next morning to discuss an important matter. In the course of that private session, which ran for several hours, Long produced a bundle of papers on German labor, finance, and raw materials and had Brüning read them. Brüning readily identified these as copies of analyses he had been regularly receiving from a German informant.[30] He explained to Long that the author of these reports was a person whom he knew well and whose opinions he trusted.[31] As an indication of their importance, Brüning pointed out that these documents were regularly prepared for major German industrial firms, occasionally made available to the Führer's "intimate advisor" (presumably Goering), and even "presented to Hitler himself."[32] But he did not disclose Respondek's name.

After this lengthy conversation Long felt relieved: Sam Woods's Berlin informant was obviously a knowledgeable and reliable source.[33] (To back up what he had said, Brüning later forwarded to the State Department copies of earlier reports from Respondek, with the observation that these could not have been compiled "without knowledge of very secret official statistics."[34]) If Long needed any further strengthening of his belief that Germany was going to attack the U.S.S.R., it came in the form of a second report received from the War Department in early March.

This was a wide-ranging assessment of German military plans for 1941, based upon Respondek's extensive questioning of party and government officials, "liaison officers," and military officers.[35] Unaccountably, this militarily most crucial of Respondek's 1941 reports had taken over two months to reach Long's desk. Sam Woods had originally shown this 16-page, German-language memorandum in January to two military attachés at the Berlin embassy, Captain John R. Lovell and his superior, Colonel B. R. Peyton.[36] The two officers knew Respondek only slightly, and though finding his previous information reliable, they feared this latest document might be a plant. On the 17th they had forwarded to G-2 an English translation opining that the report might be "of some interest or value to the War Department," even though they did not give it "any too much credence."[37] These papers arrived from Europe on January 27th but were not passed on to the State Department for over a month.[38]

Although feeling he was in possession of an extremely valuable piece of intelligence, confirming the previous Berlin reports ("It envisions very definitely war against Russia"[39]), Long, too, worried that this summary of German war strategy might have been "planted upon us with the idea of frightening" the U.S. government, especially by its disturbing mention of Nazi plans to use poison gas. To allay these fears Secretary Hull asked

J. Edgar Hoover to have Federal Bureau of Investigation (FBI) agents
do a comparative analysis of the typewriters used in preparing the various Berlin reports: this established that they had all stemmed from the
same machines.[40]

This latest document described Germany's military moves in the east
as contingent upon a satisfactory outcome of the struggle against England. Writing on January 3rd, Respondek detailed Hitler's aim of launching a combined air-and-sea assault against Britain by May at the latest,
depending on the weather and the readiness of British defenses.[41] Once
it had conquered England, Germany would confiscate vital foodstuffs,
munitions plants, and industrial materials needed in the Reich.[42] Should
Britain or the United States still refuse to accept German hegemony over
occupied Europe, Hitler intended to starve his adversaries into submission.

In this document Respondek stressed the general staff's fear of a two-
front war and indicated that the Wehrmacht would move eastward only
after the English had been subdued and negotiations with the Soviets
about increasing vital supplies of food, fodder, oil, gasoline, textiles, and
other war-critical supplies completed.[43] Then the German lines of attack,
already "worked out to the last detail," would strike at Soviet forces along
the Baltic and at Kiev, Odessa, and Rostov. Following what he expected
to be a quick victory against the Red Army, Hitler would establish a
"new order, stretching from the Atlantic to the Pacific."[44]

Respondek was remarkably accurate in spelling out German plans on
both fronts.[45] Where he erred, contrary to his postwar assertions, was
in believing that Sea Lion was still in the cards. In fact, Hitler had
abandoned any thoughts of invading Britain the preceding fall, certainly
by November 12th, when he issued an official go-ahead to Barbarossa
just hours before Molotov arrived in the German capital. To conceal his
real goal of conquering the Soviet Union, Hitler had led his own military
leaders to think Operation Sea Lion was for real, and this deception had
apparently fooled Respondek, too.

Rashly, Breckenridge Long and other officials in Washington down-
played the conditionality of Respondek's analysis and seized upon its
tentative conclusion: the Soviet Union was going to be Nazi Germany's
next target. On March 6th, Secretary of the Treasury Henry Morgenthau
noted in his diary that the president had told him in strictest confidence
about a tip-off that the Germans had determined they were not going
to be able to defeat England and, therefore, were going to attack the
Soviet Union.[46] Hull himself was just as unequivocal, at least in his *Memoirs*, published in 1948, where he stated that Respondek's report dismissed the Channel invasion as a "blind for Hitler's real and well
calculated plans and preparations for a sudden, devastating attack on
Russia."[47] Most emphatic of all, Undersecretary Sumner Welles claimed

in his 1944 *The Time for Decision*, "In the first days of January 1941 information was handed to me which in my judgment proved beyond a shadow of a doubt that the German General Staff had agreed with Hitler that an attack should suddenly be launched in the coming spring."[48] (On March 5, 1941, Assistant Secretary of State Adolf Berle recorded the more accurate observation that "we have pretty clear information that the Germans propose to attack Russia this summer," conceding it was not certain whether this would come after an invasion of England or not.[49])

It appears that some U.S. leaders wanted to read Respondek's reports as more definitive than they actually were.[50] And they had good reason to do so. Long wanted to edge the Soviets into the war and turn them against Hitler, and these motives may have been shared by his colleagues at the State Department, and even by the president.[51] More sympathetic toward the Soviets, Welles wanted to sound the alarm as soon as possible as a gesture of American good will at a time when relations between the two countries were strained.[52] In this diplomatic climate, the reservations voiced by military intelligence officers in Berlin and Washington were largely overlooked.

By the final week of February the president and top State Department officials were sufficiently convinced of the import and urgency of Respondek's reports that they decided to notify the Soviets—even before confirming their authenticity with Heinrich Brüning. Without bothering to ponder the effect this warning of a Nazi attack might have on ongoing negotiations between the Soviets and the Japanese pointing toward trade and political agreements,[53] Hull, Roosevelt, Long, and Welles first agreed to have the U.S. ambassador in Moscow, Laurence Steinhardt, break the news to Molotov. A cable was dispatched on March 1st stating that the U.S. government had acquired reliable information

clearly indicating that it is the intention of Germany to attack the Soviet Union in the not distant future.... It would appear that the plan ... is contingent upon the extent to which England, supported by American endeavor, will be able to oppose not only the military strength but also the economic efforts of Germany.[54]

On the same day this message was cabled to Moscow, the Soviet ambassador in Washington, Constantine Oumansky, was summoned to the State Department and also informed.

Controversy—hardly a rarity in the faction-torn State Department—shrouds this warning. After the war, Hull insisted it was he who had decided to reveal the contents of Respondek's report to the Soviet ambassador.[55] But Welles claimed the credit for himself: Hull and the president had merely given their "hearty" approval.[56] In any event, on the afternoon of March 1st, with Hull home in bed with the flu, Welles spoke with Oumansky and conveyed Respondek's bad news. The ambassador was dumbfounded. According to Welles, Oumansky "turned very white"[57] and promised to tell his government immediately. (By contrast, Hull later told Woods the Russian "did not believe the report could be true."[58])

This was the first invasion warning the Soviets had received from a foreign government,[59] and it was treated seriously in their diplomatic channels until it was eventually presented to Stalin by his chief of intelligence, F. I. Golikov. Ever wary of attempts to sow seeds of dissension between his government and Hitler's, the Soviet leader scanned the message, wrote the word "provocation" on it, and handed it back to Golikov without saying anything.[60] With that, Respondek's long months of intelligence work had come to naught.

In one sense, Stalin was right: the Americans did have ulterior motives for wishing to inform him. But, of course, he was also tragically wrong in supposing there was no truth to their warning.

Respondek's report was the first but hardly the last reliable tip-off about Barbarossa that Stalin would ignore. Richard Sorge, Moscow's master spy in Tokyo, transmitted a similar warning, as did Alexander Rado and Rudolf Roessler in Switzerland. The Swedes also put together details of the invasion and passed these to Ambassador Steinhardt on March 24th.[61] A week later Yugoslav authorities warned the Soviets as well. The Americans informed Moscow of substantiating statements contained in intercepted Japanese diplomatic cables.[62] Through their "Ultra" intercepts, British intelligence picked up movements of German tanks and troops toward the Soviet frontier, and Churchill told Stalin about them.[63] But all these numerous warnings[64] were discounted. Even signs detected by his own intelligence service did not change Stalin's mind: at worst he had no cause to fear until the fall, after the Wehrmacht had crushed England. (The Soviet military attaché in Berlin reported an eastern attack was slated for mid-May. An anonymous tipster had apparently sent the attaché, Major General V. I. Tupikov, a copy of Hitler's Directive No. 21, issued December 18, 1940, which called for the German army to be prepared by May 15th to "crush Soviet Russia in a quick campaign before the end of the war against England."[65])

In Berlin, where rumors of an eastern Blitzkrieg were rampant in the spring of 1941, the truth was difficult for diplomats to discern. Even though it had relayed Respondek's warning, the U.S. embassy remained puzzled about Hitler's aims. As late as June 8th, chargé d'affaires Morris was still loathe to believe the "rather impressive testimony" he had heard about an invasion being scheduled for sometime during the next two weeks. "It is quite possible," he advised Hull, "that the tremendous preparations on the Russian border are a form of final pressure on Russia or a mask for action in some other area."[66]

The person on the embassy staff most knowledgeable about Soviet affairs, George Kennan, was preoccupied with his demanding administrative duties[67] and with an informal study of German occupational policies.[68] He, too, failed to predict a forthcoming invasion. (Years later Kennan would admit that he and other Berlin-based diplomats had been "slow to recognize that in Hitler's logic the inability to invade Britain would inevitably spell the necessity of invading Russia."[69]) The night before Germany attacked, on June 21st, the journalist Alvin Steinkopf told Kennan the Associated Press staff planned on being up early to report the expected news of an invasion, but the diplomat "pooh-poohed" the idea.[70]

Neither Morris nor Kennan enjoyed the confidence of officials in Berlin who might inadvertently have revealed Hitler's war aims. U.S. military attachés were in no better position to penetrate Hitler's elaborate web of deception: they were supposed to gather intelligence only from "legitimate" sources, that is, newspapers, conversations with counterparts at other embassies, and officially sanctioned visits to military installations and battlefields.[71] With Germany at war, for most of their hard military intelligence the U.S. attachés had to rely heavily on tips from American correspondents.[72]

The remaining American reporters in Berlin had opportunities to sniff out military secrets but risked being kicked out of the country if they published or broadcast them.[73] Although the Nazis shrewdly tolerated freedom of the press and even pampered journalists to bolster their image abroad, foreign correspondents soon discovered they were walking a dangerous tightrope.[74] A vivid example of what might happen to them was provided by the case of United Press's Richard C. Hottelet. Fluent in German and an outspoken opponent of the Nazis,[75] Hottelet wrote perceptively critical pieces on the local scene, quickly becoming a thorn in the regime's side. Without warning, around dawn on March 15, 1941, he was arrested by the Gestapo on "suspicion of espionage for an enemy power"[76] and hauled off to the nefarious "grey dungeon walls"[77] of the Alexanderplatz prison. There he was kept in solitary confinement and denied visitors for several months, until finally being released in exchange for German correspondents who were suspected of spying on the United States. Although the reasons behind his arrest remain cloudy to this day,[78] Hottelet's treatment had a chilling effect on his fellow journalists. So when they picked up indications of a German move eastward, they hesitated to tell their editors.[79] (The only American reporter to get out word of the imminent invasion was Stephen Laird, a writer for *Time*. He did so by traveling to Switzerland and cabling back his information from there. Laird's last-minute story predicted that the Wehrmacht would march eastward on June 15th.[80])

On the other side of the Atlantic, a debate over Germany's intentions went on. Most State Department officials remained in the dark about Respondek's warning because Secretary of State Hull wanted to protect his source. One who was privy to the documents, Raymond Geist, chief of the Division of Commercial Affairs, speculated in May that the Berlin reports of a forthcoming Soviet invasion might be "deliberately circulated by the Germans as a part of the war of nerves."[81] The highest military circles in Washington tended to think an attack "in the near future" was likely, but General Sherman Miles, head of G-2, would go no further than to say that a showdown between Germany and the Soviet Union was a "probability."[82]

More word from Respondek reached Washington in May and early June. The first of these reports was passed along to Roosevelt by Hull on May 12th, bearing his endorsement that the "whole series represents an authoritative disclosure of the situations" presented.[83] This document discussed shortages in raw materials, industrial labor, and credit,[84] and it provided specifics about German troop movements in the Balkans and along the Soviet border.[85] In these memorandums Respondek correctly stated that the massing of forces for an onslaught against the Soviet Union was to have been completed in May but had to be postponed because of unanticipated developments in the Balkans.[86] Pondering the German build-up in the east, he continued to view this development in the context of continuing preparations for a possible "trial invasion operation against England." Respondek concluded that German offensive operations in 1941—on both fronts—would be carried out "in stages":[87] Hitler still wanted to avoid a two-front war. Yet he did not venture a guess about which invasion would occur first, or when. Thus, even at this late point the professor of economics did not know that Operation Sea Lion had been scrapped. It was not until June 5th—barely 17 days before Operation Barbarossa was launched—that President Roosevelt was finally given a more precise and accurate prediction.

Writing in late April, Respondek now declared it was necessary for the Nazis to conquer the Soviet Union "from the standpoint of the internal economic situation and from that of the coming military problems in the west."[88] An eastern offensive had become more plausible because of the perceived military weaknesses of Great Britain and the United States, particularly their inability to bomb the "highly sensitive industrial centers of western Germany." No longer worried about the western front, Hitler's generals now felt free to proceed with the "liquidation" of the Soviet Union. Respondek supplied additional details about Germany's planned use of armored divisions, motorized units, and of the Luftwaffe, but he still gave no estimate of when the invasion would take place.[89]

Meanwhile, the greatest military operation of all time was about to begin. By giving his final approval to a revised Barbarossa plan on February 3rd,[90] Hitler had started the countdown for a devastating surprise attack in June—an attack that would, he vowed to his generals, cause the world to "hold its breath and keep still."[91] By the second half of June over 2.5 million German soldiers, arrayed in 76 infantry divisions and supported by some 600,000 vehicles, 750,000 horses, and 7,184 artillery guns,[92] were amassed near the Soviet frontier, ready to strike.

At 3:30 A.M. on the 22nd, exactly 129 years to the day after Napoleon had crossed the Nieman River on his ill-fated march toward Moscow, the Germans attacked, taking the farflung Red Army totally by surprise: "the greatest piece of deception in history"[93] had succeeded. To the north Field Marshal von Leeb's army group pushed across Lithuania toward Leningrad. Field Marshal Bock's forces struck out for Moscow, and in the south Field Marshal von Rundstedt's troops moved across the Ukraine toward Kiev and Rostov. It was all happening just the way Erwin Respondek had said it would.

6

THE MASTER SPY
AT WORK

When he heard the news broadcast on the morning of June 22nd, Erwin Respondek was both delighted and dismayed: delighted that Adolf Hitler had at last committed his long-anticipated blunder; dismayed that the Wehrmacht had caught the Russians unprepared. All along the border the Red Army was retreating in rout. What had gone wrong? Why had his warning been ignored?

Of course, Respondek had no idea how his reports had been received in Washington. Neither Breckenridge Long nor Cordell Hull had informed Sam Woods of their confidence in the Berlin documents or of their having notified the Soviet ambassador. Messages ran only one way along the Respondek–Woods–Long pipeline. From what was happening on the eastern front it could only seem to Respondek that his arduous efforts to unearth and verify Hitler's most closely guarded secret had been in vain. To say the least, he was sorely disappointed.

America's informant in Berlin could have no way of knowing how much his intelligence had helped State Department diplomacy, even if it had not saved the Red Army. Just over a week before Respondek's first memorandum mentioning a Soviet invasion crossed Cordell Hull's desk, the secretary was approached by the Japanese ambassador in Washington, Admiral Kichisaburo Nomura, about opening secret, private talks with the aim of averting a Pacific war between the United States and Japan.[1] Starting on March 8th, the two diplomats held over 40 evening discussions in Hull's suite at the Carlton Hotel. During these talks the Japanese ambassador repeatedly stressed his country's desire for peace. Hull could afford to be forceful in taking positions with Nomura (and not worry about the prospect of Japan signing a nonaggression pact with the Soviets, as it did in April) because of what he already knew about the Nazis' forthcoming aggression.[2] (An invasion of the Soviet Union by Japan's chief ally would, he reasoned, automatically scuttle any existing treaty between the two Asian nations.)

Although Respondek would not learn about these diplomatic consequences for some time, he would, nonetheless, continue to gather information for the United States. And what he would be able to share with Sam Woods would have an impact on the course of the conflict.

Early in the Second World War, nations threatened by the Nazis dreaded above all else one terrible weapon—poison gas. Talk of gas warfare conjured up haunting memories of soldiers clawing for breath, blinded, in the dank, muddy trenches of the Somme. Since Germany had been the first to use chlorine and mustard gas during the Great War, her adversaries had good reason for even greater fear now, with Adolf Hitler in power.[3] Even groundless rumors of the Führer's having stockpiles of lethal gas could intimidate his enemies and undermine their resolve to fight. Fully cognizant of the propaganda value of such rumors, Hitler decided to start one himself in March 1940.[4] At that point Germany did not possess any new poison gas. In fact, its scientists would not concoct a lethal nerve gas until late in the war, although large quantities of mustard gas were accumulated for possible battlefield use.[5]

Berlin representatives of neutral nations were informed by members of Hitler's staff that Germany had stocks of gas on hand and intended to use them to "poison the whole population of England." To lend credence to this threat, Hermann Goering arranged for several foreign military attachés to tour chemical laboratories in Gatow, on the western outskirts of Berlin.[6] This visit to purported gas storage sites was followed by another wave of rumors. (In early May, a well-connected military attaché informed the U.S. embassy that the Germans had manufactured a large supply of mustard gas.[7] Just after Christmas an anonymous, hand-written note warned that Hitler intended to use gas in the assault across the Channel.[8]) Steeled for a German landing that fall, the British expected the worst. Wrote Churchill afterward: "They would have used terror, and we were prepared to go to all lengths."[9]

By one of those improbable coincidences that made him such an invaluable intelligence source, Erwin Respondek was in an excellent position to assuage these Allied fears. For years he had enjoyed close professional ties with IG Farben, Germany's leading chemical concern. Furthermore, he had a direct personal link to German chemical research laboratories through his son-in-law.

While studying nursing in Würzburg, Respondek's older daughter, Valeska, had met and married a Frankfurt chemist, Dr. Friedrich Hoffmann. Even though he was opposed to the Nazis, Hoffmann was drafted to conduct experiments involving chemical weapons.[10] He was sent to a laboratory in Gatow, where he performed this work until the end of the war. (In 1947 he was brought out of Germany by U.S. occupation forces and relocated in Maryland, where he was to continue his research on poison gas for the U.S. military.[11]) In the spring of 1941 Hoffmann disclosed to his father-in-law that Hitler's talk about using a new, more deadly gas was just a "bluff": no such weapon existed.[12] Later that year Respondek obtained, either from Hoffmann or from his contacts at IG Farben, a copy of a secret report on "chemical war materials" and gave an excerpt from it to Captain Lovell and Colonel Peyton.[13] This document confirmed that German researchers had made no real progress in developing new, more deadly forms of poison gas or other chemical weapons. Experiments involving prussic acid, mustard gas, and various suffocating gases had not succeeded. The report did mention a "Most" or "117" gas that could cause death within 20 minutes. This chemical agent could be dropped from aircraft in 550-ton bombs capable of contaminating a square kilometer to the height of 100 meters.[14]

This disconcerting information was transmitted back to the War Department without any comment from the two military attachés. Respondek had even more alarming news in his memorandum of January 3rd. In describing Operation Sea Lion, he mentioned that German assault troops could be expected to use mustard gas.[15] As was noted earlier, this "sinister reference" greatly upset Breckenridge Long,[16] who wondered at first if it might not have been planted to frighten the British and Americans. It did so, but unnecessarily.

Respondek's warning about another German "secret weapon" proved more significant. This was no propaganda ploy, but a real, potentially devastating device—one that might have spelled defeat for the British on the high seas: the magnetic mine.

Naval mines were first widely used during the First World War to disrupt shipping and destroy enemy vessels of war. But these explosive devices floated on the ocean surface and could be easily spotted and plucked out of the water by minesweepers. To improve the mine's effectiveness, British scientists worked on developing one that could be activated magnetically—from below the surface, or from a shallow ocean bottom—by the force field of a passing ship's hull. In 1918 mines of this type were first tested, and a few were exploded near German warships off the coast of Belgium.[17] On their own the Germans were arming some of their U-boats with magnetic torpedoes and exploring ways of perfecting a magnetic mine.

After the war ended, this research continued inside a secret naval testing station at Kiel. There, in 1929, ground-laid mines with magnetic detonators were first manufactured under the supervision of a professor of physics, Adolf Bestelmeyer. Over the next few years the Germans learned how to drop these explosive devices by parachute and from high-flying aircraft. When war broke out in 1939, the highly classified magnetic mine constituted Germany's only bona fide "secret weapon." It was a weapon Britain had neglected to develop, and against which it had no defense.[18]

The danger to Allied shipping was obvious: mines scattered throughout the coastal lanes off the British Isles could form an invisible blockade, cutting off supplies of war matériel and foodstuffs and eventually forcing England to surrender. This fear became a stark reality on September 16th, when the steamship *City of Paris* was damaged by a mysterious underwater explosion, thought to be caused by a magnetic mine. German mining operations—carried out largely by U-boats and destroyers, but also from the air—in harbors from the Firth of Forth to the Thames estuary caused considerable damage and disruption of British shipping: a total of 76 vessels were sunk during the first few months of the conflict.[19]

The British were caught completely off-guard. As Churchill later conceded, "The terrible damage that could be done by large ground mines had not been fully realized."[20] He feared this new threat to shipping might "compass our ruin."[21] Fortuitously, one of the German magnetic mines dropped by parachute washed up on the mudflats of the outer Thames in late November and was recovered by British ordnance experts.[22] This was the biggest "catch" of that first war year.[23] The British were able to examine the mine's firing mechanism and, armed with that knowledge, start work almost immediately to devise defensive measures. Within several months a method of degaussing, or demagnetizing, steel hulls was developed, making the magnetic mine ineffective. But dealing with this threat consumed a great deal of Britain's defensive energies at that stage of the war.[24]

Erwin Respondek found out about Germany's magnetic mine late in 1940, most likely from his former mentor, Hermann Bücher. (It was Bücher's firm, the AEG, that had modified the mine for seadrops in 1937.[25]) By then the British knew a great deal about this "secret weapon," but it was still news to the Americans.[26] When Major Lovell read Respondek's report of a new mine "of unusual size and high explosive content" on February 24, 1941, he was surprised.[27] So was the Navy Department. A mine expert in Washington expressed "great interest" in this report of a German magnetic mine, opining that it sounded technically feasible.[28]

Previously ignorant of both German and British progress in mine development, the United States Navy came to realize the offensive capability of the magnetic mine and ordered its ordnance laboratory to begin manufacturing one, as well as to come up with methods of neutralizing it. Mine specialists were sent to Great Britain to learn more about the construction of these mines. By copying the German design, these researchers were able to produce the first American magnetic mines as early as 1942, and they were used that summer in combat in the Pacific.[29]

Respondek's other major intelligence "scoop" in his February report was greeted with more skepticism. Through Woods, the former professor of economics had passed on to the U.S. military attachés in Berlin word that the Nazis were planning on building 400 submarines during 1941. This translated into a highly ambitious construction goal of over 33 U-boats a month—to be met by siphoning off some 250,000 skilled laborers from other industries, the army, and Axis-occupied countries.[30] Major Lovell found this information "interesting," corresponding to other reports he had received about proposed manpower increases for submarine construction.[31] Unknown to Lovell, his counterpart in the naval attaché's office, Lt. Commander Arthur "Speedy" Graubart, had also arrived at an estimate of U-boat production for 1941 that nearly matched Respondek's. He based his figures on visits to submarine yards, conversations with German naval officers, and analyses of parts shipments. A submarine specialist who had studied diesel engines at the Technische Hochschule in Dresden, Graubart put the target at 25 per month, or 300 for all of 1941.[32] This coincided exactly with the figure Admiral Raeder had established the previous August, after convincing Hitler to support a major U-boat build-up as a means of turning the tide in the Battle of the Atlantic.[33]

The Navy Department was not buying any of this, however. Lt. Colonel H. E. Maguire told his superior, General Miles of G-2, that Respondek's figure of 400 submarines was "exaggerated and fantastic."[34] Because of its disbelief in these estimates and the absence of formal intelligence cooperation with the British, the navy probably did not share either Graubart's or Respondek's prediction with the Royal Navy. United States naval intelligence's own projection for German submarine construction was far more conservative—just 12 submarines a month.

In fact, German submarine yards turned out an impressive monthly average of 19 new U-boats in 1941. British intelligence was considerably off this mark, and as a consequence the Royal Navy was poorly prepared to meet this burgeoning threat to merchant convoys and warships. Without adequate air cover or sea escorts, Great Britain suffered heavy ship losses up to September, when President Roosevelt agreed to have U.S. destroyers protect foreign vessels passing through the vulnerable mid-Atlantic belt.[35]

In the beginning of February 1941 Respondek's quiet, unobtrusive gathering of military intelligence suddenly came to a halt. One morning Gestapo agents appeared unannounced at his office, now located at

Charlottenstrasse 54, near Lichterfelde, and demanded to be shown Respondek's files. His secretary, a Fraulein Nowka, obligingly, if somewhat nervously, ushered the secret police inside. For a moment, Respondek must have inwardly panicked: somehow he had been found out. But the Gestapo were not looking to catch a spy that morning. Instead, they were curious about Respondek's representing of Jewish clients whose property had been confiscated under the Nazis' Aryanization laws. This work was viewed as suspect, if not outright illegal. With Respondek grimly looking on, the Gestapo agents packed together all his files dealing with Jewish firms and individuals in Bavaria and carted these away.[36] They took Respondek with them, too. At the administrative headquarters of the SS-Reichssicherheitshauptamt he was thoroughly questioned about complaints brought against him by party Gauleiter in Würzburg, Bayreuth, and Nuremberg. While other agents sifted through his papers, Respondek defiantly defended himself:

I pointed out that I had been banned from speaking or writing by the *Gauleiter* in Berlin [end of 1933] and that I was not a member of either the Nazi Party or any of its organizations. Nor was I a member of the Nazi Lawyers' Association. As an independent financial advisor I was entitled, by virtue of my notarial power of attorney, to represent my Jewish clients before government officials. ... It was not at all forbidden by law for a German citizen to represent German citizens of the Jewish faith.[37]

These arguments did not sway his Gestapo interrogators, and Respondek was held in custody, behind the high iron fence of the infamous Prinz Albrechtstrasse headquarters, for several months, until May 1941. Before being taken away, he had had the presence of mind to ask his secretary to notify Hermann Muckermann about his detention.[38] Muckermann had immediately telephoned Heinrich Wienken, the Catholic priest who ran the Berlin office of the Deutscher Caritas Verband, a Catholic welfare organization. In this capacity Wienken rescued hundreds of persons from the hands of the Gestapo and saved countless others from death in the concentration camps.[39] He did what he could to arrange for Respondek's release, apparently to no avail. In the end, the Gestapo simply concluded they had no real case against this friend of German Jews and let him go, with Respondek's written promise to work for the "victory of the Führer." But this would not be the last time they would get their hands on Erwin Respondek.

As soon as he was free again, Respondek resumed his gathering of intelligence for the Americans. From officers he knew within the Army High Command, he turned up evidence that spring of another important new German weapon: the glider plane. This is how he described it to Woods:

The (German) transport planes are combined with several rather large gliders. As a result of new inventions, the latter are hooked onto the transport planes. Take-off, transportation in the air and release are effected by automatic devices and releases. In February these landing planes were tested with positive results. The construction procedure is that of Messerschmidt, of Augsburg and Regensburg.[40]

Glider planes had been a big plus for the Germans early in the war. A favorite of Hitler's, this novel combat-support aircraft was first dramatically deployed on the night of May 10, 1940, when nine gliders, towed by JU-52 transport planes and carrying a 78-man commando assault team, landed noiselessly on top of the seemingly impregnable fortress of Eben Emael in Belgium and subdued its garrison of 850 flabbergasted soldiers with a loss of only six lives. A delighted Führer then ordered the use of gliders in other combat assaults, including his contemplated invasion of England.[41] For the time being, the Germans kept this weapon tightly under wraps. It was believed Eben Emael had been overwhelmed by parachutists, and the Allies gave little thought to the possibility that gliders might have been used.

This view changed as a result of more accurate intelligence, including that supplied by Respondek. On February 25, 1941, barely a week after his memorandum describing German gliders reached Washington, General Henry H. Arnold, head of the Army Air Corps, decreed, "In view of certain information received from abroad a study should be initiated on developing a glider that could be towed by aircraft."[42] Soon the army was designing and testing this new kind of plane. The first U.S. combat gliders went into full production in October 1942. Later in the war, the Americans used gliders in operations across the Channel and into Sicily, Holland, and Burma.[43]

The Germans themselves never repeated the grand success of their first glider assault. The aircraft described by Respondek in his April report—the Messerschmidt ME 321—was satisfactorily tested in February, but because of its enormous size (a wingspan exceeding 180 feet) it proved ungainly in the air and difficult to tow. When finally deployed in North Africa, the slow-moving behemoths fell easy prey to RAF fighters.[44] On May 20, 1941, the Germans once again used a force of 80 of the much smaller DFS 230 gliders in their biggest airborne assault of the war, against the island of Crete, but suffered heavy losses.[45] From then on gliders were of only marginal help to the Wehrmacht.

Through the spring of 1941, Respondek's High Command sources also told him about "swimming" or amphibious tanks[46] (which were to be used in the Russian campaign); increased German reliance on long-range bombers in the North Atlantic (which took place during the second half of the year[47]); the sites of vulnerable war industries in western Germany[48] (which were subsequently bombed with more frequency[49]);

and the existence of a secret German–Japanese military commission.[50] All this information was sent on to Washington. From his son-in-law and other contacts in industry Respondek also compiled a wealth of material regarding the German testing of synthetic substances, such as plastics and textiles. These would help sustain the Nazi war economy in the face of shortages of more conventional materials.[51]

Finally, turning to his informants within the Kaiser Wilhelm Society, Respondek prepared a summary of the "status and recent activity of German scientific developments" and handed this over to Woods, who in turn gave it to Colonel Peyton for forwarding to the War Department.[52] This document referred to ongoing German work on splitting the uranium atom. These scientific experiments would later arouse the intense interest of senior U.S. government officials.

The impact of wartime intelligence is always difficult to gauge. In Respondek's case there are some indications of the value placed on his information. Labor statistics approximating his were disseminated by the Office of the Coordinator of Information (COI)—forerunner of the Office of Strategic Services (OSS). The German's data on shortages of war-critical metals, food, and other raw materials also resembled those published by the COI.

Ironically, Respondek's single most vital piece of intelligence for the Americans that spring appears to have fallen on deaf ears in Washington. Indeed, it may never have been transmitted from Berlin. There is scant evidence of its existence. But it was a warning that, had it been relayed and heeded, might have saved thousands of American lives and helped avert one of this country's great military debacles. This tip-off involved not Germany but its Axis partner halfway round the world, Japan.

Early 1941 was a time of complex diplomatic maneuvering—and secret military planning—for the Japanese. Hitler's smashing European victories were encouraging bellicose circles in Tokyo to seize the opportunity for similar conquests in Southeast Asia, thereby securing vital raw materials for the expanding Japanese empire. Other Japanese officials hesitated, fearful of a clash with the powerful United States over hegemony in the Pacific.[53] A principal figure in these deliberations was Japan's foreign minister, Yosuke Matsuoka. An autocratic, mercurial, and somewhat erratic personality, Matsuoka wavered back and forth on Japan's war options, such as attacking the Soviets.[54] Toward the United States, where he had studied (at the University of Oregon) and lived for over 16 years, Matsuoka tended to be conciliatory, hoping some kind of accommodation could be worked out.[55] He saw the Tripartite Pact, signed by Italy, Germany, and Japan on September 27, 1940, as a step in that direction.[56]

In February the Japanese foreign minister was authorized by his government to visit Berlin, Moscow, and Rome in order to strengthen Japan's ties to the Axis powers, but primarily to neutralize any potential threat from the Soviets in Asia.[57] Meanwhile, without Matsuoka's knowledge, Admiral Yamamoto was proceeding with a scheme of his own, designed to gain Japan supremacy in the Pacific at one fell swoop by annihilating the U.S. fleet—if and when negotiations with the United States broke down. Announced with great fanfare, Matsuoka's trip to the Soviet Union and Europe was eyed anxiously by Western diplomats. Those concerns grew when the train bearing the diminutive, blustery foreign minister pulled into Berlin from Moscow on March 26th, amid a sea of waving Japanese flags. Matsuoka's scheduled meetings with Joachim von Ribbentrop and Adolf Hitler came on the heels of an exceptionally warm reception by Joseph Stalin, who had affirmed his support for the Axis powers in the European conflict.[58]

The exact purpose of Matsuoka's celebrated visit to Berlin is unclear. He had no firm agenda. He did not want to commit Japanese troops against Singapore, or against U.S. bases in the Pacific, as his hosts were sure to urge. Nor was Matsuoka, no great friend of the Germans,[59] seeking a military alliance with the Nazis. For their part, the German leaders wanted to see Japan enter the war, arguing England was already defeated, but were reluctant to take Matsuoka into their confidence about their own military plans, such as Operation Barbarossa. For both sides, this was more of an exploratory get-together than a chance to plot strategy.[60]

The Japanese foreign minister was accompanied on this long diplomatic odyssey by his thirty-eight-year-old *chef de cabinet*, Toshikazu Kase.[61] Like Matsuoka, Kase was American-educated, a 1927 graduate of Amherst who had gone on to earn a master's degree in history at Harvard. Politically he was pro-American and anti-Soviet. Helped by his fluency in English and ease with Westerners, Kase had held embassy posts in Washington, Berlin, and London prior to 1941,[62] when he was called home to work first for the foreign minister and then to oversee Japan's diplomatic overtures to the United States.[63] Kase was by now a seasoned foreign service officer who enjoyed Matsuoka's trust and liking and who could exert some stabilizing influence over his often contradictory superior. (Kase would later serve as secretary to foreign minister Togo and then become deeply involved in negotiating Japan's surrender.[64] In the 1950s he was named Japan's first ambassador to the United Nations.)

Exactly what Kase may have known about his country's aggressive designs against the United States is difficult to ascertain. From Matsuoka he could not have acquired any authoritative information. It is entirely possible the foreign minister had heard rumors about a surprise attack, or deduced this on his own. It is also possible that the unpredictable Matsuoka may have simply speculated out loud in Kase's presence.[65]

In any case, while he was staying in Berlin during April 1941, Kase met privately more than once with Erwin Respondek and discussed these matters.[66] On the basis of these conversations Respondek concluded that Japan intended to declare war on the United States and attack its Pacific fleet.

How—and how well—Respondek knew Kase remains a question mark.[67] Japanese visitors periodically came to dinner at the Respondek home in Lichterfelde during the 1920s and early 1930s,[68] and because of his diplomatic status in the German capital Kase may have been among them. Most of these guests were either business associates or individuals Respondek had met through his government service, particularly at international conferences. It is entirely possible that he first met Kase at meetings of the League of Nations. Knowing Respondek's political connections and views, Kase would hardly have spoken casually about Japan's military intentions. More probably, he deliberately divulged whatever information he had, with the hope that it might alert Washington.[69]

Did this ever happen? Available historical records indicate it did not. None of the published accounts of warnings about Pearl Harbor refer to a message received from Berlin.[70] The signs the United States is known to have overlooked or misread are those yielded by "Magic" intercepts of Japanese diplomatic cables, those suggesting military movements and intelligence gathering in the Pacific, and Ambassador Joseph Grew's report of January 27, 1941, which stated that Pearl Harbor was to be the Japanese target.[71] Breckenridge Long made no mention in his diary of a Berlin tip-off. Neither Cordell Hull, in his postwar memoirs, nor Sam Woods, in reconstructing his wartime collaboration with Respondek, ever described such a warning. Neither the State Department files for April and May 1941, nor the Military Intelligence Division reports for the same period, nor corresponding White House files contain any reference to it.

Did Respondek simply make the story up? The former professor *was* supremely confident of his abilities and accomplishments, even arrogant. On occasion he was prone to exaggerate his own importance.[72] But Respondek never sought to publicize or capitalize upon his role in this purported warning about Japan. He described his alleged meetings with Kase only in a letter to Cordell Hull written some three years after the war's end, a letter not intended for others to read. Why would he have lied?[73]

If Respondek did send a warning to Washington, how did it get there? Why is there no surviving record of it? Why did Sam Woods not mention it in recalling Respondek's wartime accomplishments? These questions

all beg answers.[74] It is certainly peculiar that a tip-off about Japanese
war plans in the Pacific, coming from such a reliable source, would be
lightly dismissed. Nevertheless, this seems to have been the case. The
urgent, horrifying news flash from Hawaii on Sunday, December 7,
1941, shocked U.S. officials listening to their radios in Washington as
much as it did those 4,000 miles farther away in Berlin.

Sam Woods, as a manual arts student at Valparaiso University, 1919.

Courtesy Valparaiso University

Erwin Respondek (fourth from left, standing) with other Finance Ministry officials and Lord Balfour (front center), Berlin, 1926.

Reprinted from Hans Schäffer: Steuermann im wirtschaflichen und politischen Krisen, *by Eckehard Wandel. Courtesy Leo Baeck Institute*

Sam Woods (fourth from left), then U.S. commercial attaché in Prague, at a 1934 hunting expedition with Bernard Baruch (second from left), Sen. Joseph T. Robinson (third from left), and Breckenridge Long (sixth from left).

Courtesy H. Grady Miller, Jr.

Charlotte Respondek, circa 1935. A convert to Catholicism, she had private audiences with both Pius XI and Pius XII on behalf of her husband's resistance activities.

Courtesy Valeska and Gabriella Hoffmann

Respondek with his daughters, Dorothea (in his lap) and Valeska, in the garden of their Lichterfelde home, circa 1928.

Courtesy Valeska and Gabriella Hoffmann

Charlotte Respondek and her children, Valeska (standing), Dorothea, and Peter, around the time of the Nazi takeover.

Courtesy Valeska and Gabriella Hoffmann

Hermann Muckermann, 1935. Banned by the Nazis for his views on eugenics, this worldly priest helped Respondek establish key contacts within Germany's elite scientific and Catholic circles.

Courtesy Valeska and Gabriella Hoffmann

Heinrich Brüning, German chancellor, 1931. In American exile he vouched for the reliability of reports Respondek forwarded to the State Department. He thus lent credibility to the Barbarossa warning.

Courtesy German Information Center

Sam Woods, circa 1940. Underestimated by both his U.S. embassy colleagues and the Gestapo, he carried out his unofficial intelligence gathering in Berlin with deceptive nonchalance.

Courtesy Milada Woods

Erwin Respondek, circa 1939. Convinced that the Nazis were bent on destroying Germany, he threw himself wholeheartedly into collecting war-related information for his American friends.

Courtesy Valeska and Gabriella Hoffmann

Sam Woods (far right) at a dinner in his honor in Zurich in November 1942. Appointed consul general by Cordell Hull, Woods used his post to communicate with Respondek and aid interned U.S. airmen.

Courtesy Stadtarchiv Zurich

Secretary of State Cordell
Hull in his office. He considered Respondek's and
Woods' reports among the
most valuable he received
during the early years of
the war.

Courtesy Franklin D. Roosevelt Library

Assistant Secretary of State Breckenridge
Long, circa 1935. A friend of Woods, he
served as the chief link to Hull, President
Roosevelt, and the War Department for
alarming reports on German atomic research
and other "secret weapons."

National Archives 208-N–5558-P

Col. Gen. Franz Halder (right), the German army's chief of staff, plotting strategy with Hitler and Marshal Ion Antonescu (front left), the Rumanian dictator, in 1940. Evidence suggests that Halder revealed details of the Barbarossa plan to Respondek.

Courtesy Buchverlage Ullstein Langen Müller, Munich

The U.S. embassy staff, Berlin, 1940. Jacob Beam, Respondek's U.S. contact prior to Woods, is the third from the left (standing) and George Kennan is standing immediately to his right, with his hand on the desk. Woods is seated at the left, opposite Chargè d'Affaires Alexander Kirk (seated at right).

Courtesy Dagfin S. Hoynes collection

Sam Woods outside the U.S. embassy in Berlin, 1940. On rare occasions Respondek would climb inside Woods's Buick and confer with him as the car sped off through the city's traffic.

Courtesy Alex Dreier

Sam and Milada Woods with fellow internee Julian Foster (center) at Monte Estoril in 1942, a few days after their release from Bad Nauheim.

Photo by Dagfin S. Hoynes. Courtesy Dagfin S. Hoynes collection

Max Planck, 1944. One of Germany's most eminent physicists, Planck served as Respondek's surrogate father after World War I and then briefed him on German progress toward development of an atomic bomb.

Courtesy Archiv zur Geschichte der Max-Planck-Gesellschaft

Charlotte Respondek and Herbert Müller, mid 1950s. During the war Müller supplied Respondek with high-level information about German atomic research while he sought to block work on a bomb. After the war Müller and Charlotte lived together.

Courtesy Valeska and Gabriella Hoffmann

Wilhelmina Busch Woods and Sam Woods during a Fourth of July celebration at their Bernried estate, circa 1950. While his former collaborator struggled after the war, Woods lived his final years in opulent splendor.

Courtesy Kenneth J. MacCormac

Thomas B. Stauffer as a lieutenant in the U.S. Army, 1945. Tasked with identifying Germans who had been sympathetic to the Allied cause, Stauffer tried in vain after the war to find work in the United States for Respondek.

Courtesy Lucia C. (Stauffer) Savage

Erwin Respondek with his second wife, Elsbeth, circa 1970. Unable to earn a steady income or gain public recognition for his wartime deeds, Respondek grew bitter toward the U.S. government for having "betrayed" him.

Courtesy Henriette Respondek

Schloss Höhenried, the Woodses' home in Bavaria after the war.

Photo by John V. H. Dippel

The graves of Sam (left) and Wilhelmina Woods on the shore of Lake Starnberg outside Munich.

Photo by John V. H. Dippel

Erwin Respondek's grave at Parkfriedhof, Berlin.

Photo by John V. H. Dippel

7

THE SCREW TIGHTENS

The Americans still living in Hitler's Berlin spent the remainder of 1941 in a state of disquieting limbo. They endured each passing day like prisoners awaiting sentence to be passed—bored and testy. Gradually their numbers dwindled. The once-favored hotels and pubs lost most of their garrulous and amusing habitués, victims of the infamous Berlin "blues." For those who opted to stay on—out of a sense of duty, sheer inertia, or a fascination with what was to come—the city lost its glitter and its panache. Once friendly Berliners now turned the cold shoulder when they heard English, the *Feindsprache*, spoken on a bus or street corner. To the Nazis, these American hangers-on became an annoyance—unwanted houseguests who would not leave, and who could not be thrown out on the street. This was especially true of the unintimidated correspondents who kept churning out unfriendly stories night after night for their readers across the Atlantic.

Over the German capital intimations of war hovered like a rain-laden storm cloud. With its Ost-West Achse covered "like an enormous, over-grown green circus marquee,"[1] with flak guns bristling on rooftops, Berlin was girded for that war, but little of it came, only an occasional RAF bomber on a nuisance run. The rationing of food, gasoline, and clothing increased, and so did the Berliners' grumbling. The young, dashing Herbert von Karajan came to town to conduct *Tristan* and thrilled a full house at the Staatsoper,[2] but even a magical moment like this could not shake a deepening gloom. The news from Russia was bad and growing worse. Moscow did not fall, as shrill Nazi propagandists had insisted it would,[3] and antiparty graffiti mysteriously cropped up overnight on walls and kiosks, asking where it would all end.[4] With each morning's paper the lists of soldiers who had "fallen" in the east grew longer—an endlessly growing litany of death.

For the conspirators Erwin Respondek and Sam Woods these were tense and dangerous days. Ever since Respondek's arrest, the Gestapo had trailed the two men more diligently, making it more difficult and more risky to meet. Perhaps for this reason no new messages were transmitted to Washington. Toward the end of the year, Woods's superiors in the State Department became worried about his safety, diplomatic status notwithstanding. An urgent "triple priority" cable was dispatched, ordering the commercial attaché home at once.[5] But it came too late. Events in the Pacific were rapidly coming to a head, and there was no time left for an American in Berlin to cross the borders of the Third Reich. Late on a cold and rainy December 7th a stunned George Kennan listened to the news from Pearl Harbor on a crackling embassy radio.[6] Now it would be only a matter of days before Germany followed suit and declared war on the United States. The Americans marooned inside the Reich could only grimly steel themselves for the inevitable.

But Woods and Respondek could not afford to sit around and wait. They had to act quickly to ensure that their intelligence link would not be cut once the U.S. embassy was vacated. Taking advantage of Berlin's eye-of-the-hurricane calm following Pearl Harbor, the two men met one more time, on December 10th. Respondek brought along a beautiful collar of Belgian lace as a gift for Woods's wife, Milada. He pointed out its unusual design and said he had had an identical collar made for his own wife. They were the only two of their kind in existence. Respondek then made a proposition, recorded in this way by Woods:

if I could secure an assignment near the German frontier perhaps it would be possible for us to continue our collaboration. He emphasized that if I received such an assignment, and he had news for me, he would attempt to send a messenger to me with his wife's lace collar, and if I, in turn, sent a messenger to him, he should bring my wife's collar.[7]

In case Woods needed to send him another note, Respondek produced a small wooden statue of St. George the Dragon-Slayer.[8] This exquisite, seventeenth-century carving already had quite a history.[9] According to Respondek, it had once belonged to the Bernheimer family in Munich, owners of a renowned antique store patronized by wealthy Germans, including top Nazis, until it was finally put out of business.[10] As a connoisseur of art and antiques Respondek had come to know Otto Bernheimer and his wife long before Hitler came to power.[11] Out of gratitude for Respondek's helping his wife, son, and himself to flee the country in 1939, one of the Bernheimers' sons, Ludwig, had given Respondek this five-inch high statue of St. George.

At their final meeting Respondek handed over the carving to Woods, to be presented to President Roosevelt "as a symbol of struggle and victory" over the Nazis.[12] Naively Respondek was to place his complete trust in this gesture of solidarity between himself and the U.S. leader. As he recounted many years afterward, "Woods reported to me after 1945 that the President was very pleased [by this gift], sent his thanks, and told him that he [the president] would invite me to Washington as 'the first German' after the war ended."[13] (As late as 1961, Respondek thought the statue was on display at the Roosevelt family museum at Hyde Park. But it is not there today, and there is no record of its ever having been there.)[14] Did Woods simply make up this story to spur Respondek on to greater feats of espionage? This seems more likely than not. For one thing, Woods never spoke personally with Roosevelt, as he implied to Respondek. For another, Respondek's "invitation" to Washington was never issued. The statue itself has long since disappeared.[15]

Before departing from Berlin, Woods took steps to forge another bond with his German confidant. He told Respondek they could stay in touch through a Swiss diplomat in the German capital by the name of August Ochsenbein.[16]

Born in 1901, Ochsenbein was descended from one of the oldest families in the medieval Swiss city of Solothurn. After obtaining his doctorate at the University of Bern, Ochsenbein had embarked on a diplomatic career that had taken him to Manchester, Danzig, Breslau, and then, in March 1933, to Berlin. At the Swiss embassy he dealt with economic treaties, agricultural exports, and other trade matters.[17] As the Swiss commercial attaché he naturally ran across his U.S. counterpart, Sam Woods, shortly after arriving in Germany.[18] Like Woods, Ochsenbein appreciated fine wine and art. (In his apartment, as a private protest, he hung paintings of German artists banned by the Nazis.[19]) He was also no great admirer of Adolf Hitler. While Ochsenbein's dealings with Woods appeared to be strictly social in nature,[20] he was actually being drawn into the American's network. This involvement evolved with the approval of the Swiss ambassador to Germany, Dr. Hans Frölicher.[21] Once Woods left Berlin, Ochsenbein was to help arrange for Respondek's documents to be slipped out of the country.

The circumstances of Ochsenbein's first meeting with the German financial expert are cloudy, but Agnes Dreimann, a close friend of the Respondek family, recalls his being a wartime dinner guest at their Lichterfelde home. She also remembers Ochsenbein's receiving documents for Woods.[22] Respondek himself described their initial contact as taking place in May 1942.[23]

Ochsenbein was stepping into a dangerous role. In a Nazi-dominated Europe, Swiss independence hinged upon not provoking the Germans. (The Swiss government accommodated Hitler in numerous ways—by restricting trade with Great Britain,[24] by tolerating what amounted to German censorship of its press, by darkening its cities at night to deny British bombers useful orienting points, and by preventing British propaganda from being mailed to Germany from Switzerland.[25]) Still, despite the presence of a strong Nazi movement within their borders, the Swiss were generally sympathetic to the Allied cause and willing to incur some risk to help defeat Hitler. For instance, Swiss factories continued to ship the British spare watch parts, which could be used to manufacture timing mechanisms for explosives. Swiss air defense units also refrained from attacking stray RAF bombers bound for targets in Germany and Italy, while their security forces allowed the Soviets' spy Rudolf Roessler to transmit intelligence from his "Viking Line" headquarters in Lucerne.[26] In this delicate climate, Swiss diplomats had to walk a very narrow line. For this reason, Ochsenbein's participation in the passing on of Nazi secrets to the United States is most surprising. At all costs his deeds had to be well concealed.[27]

No sooner were these arrangements made than the Nazi regime moved quickly against Sam Woods and his embassy colleagues. In the early morning hours of December 11th, the day Hitler declared war on the United States, Gestapo agents came knocking on the doors of American correspondents and remaining embassy staff and rounded them up at the Alexanderplatz prison.[28] After being confined in a hotel outside Berlin for three days, the Americans were shunted on board a special train that took them to the southern German spa of Bad Nauheim, outside Frankfurt. They were to be held there indefinitely in retaliation for the detention of German diplomats in the United States. Sam Woods and his wife Milada were among the 134 Americans who, bone-weary and cold, arrived at the once-luxurious but now-abandoned and unheated Jeschke's Grand Hotel, facing an uncertain future.[29]

Hoping to be quickly exchanged, the journalists and Foreign Service officers instead languished for five tedious months at Bad Nauheim, neglected and seemingly forgotten by their government. An American island inside Hitler's wartime Reich, they faced a peculiar fate. Entrusted to the care of a solicitous Gestapo officer, the internees were treated courteously (served at dinner by waiters in tails) and reasonably well, given the spartan state of their quarters. The Americans were even allowed to leave the spa hotel for supervised winter hikes, sports, and church services.[30] Within the Grand Hotel they could run their own affairs. Under George Kennan's supervision, strict rules of decorum befitting "normal times in any first-class hotel with a high-class clientele" were enforced: gentlemen were expected to wear coats and ties and conduct themselves civilly, and the rooms and lounge were to be kept immaculate (a task left to Sam Woods to oversee).[31] To make up for the poor fare served in the dining room, Woods, the group's acknowledged "trencherman," somehow procured two trunkloads of provisions from the embassy's canteen.[32]

As the weeks slowly passed, not the Nazis but boredom became the Americans' greatest enemy. To ward this off, some of the journalists tossed empty wine bottles at their guards' feet and once dropped a cuspidor down several flights of stairs in a prank worthy of a college fraternity.[33] (The Germans dourly noted this as a sign of "prison psychosis."[34]) Now and then the internees got under the Germans' skin, as when Woods and a few reporters flew a kite outside the hotel. They were sharply reprimanded for trying to communicate with "enemy aircraft."[35]

In fact, the internees were secretly keeping in touch with the outside world. Edwin Shanke, an Associated Press correspondent from Milwaukee, had managed to slip a battery-operated RCA Victor radio past the Gestapo.[36] Each evening a small knot of Americans, including Woods, would gather in Shanke's room, ostensibly for choir practice but actually to listen to the nightly BBC news broadcast.[37] When the batteries were almost used up, Woods had his wife Milada obtain new ones by writing to relatives in Prague, saying they were needed for a flashlight. Unsuspicious, the Nazis allowed the batteries to come through—and with them, more news about the war that was raging all around them.[38]

Woods himself did not attract any particular Gestapo attention. (He secretly expressed his hatred of the Nazis by pouring water on the hotel carpets nightly, to make them turn moldy.) And among his compatriots at Bad Nauheim, the friendly commercial attaché preserved his image as a jovial and generous *bon vivant*, appreciated for keeping others' spirits up, lending a pair of shoes to a needy reporter,[39] and looking after the group's culinary needs. (In one of the Americans' skits, the dining room was dubbed the "Sam E. Woods Memorial Hall" in ironic tribute to his reputation as a gourmand.[40]) There was some gossip about Woods's being mixed up in espionage, but Jeschke's Grand Hotel was rife with implausible rumors that spring, and no one really paid them much heed.

For Erwin Respondek, life in Germany was far more perilous. He was a marked man, alone without his American friends. After observing his movements and dealings with Woods for many months, the Gestapo was ready to pounce. In the chilly predawn darkness of January 10, 1942, secret police agents rang the doorbell at Mariannenstrasse 3, rousing everyone. By a stroke of nearly disastrous bad luck, they had come at precisely the wrong time.

The night before Respondek had worked late at his large, cluttered desk on the first floor, finalizing documents to be sent on to Woods.

Tired and foolishly incautious, he had slipped these papers inside a briefcase, carried it down to the basement, but then neglected to return the case to its usual hiding place. Realizing this, with the Gestapo standing literally on her doorstep, Charlotte Respondek did some fast thinking. Somehow she had to gain some time. Would the gentlemen mind waiting just a minute? The two maids, she said, were still asleep down in the basement. They would be badly frightened if strangers were suddenly to appear in their bedroom. Could she go downstairs first and wake them? The Gestapo agents consented to this. Charlotte hurried down the cellar steps, grabbed the incriminating briefcase, and took it up the back stairs and out into the yard, where she concealed it inside a garbage can. Then she alerted the maids and returned to the front door. They could start their search now, she told the Gestapo.[41]

While his house was being searched, other secret police agents placed Respondek under arrest and drove him away to prison. Files in his Charlottenstrasse office were pored over for evidence of his association with the U.S. embassy. Inside the Alexanderplatz prison, Respondek was led down a series of long corridors, with heavy steel doors clanging shut behind him, until he reached an interrogation room.[42] A crisply uniformed Gestapo officer was waiting for him, and he came straight to the point: "Do you know Sam Woods?" he demanded.[43] Keeping his composure and managing not to turn pale, Respondek admitted that he did. "You don't deny this?" shot back his startled interlocutor. "No," replied Respondek. "You know that you have stood in connection with the enemy number one of our state?"[44] Respondek made no attempt to deny this accusation either. His Gestapo questioner then pointed triumphantly to a thick stack of red-tinted portfolios lying on the table, each bearing the ominous insignia of the SS. "You can see that your file is very voluminous," he said. "Everything—all of your visits to the embassy and your personal meetings with Woods—is there. We have photographs and other materials. The documentation, you see, is very complete."[45]

Confronted with this damning evidence, Respondek coolly explained that his contacts with Woods and other Americans related to his professional work and, ultimately, to the "interest of Germany," since they touched upon such matters as U.S. export policy.[46] Inwardly confident that Woods had not betrayed him, and not intimidated by the Gestapo,[47] Respondek calmly stuck to his story. He gave nothing away, named no other names. The search of his office turned up nothing incriminating. All the Gestapo had uncovered were some documents describing Respondek's labors on behalf of German Jews, correspondence with his industrial clients, and other innocuous business papers. Repeated interrogations of Charlotte Respondek and her fifteen-year-old daughter, Dorothea, turned out to be just as fruitless. Finally, after holding him for several weeks, the secret police curtly informed Respondek they could not prove that his dealings with Sam Woods amounted to "high treason," and so they were letting him go.[48] Safe back home on the Mariannenstrasse, Respondek was immensely relieved. After this grueling experience he knew he had nothing to fear from the Gestapo as long as he made no mistakes in the future.

Several months later, in May 1942, Respondek ventured to approach the Swiss diplomat, Ochsenbein.[49] For the time being, Sam Woods was in no position to receive any reports from Berlin, as he was still a guest of the Gestapo at Bad Nauheim. But that situation was about to change. In the middle of the month the interned Americans were released and transported by special sealed trains across France and Spain to the neutral port of Lisbon. From there they sailed for home on board the SS *Drottningholm*.

When the liner docked in New York harbor on a cool, drizzly June 1st, it was placed under quarantine. One of the first persons allowed on board was Jack Erhardt, head of foreign personnel for the State Department. He located Woods and told him that he and Milada were to take the first train straight to Washington. The commercial attaché assumed he must be in some kind of trouble with the government. But, no, he was being summoned to see his boss, Secretary of State Cordell Hull. At Union Station the Woodses were met by an old Washington friend, Congressman Luther Johnson of Texas.[50] Johnson was a staunch New Dealer, then the second-ranking member of the House Foreign Affairs Committee. This is how Woods described what happened next:

After breakfast, Congressman Johnson accompanied me to the Department, where I was informed that Assistant Secretary of State Long wished to see me. After a short conversation with him he stated that the Secretary wished to speak to me, and he, Congressman Johnson, and I went to the Secretary's office. The Secretary greeted all of us very cordially and then said he wished to congratulate me on the reports I had sent him from Berlin before the outbreak of hostilities, which, he was good enough to say, were among the most helpful received from the entire Foreign Service during the year.... Mr. Hull was then kind enough to say that he was thinking of recommending my name for a citation, whereupon I asked him not to do this, as it would possibly arouse a certain amount of curiosity, with consequent publicity. (I did, however, ask him to prepare a personal memorandum for my file with the Department.) Then, after explaining the arrangement I had made for communicating with Ralph [Respondek's code name], I suggested that I might be assigned to some post near the German frontier. Mr. Hull replied that he thought this should be done and said that I could go to Stockholm, Bern, Lisbon, or Madrid. As I had always worked in a Legation or Embassy, I asked to be assigned to a Consulate. Mr. Hull then inquired which was the nearest Consulate to the German frontier and was informed that Basel was on the border between Switzerland and Germany. He then asked which was the nearest Consulate General and when he was told that this was Zurich, he stated that I would be assigned there as Consul General. He then suggested that I speak to Secretaries Long and [Adolf] Berle about the details of my return and added that any reports which I might receive from Ralph should be sent to the Department through the Legation in the most secret code, marked for the attention of Assistant Secretaries Berle and Long.[51]

Before he left Washington for a vacation with relatives and friends in Mississippi, Woods also spoke with Adolf Berle. A onetime corporate "whiz kid" who had drafted much of the New Deal's banking and securities legislation, Berle was then overseeing Latin American affairs. He proposed to Woods that Respondek's statistics on German strategic supplies be leaked to neutral countries, with hints that this information had fallen into Allied hands as a result of Goering's carelessness.[52] Berle's idea was to drive a deeper wedge between Hitler and the Reichsmarschall, so that Goering might be dismissed or shot. Woods rightly pointed out such a ploy would almost certainly lead to Respondek's arrest and removal as an intelligence source,[53] and so this scheme was shelved.

After a month's rest in the South, the peripatetic commercial attaché returned to the capital for a final briefing before sailing for Europe. In the interim, tensions within the State Department had reached the boiling point. Hull had intimated to Long that he could no longer trust Sumner Welles, who was "laying plans for himself," namely to take over Hull's job.[54] In this rancorous atmosphere Woods conferred again with Long and the secretary of state, and he was assured he would receive the full cooperation of the U.S. minister in Switzerland, Leland Harrison, in carrying out his intelligence work. Then, on July 29th, his instructions firmly in mind, Woods caught a train out of Washington for New York to start the next chapter in his remarkable wartime career.

His departure came at a momentous juncture in the war. In the deserts of North Africa, Rommel's Afrika Korps had captured the British stronghold of Tobruk. On the Russian front, General von Kleist's Army Group B was converging on Stalingrad. But the Germans' glory days of lightning-quick conquests were over. Everywhere the once-invincible Wehrmacht was bogged down, opposed by stiffening resistance, its losses mounting. The war was going to drag on longer than Hitler had predicted, and the Allies now had opportunities to seize the upper hand. Intelligence gathering would play a significant role in this, and Sam Woods, at his diplomatic listening post in Zurich, would be one of the more important practitioners of this clandestine craft.

Mountainous, landlocked, neutral Switzerland had made itself a free zone where agents from both sides could discreetly set up espionage operations, monitor developments in the war, collect information—and keep an eye on each other. Under cover of wartime blackouts, shadowy intrigues were ubiquitous and plentiful, involving spies sent there by

Admiral Canaris's Abwehr (military intelligence) and Walter Schellenberg's rival Sicherheitsdienst (security agency), upper-crust British agents, French resistance fighters, well-to-do German émigrés, seasoned Polish and Russian intelligence officers, rabidly pro-Nazi Swiss Frontists, lone figures like Rudolf Roessler, and a host of dubious characters of every description and nationality who thrived in this tangled web of ambiguous loyalties, heroic daring, greed, stealth, and raw cunning—all watched over by the superb Swiss intelligence service. Now the Americans were joining in, too.

Before the Second World War, U.S. espionage was largely an amateur affair. An intelligence buff, Roosevelt had simply asked several of his wealthy, well-traveled friends, such as Kermit Roosevelt, Vincent Astor, and Nelson Doubleday, to keep him posted on secret military, political, and economic developments.[55] The outbreak of war in 1939 had rendered this informal information-gathering network obsolete: what the United States needed now was a professional organization capable of systematically collecting and evaluating vital military intelligence, to protect U.S. interests around the world and, eventually, to aid the U.S. war effort. To achieve this end, the president summoned his former Columbia Law School classmate William "Wild Bill" Donovan to the White House in June 1941 and persuaded him to head up a new Office of the Coordinator of Information.[56] An ex-Wall Street lawyer and the most highly decorated American soldier in the First World War, Donovan set about assembling his intelligence apparatus, relying heavily at first on assistance from the British Secret Intelligence Service.[57] Soon he was recruiting his own elite corps of young, "calculatingly reckless" agents.[58] Within little over a year the COI had acquired another innocuous title— the Office of Strategic Services (OSS)—and become a highly active, if flamboyant and controversial, arm of U.S. intelligence. Its Yale- and Harvard-educated agents were dispatched to far corners of the globe, where they spent bales of money, performed daring feats of infiltration, and wired back mounds of cables to OSS headquarters. Donovan had a flair for the bold and the outlandish, and many of his wartime schemes displayed a kind of boyish exuberance about what it was possible for secret agents to accomplish. All too often, the OSS's yield of solid, useful intelligence fell embarrassingly short of its claims and expectations.

Where Donovan was undoubtedly successful was in building a corps of bright, colorful, and capable young men to carry out his clandestine operations. Representative of their high caliber was the dapper, forty-nine-year-old Allen Welsh Dulles, tapped by his old friend Donovan in 1942 to run an OSS spy network based in Switzerland. As a State Department official Dulles had dabbled in cloak-and-dagger games decades before, when he had been sent to Bern tasked with collecting political information out of Germany and the collapsing Austro-Hungarian empire.[59] So when he boarded a transatlantic steamer with a bank draft for a million dollars tucked in his billfold and with the mission of establishing ties with Germans opposed to Hitler, the Princeton-educated international lawyer was returning to a line of work he knew and enjoyed.

Arriving in the Swiss capital, Dulles took up residence conspicuously in a four-story, seventeenth-century patrician house atop the cobblestoned Herrengasse, commanding a panoramic view of the Alps and the swift-flowing Aare River far below. From this headquarters Dulles began putting out feelers for useful informants and collaborators.

Roosevelt's "special representative" was not the only American in Switzerland bent on obtaining valuable information from inside the Third Reich. Sam Woods had preceded Dulles by three months, and his well-connected and highly reliable source was already firmly in place. Accompanied by his wife, Woods had arrived on August 19th, eager to carry out the secret mission given him by Cordell Hull. Unfortunately, the newly appointed consul general got off to a bad start. Before going on to Zurich, Woods stopped off in Bern to pay a courtesy call on the U.S. minister, Leland Harrison, and brief him on the reason for Woods's being assigned to Switzerland.[60] Poles apart in temperament and background, the two men did not hit it off.

Harrison was a New York blueblood, a career diplomat on affectionate, first-name terms with the president (who called him "Nemo") and with such prominent members of the State Department's "old-boy" network as Sumner Welles, Alexander Kirk, and Harrison's predecessor at the U.S. legation, Hugh Wilson. Harrison had assumed his ministerial duties in 1937, after serving in Tokyo, Peking, London, Bogota, Paris, Stockholm, and Bucharest, and had found the pace of diplomatic life in this European haven sufficiently civilized and leisurely for him to want to stay on, despite the president's offer of an ambassadorship in Canada.[61] Now, with war engulfing Europe, Harrison found himself immersed in the more serious business of collecting intelligence. In the fall of 1941, for example, he sent Sumner Welles reports on German troops on the Russian front and on conditions inside the Reich.[62]

Known for what one acquaintance has termed a "Skull and Bones" snobbishness,[63] the senior U.S. diplomat in Switzerland might have been expected to size up this inexperienced, upstart new consul general from Mississippi with a jaundiced eye. And, indeed, their relationship began with a misunderstanding. Mistakenly believing that Harrison already knew why Washington had sent him,[64] Woods waited patiently over lunch for the minister to dispense with the small talk and get down to business. Harrison, for his part, wondered when the genial Southerner was going to brief him about his secret mission. Finally the two men did talk about it,[65] but a foundation for future cooperation was not firmly laid. The only advice Harrison gave Woods was not to contact Respondek right away—advice that the consul general wisely chose to heed.[66]

In 1942 Zurich was coping in a characteristically Swiss manner with the contradictions of its precarious wartime predicament. Situated flush against sausage-shaped Lake Zurich, its slender church spires, expensive boutiques, and elegant cafés crowded along the water's edge, its broad, tram-railed streets curving lazily uphill, this stolid center of world commerce and banking showed few visible signs of the conflict that was devastating the rest of Europe. Precisely at ten o'clock each night, in deference to the Germans, the city was plunged into darkness, but otherwise there was little to remind the newly arrived Woodses of embattled Berlin. Pork, eggs, chocolate, and other goods were rationed, but the windows of Zurich's butcher shops and grocery stores looked like a cornucopia compared to what could be found elsewhere on the continent. Zurichers' fears of a German invasion reached a fever pitch following the fall of France but then subsided as Hitler elected to use threats and intimidation to get his way with the Swiss.[67]

Zurich was bombed once, by accident, just before Christmas that year, leaving one person dead and several buildings damaged, but other than that the city experienced the war vicariously, through cinema newsreels depicting the fighting in Russia, followed by the latest comedy from Laurel and Hardy.[68] Mostly, Zurichers felt the conflict's impact through the stream of tattered, suitcase-toting refugees who sought a temporary haven there, escaping from France and other occupied countries,[69] bringing with them lurid tales of a growing European nightmare.

German influence on Zurich was strong, but there was no great local enthusiasm for the Nazi cause. A rally of several thousand Reichsdeutsche on October 4, 1942, marked the high point of Nazi efforts to indoctrinate the Swiss, but it only ended up causing a storm of protest.

As America's chief envoy in the city, Sam Woods was warmly welcomed. His outgoing, big-hearted manner and Southern charm quickly won him the friendship of many of Zurich's civic and business leaders, none of whom had any inkling of Woods's real reason for being in Switzerland. Along with Milada, his mother-in-law, and a prized Airedale, the fifty-year-old consul general settled down in a stately, doric-columned house on the quiet, treelined Toblerstrasse, high on the slope of the Zürichberg, looking down on the sparkling lake, surrounded by trees and lush gardens.[70] To the Woodses life in Zurich was "paradise" after the dreariness and dread of Nazi Berlin. The couple built up a wide circle of Swiss and American friends, entertaining them with cocktails and greatly appreciated American layer cakes. Most of these were purely social acquaintances—people for whom Woods would obtain extra ration coupons or look up relatives when he was vacationing in the

States.[71] But the new consul general also soon came into contact with individuals in Zurich who were quietly fighting against Hitler.

One of these was the publisher Emil Oprecht. Founder of the Europa Verlag, Oprecht had brought out the works of such Nazi-banned emigré German authors as Thomas Mann. Politically liberal, Oprecht became a key liaison for anti-Nazi Germans, Swiss, and other foreigners. They congregated at his apartment over his bookstore, located almost directly across the street from the German consulate, to talk politics and conspire.[72] Starting in 1942, the idealistic Swiss publisher put Woods in touch with several well-informed German refugees, as well as with Swiss working to defeat the Hitler regime.[73]

Through other ties to the Swiss police and knowledgeable anti-Nazis, cultivated with help from his German-speaking wife,[74] Woods began amassing intelligence on the German resistance, the German homefront, war developments, and Nazi scientific research.[75] In mid-November, the consul general was told by his well-connected aide, Maurice Altaffer, about the plans of dissident army officers to oust Hitler and set up a new government. This was the first news the U.S. government had of this opposition circle and its Operation Flash scheduled for March 1943.[76] Not all of Woods's reports proved to be so valuable, however. In November he passed along to Harrison inaccurate, second-hand information about Mussolini's being seriously ill with a lung ailment,[77] and the following March he forwarded erroneous news of Hitler's having been wounded during a fray at his eastern field headquarters.[78]

Reading these cables at his Bern office, Harrison was unimpressed. To him, Woods was a rank amateur, unfamiliar with Switzerland, inept at intelligence gathering. The U.S. minister was exasperated by having to sift through an avalanche of seemingly unimportant messages that kept coming out of Zurich.[79] (On one December report describing German metal shortages, a peeved Harrison scribbled, "This letter reads like an article from *Reader's Digest*."[80]) Harrison's opinion of Woods was shared by many U.S. Foreign Service officers in Switzerland, who considered him simply a political appointee, not really up to the demands of his job.[81]

Allen Dulles took a more charitable view. William Donovan's man in Bern had heard about the Mississippian's intelligence channel into Nazi Germany at some point in 1942, and he may have brought it up when he first conferred with Leland Harrison, in November. A relentlessly curious man, Dulles never disparaged or turned his back on a good source,[82] and so, overlooking their personal differences, he came to respect Woods's intelligence work. The two stayed on good terms throughout their years in Switzerland,[83] even though they had few direct dealings.[84] In his seeming naivete and garrulousness, Woods struck

Dulles (as well as the Office of War Information's chief in Switzerland, Gerald Mayer, and Dulles's American assistant, Mary Bancroft) as a bit of a "clown"—an amusing, awkward, and miscast character who, nonetheless, was doing valuable work.[85] (Mrs. Bancroft once overheard Woods deriding Swiss neutrality: "What?" he exclaimed. "You mean you are in favor of bombing babies?"[86] She also recalls a more poignant side of the consul general's personality. One afternoon she spotted a lone Woods strolling desultorily up the Bahnhofstrasse, clutching a bunch of brightly colored balloons. When she stopped him and asked whom they were for, Woods, separated from his own daughter for so many years, told her he was looking for a child who might like them.)

At times Woods's extroverted manner got him into some awkward situations. One rainy day he was driving through Zurich when he spotted a man standing at a tram stop, getting thoroughly drenched. The consul general pulled over, opened the door, and offered the man a ride. The stranger looked painfully embarrassed, shook his head, and refused to budge. But Woods insisted, and finally the man climbed in. It turned out this reluctant passenger was the German consul general, Carl Dienstmann.[87]

The Germans in Switzerland did not take Woods all that seriously. In part, this was because neither the Abwehr nor the Sicherheitsdienst understood U.S. intelligence operations in Switzerland. For instance, although the Germans knew that Dulles was a key player, as late as 1944 they still believed his role was to lay the groundwork for a new "economy of Europe after the war."[88] Underestimating the Americans' wide circle of contacts, German intelligence officers concluded their information came chiefly from Swiss journalists.[89] The Germans did figure out that Woods was gathering intelligence, but they believed this was limited to economic matters.[90]

Characteristically, the consul general did all he could to throw the Germans—and everyone else—off his tracks. A dozen years of diplomatic service in sophisticated European capitals had not diminished Woods's ability to play the country bumpkin when it suited his purposes to do so. Mary Bancroft remembers asking Woods about a weekend he had spent away from Zurich. He told her he had gone to Lugano, when, in fact, he had visited Locarno, presumably to pick up information. Woods made a point of mixing up names and other facts deliberately to create the impression he could not keep them straight.[91]

All this intelligence work only served as a prelude for Woods's resuming his contact with Erwin Respondek. This did not happen right away. Taking Harrison's advice, Woods made no attempt to send a message to Berlin. He had to assume Respondek had discovered, via Ochsenbein, where he was and how to reach him. For the next several months Woods impatiently waited for a sign from Respondek, not knowing anything about the latter's arrest by the Gestapo in January or about the extra precautions his German friend had had to take since then.

In October of 1942 Respondek received what he was to describe as an intriguing offer from Washington. Returning from a summer vacation in Switzerland (where he likely met with Sam Woods[92]), Ochsenbein got in touch with Respondek and told him the U.S. State Department intended to reward him after the war with a high-level position commensurate with his stature "as a distinguished politician and former member of Parliament."[93] This promise filled an emotionally and financially drained Respondek with pride and hope and inspired him to redouble his information-gathering efforts.[94]

Drawing upon his usual high-level sources within various Reich ministries and his conversations with other officials, Respondek put together for Woods a status report on current conditions inside Germany. He then approached Ochsenbein about ferreting this information out of the country. The two came up with the scheme of using Catholic priests—or men posing as priests[95]—as couriers between Berlin and Zurich.[96] One raw December day, with papers for Sam Woods concealed on his person, the first of these messengers slipped out of Berlin, bound for Zurich.

Just before New Year's, Sam Woods donned his bulky overcoat, left his consular offices at Bahnhofstrasse 3, near the quays, and started walking toward his car for the short drive home. On the way he had a strange encounter:

As I approached my car I noticed a priest standing near by, who came towards me after I had entered the car and asked in English if I were Sam Woods. When I replied in the affirmative he said that he had a message for me from my friend in Berlin. I told him that I had many friends there when I left, whereupon he asked if I did not have a special friend whose name began with "R." I said "Yes" and asked if he had any way of identifying himself, to which he answered: "I have a piece of lace."[97]

Convinced by this, Woods beckoned the "priest" inside his car and drove him in silence up the Zürichberg to his home on the Toblerstrasse. There, to overcome the courier's own wariness, Woods produced his matching lace collar, given to Milada before they left Berlin. The "priest"—who refused to reveal anything about his identity, for fear of compromising others[98]—then handed the American a sheaf of papers.

As soon as the messenger departed Woods eagerly sat down and read through this long-awaited report from his German confidant. In it, Respondek sounded a sobering note: tighter security controls, especially within the military and Nazi Party, were making it much harder for him to obtain reliable information. Conditions had changed dramatically since he had last seen Woods in December 1941. A prolonged war was "seeping up the vital assets and life of Germany." Hitler's strategy now "centered on savage and unrestrained warfare to the finish."[99] Respondek's two "most trusted associates" in the German military did not expect peace any time within the near future. Stymied by the "undefeatable" Russians in the east[100] and pressured by the Americans in the west, the Wehrmacht was going to withdraw gradually on all fronts. As Respondek correctly foresaw, this deliberately brutal retreat would "mean millions dying of hunger, general destruction of Europe through the scorched earth policy, and unbelievable persecution and death."[101]

Respondek's intimates within the NSDAP feared Italy would soon quit the Axis alliance, thereby greatly weakening Germany's southern defensive perimeter. If Mussolini failed to prevent this from happening, the Germans would resort to carrying out actions on their own, murdering all Italians who were not firmly pro-Nazi, including, as Respondek laconically put it, "the Pope and his personnel."[102] In realigning his troops, a desperate Hitler would no longer respect neutrality: the Swiss could expect a German invasion. Respondek was sure this was how the Nazis intended to protect their vulnerable "underbelly."

With New Year's celebrations in full swing in Zurich, Woods's secretary dashed off an English paraphrase of this alarming report. Aided by his close associate and fellow Southerner Robert T. Cowan, the consul general had it typed and encoded for transmission to Leland Harrison, to be forwarded to the State Department.[103] Sadly, it would prove prophetic: its stark picture of a tenacious German resistance was exactly what Allied forces in late 1944 would encounter.

At great personal risk, Respondek had succeeded in restoring his intelligence channel to Sam Woods and Washington. Important as this latest news was, it would pale by comparison with what he would have to report during the coming year. Then he would tell of progress toward a new German secret weapon so powerful it might miraculously change the course of the war in Hitler's favor: the atomic bomb.

8

PURLOINING GERMANY'S ATOMIC SECRETS

The early twentieth century was a revolutionary epoch for physics. And no nation dominated scientific advance in this field as did Germany. For there it was, in 1900, that Max Planck laid the groundwork for all of modern physics by formulating his quantum theory of energy transfer. It was there, too, that Albert Einstein was born and first schooled, and where, at the height of his international fame, he returned, at Planck's urging, to assume a prestigious post at the University of Berlin.[1] And it was the scientifically progressive Weimar Republic that spawned, or nurtured, most of the century's most illustrious physicists: Max von Laue, who devised a way of measuring X-ray wave lengths; Wolfgang Pauli, "father" of the neutrino; Werner Heisenberg, formulator of the "uncertainty principle"; Max Born; Lise Meitner; Edward Teller; and, as a graduate student, J. Robert Oppenheimer. With its peerless Kaiser Wilhelm Gesellschaft (boasting 15 Nobel prize winners), Prussian Academy of Sciences, and illustrious university, Berlin occupied center stage in German physics.

To these elite scientific bastions Erwin Respondek enjoyed a privileged access. Through a variety of personal connections, he was able to keep abreast of German experimental progress—knowledge shared with few persons outside the scientific community. After 1939, this knowledge would extend to war-related projects. Those would include research relating to an atomic bomb. From Respondek, the Americans would receive news about German progress in the race to produce the most devastating explosive device the world had ever seen.

Respondek's oldest and principal scientific tie was to Max Planck. His brother, Georg, was one of the few students selected to study and earn a Ph.D. under the bald-headed, reserved classical physicist at the University of Berlin.[2] He introduced Erwin as a young schoolboy to the famous scientist and his family. When Respondek was working for the Finance Ministry immediately after the First World War, he lived for nearly two years in Planck's spacious Grunewald villa.[3] He also served as a surrogate son during a time of tragic personal loss for Planck.[4] (One of the physicist's sons was also named Erwin.) Their friendship would endure until Planck's death in 1947. Through the world-famous physicist, Respondek came to know other eminent German scientists, including Otto Hahn and Werner Heisenberg, who were deeply involved in atomic research.[5] But it was from Planck himself that he first heard about German advances in this area.[6]

Hermann Muckermann was a second valuable source. From his years at the Kaiser Wilhelm Society prior to 1933,[7] the onetime Jesuit knew numerous scientists all over Germany. Many of these colleagues he may well have introduced to Respondek before the Nazis came to power. Now semiretired, Muckermann participated in the resistance activities of Respondek's circle. (Once the Gestapo nearly caught him with some highly sensitive papers. Muckermann had received a list of the persons slated to take over ministerial posts after a successful coup against Hitler. That same day secret police came calling at his home in Frohnau. Luckily, Muckermann's Scotch terrier began barking at the approaching Gestapo agents, and his housekeeper was able to toss the papers into the furnace just in the nick of time.[8])

But Respondek's most valuable confederate in purloining German atomic secrets was Herbert (Rainer) Müller,[9] one of his few close friends. To this day Müller remains a mysterious, shadowy figure. Little is known about his life and career, other than that he was born, a Protestant, on August 29, 1907, studied law at the University of Berlin, and then married and established a home in Charlottenburg. He was an easy-going, quiet, intelligent man with a love for literature and music and something of a romantic temperament.[10] He was also crafty and duplicitous, a person who could easily blur his loyalties, both personal and political. (During the war he and Charlotte Respondek carried on an affair, more or less under their spouses' noses.[11] Many years later his secretary would remember Müller as a person who could easily have worked "for both sides."[12]) In June 1934, at the age of twenty-six, Müller joined the Institute for Foreign and International Civil Law, a center for legal research affiliated with the Kaiser Wilhelm Society. Subsequently, Müller served as temporary director of this institute while advising the central administration on legal matters.[13] He published papers on such topics as German administration of justice in the context of international civil law and reform of guarantor law in Switzerland.[14] In his administrative role

Müller was well positioned to stay in touch with scientific progress in many fields, including atomic physics. After 1938 he also took advantage of his Kaiser Wilhelm Society posts to shield politically suspect scientists from attacks and dismissal.[15] In addition, Müller endeavored to erect obstacles for those German scientists working on an atomic bomb, while he passed on details about their research to Erwin Respondek.[16]

On top of these sources, Respondek could count on his long-standing professional ties to such scientist-industrialists as Carl Duisberg, Hermann Bücher, Wilhelm Kalle, and Carl Bosch for privileged information concerning German weaponry.[17] And as was noted earlier, his anti-Nazi son-in-law, Friedrich Hoffmann, was fully informed about German experiments involving poison gas.

Earlier Respondek had made use of these ties to prepare for Sam Woods a synopsis of scientific work inside the Reich, which touched upon ongoing experiments in nuclear fission.[18] But there was one sensational piece of news he kept from his American friends. It concerned two of the largest and most powerful industrial firms in the world—one German, the other American—and their secret pact to exchange scientific findings. It was an agreement that would stay in force until the final months of the war and remain concealed long thereafter.

The Delaware-based chemical giant Du Pont had long sought a cooperative arrangement with German companies. As early as 1919 Du Pont executives had broached such a proposal on dyestuffs with Carl Bosch, the inventor of synthetic ammonia, future founder of IG Farben, and then chairman of the board of Badische Anilin und Soda Fabrik.[19] But the wily Bosch, who saw little advantage in sharing German expertise with the Americans, rebuffed this bid. Undaunted, Du Pont persisted in its attempts to acquire German technical know-how after IG Farben was created in 1925. The following year, in Hamburg, Du Pont officials signed a secret "gentlemen's agreement" with two Farben subsidiaries, Dynamit Aktien Gesellschaft and Köln Rottweiler—both major explosives manufacturers—granting each party a first option on new processes and products, such as black powder and safety and powder fuses.[20]

Although unable to achieve the same kind of comprehensive cartel arrangement it had already signed with the British Imperial Chemical company,[21] Du Pont did invest some $3 million in the German armaments industry in the 1920s, thereby gaining a large lead over its U.S. competitors. In 1929, quite possibly as the result of a hush-hush Mediterranean cruise its top executives took with counterparts from IG Farben and Imperial Chemical,[22] Du Pont signed another pact with the German conglomerate.[23] In 1933, with Hitler now in power, officers of the American company went so far as to agree to sell the Germans "military propellants and military explosives"—in clear violation of both the Versailles Treaty and the peace treaty between the United States and Germany.[24] This happened despite a warning from a Du Pont executive in Germany that it was "common knowledge" that IG Farben was bankrolling the Nazis.[25] Lammot Du Pont, the company's president, wisely scrapped this agreement before it was formally signed,[26] even though he continued to hope he could circumvent these legal restrictions.

Reports of Du Pont's secret cartel pacts with IG Farben and other European firms were aired at the Senate's munitions hearings in 1934. A solemn and dignified parade of Du Pont family executives—Lammot, Felix, Pierre, and Irénée—flatly denied the existence of any such arrangements until documents were introduced in evidence that described a cartel pact on explosives with Imperial and several German firms.[27] These embarrassing revelations notwithstanding, Du Pont cultivated further ties with IG Farben during the Nazi years, making available licenses in acrylates and nitrogenous products, and then, in 1938, giving the German chemical manufacturer important processes necessary for the manufacture of buna rubber[28]—an important, newly developed synthetic substance for making tires. These exchanges of strategically important industrial know-how continued even though they violated U.S. neutrality laws and even though President Roosevelt was warned about them by his ambassador in Berlin, William Dodd.[29] Despite the outbreak of war, Du Pont went on negotiating trade agreements with Farben until 1941, when its board finally voted to sell its stock in the German firm[30] and "suspend" patent exchanges until "the present emergency has passed."[31]

But it was soon revealed that IG Farben had kept a toehold in the lucrative U.S. market through its 90 percent ownership of the New York–based firm General Aniline and Film Corporation. This "dummy" front controlled $11.5 million of assets in American firms, including Du Pont.[32] This news caused quite a stir in the press and in Washington and led to both seizure of General Aniline's assets, under the Trading with the Enemy Act,[33] and to a 1943 indictment of Du Pont, along with two other American companies, for engaging in a worldwide conspiracy to control strategically important metals. (Du Pont was eventually convicted.) The Delaware firm was brought back into court in January 1944 charged as a co-conspirator in cartel agreements governing explosives. (All told, 15 separate legal actions were brought against Du Pont for its cartel ties. The company lost eight cases and was fined a total of $323,000, out of a possible $4 million.[34])

According to Respondek, it was in this context that Du Pont's best-concealed pact with IG Farben was forged. At some point shortly before Hitler came to power, the leadership of Du Pont worked out an agreement with their peers at IG Farben whereby the two firms would regularly exchange the results of experiments conducted in their laboratories "so that in this regard no secrets would exist between the

United States and Germany."[35] In Germany this pact was known only to Carl Duisberg, chairman of IG's Aufsichtsrat; Carl Bosch, then chairman of the board; Geheimrat Hermann Schmitz, Bosch's chief financial advisor and the person who set up Farben's "camouflaged" control of companies in the United States and elsewhere; Dr. Wilhelm Kalle; three or four other top IG directors; and the trusted financial advisor who had helped draw up the agreement, Erwin Respondek.[36]

The outbreak of hostilities between Germany and the United States in December 1941 did not affect this pact. As Respondek explained after the war, IG Farben "supplied Du Pont with information, in the greatest detail, before the war and during the German–American conflict up until January/February 1945, by means of a secure route through Basel."[37] (In all likelihood the Basel connection was IG Chemie, a Farben "cloak" for its worldwide interests, established in Switzerland in 1929 and headed by Hermann Schmitz.[38]) The highly confidential papers IG Farben sent to Du Pont—and received from it—were kept "locked in a special safe, to which no one in the company had access other than three or four special directors."[39]

This purported industrial alliance raises some disturbing questions about German knowledge of U.S. military secrets. For Du Pont and IG Farben were heavily involved in extremely sensitive war-related research and development. During the First World War, a German chemist by the name of Walter Heldt had perfected a poison gas known as Zyklon B for use as a delousing agent.[40] Production of this gas was now in the hands of the Deutsche Gesellschaft für Schädlungs-Bekämpfung (DE-GESCH, or the German Society for Pest Control), which was 42.5 percent controlled by IG Farben. When the Nazis began to carry out their "Final Solution" by setting up gas chambers in 1942, it was to DEGESCH they turned for the deadly Zyklon B.[41]

For this, Farben executives were indicted by a Nuremberg war crimes tribunal. Ultimately they were exonerated on the grounds that it was impossible to prove the German directors had known how the gas was being used.[42]

For its part, Du Pont was the leading American business partner in creating an even more terrifying weapon—the atomic bomb. General Leslie Groves, head of the Manhattan Project, had approached Du Pont officers in November 1942 to seek their help in manufacturing the uranium slugs and other materials required to trigger the bomb. By agreeing to do so—for the fee of one dollar—Du Pont eventually built and operated all the major installations in the Manhattan Project, including the Clinton Engineer Works in Oak Ridge, Tennessee, where uranium 235 and plutonium 239 were developed.

There is no known evidence that Du Pont informed IG Farben about its atomic research, or that Farben told Du Pont about its large-scale production of Zyklon B gas, but the comprehensive nature of their wartime scientific exchange makes this conceivable. Certainly Respondek implied many years afterward that information about chemical and bacteriological weapons was, indeed, exchanged.[43]

Whether or not the U.S. government ever learned of this secret IG Farben–Du Pont link remains in doubt. According to Respondek, an elderly Wilhelm Kalle spoke with him in December 1945 at the industrialist's summer home on Lake Starnberg[44] and urged Respondek to intervene with Cordell Hull to head off an anticipated prosecution of IG's directors for having knowingly furnished the SS with poison gas. At that time Kalle reminded Respondek of the Du Pont connection. Respondek promised he would notify Ambassador Robert Murphy of their conversation when he returned to Berlin.[45] Details of the Farben–Du Pont pact were then allegedly contained in a report sent by Murphy to the State Department just after Christmas of that year.[46] After some time elapsed, Respondek learned

that the report was confirmed and that satisfaction was expressed with it. The Du Pont company confirmed the statements of Dr. Kalle. This was of some importance for the announced industrial trial . . . [but] the charge against IG on account of the alleged shippings of poison gas to eliminate the unfortunate victims of Auschwitz could not be conclusively proven in any case.[47]

Given all of Respondek's connections to leading German scientists and his skill at exploiting them, it is not surprising that he should have found out about German atomic experiments. The scientists themselves, more concerned with the theoretical aspects of nuclear fission than with production of a weapon of mass destruction, did not shroud their work in secrecy. In the Third Reich, atomic weapons were not initially regarded with very much enthusiasm. For one thing, Hitler was skeptical of them. (In his memoirs, Albert Speer emphasizes that the German Führer did not grasp the scientific principles involved and only spoke once or twice about the possibility of developing an atomic bomb. Noted Speer, "Hitler was plainly not delighted with the possibility that the earth under his rule might be transformed into a glowing star."[48]) As a result, in the mid-1930s information was freely available on German progress in this area.[49]

Inexorably, atomic physics research fell victim to Nazi racial phobia about "Jewish science."[50] Einstein and other prominent Jews were fired from their research posts. Even non-Jews sympathetic to the new physics were ousted, including the venerable Planck, who was pushed out of the leadership of the Kaiser Wilhelm Society in 1937 to bring it more in line with Nazi ideology and power structure.[51] But this growing intolerance did not stop Planck and other physicists from discussing what the chemists Otto Hahn and Fritz Strassmann had achieved in their Dahlem laboratory in late December 1938: the first successful splitting of the atom.[52] Worried that a "uranium bomb" might obliterate all of humankind,[53] the normally sanguine Planck confided his fears to Erwin Respondek.[54]

The Germans began seriously thinking about such a weapon at a time when the Wehrmacht was overrunning Poland. Spurred by a report on the possibility of making a bomb[55] and by indications that U.S. military authorities were already funding experiments that might yield atomic weapons, the Heereswaffenamt (Army Ordnance Office) called together a number of nuclear physicists, including Hahn, Heisenberg, Paul Harteck, Walther Bothe, and Carl-Friedrich von Weizsäcker, and asked them to study the feasibility of Germany's building its own nuclear explosive.[56] This research program was to be housed in the newly created Kaiser Wilhelm Institute for Physics, under the direction of Kurt Diebner, a thirty-four-year-old nuclear physicist.[57] As a result of experiments conducted by Weizsäcker during the summer of 1940, these German scientists concluded that "an energy-producing pile might be used for the production of an atomic explosive,"[58] even though considerable technical barriers would have to be overcome first.

The first problem was to construct a uranium pile, or atomic reactor, to test Weizsäcker's hypothesis. This took place in the fall in a wooden barracks on the grounds of the Institute for Biology and Virus Research, codenamed "The Virus House" to keep unwanted visitors away. A second obstacle—a shortage of heavy water (deuterium) to keep a nuclear chain reaction under control—was partially solved when German troops invaded Norway and captured, intact, the Norsk-Hydro plant at Vemork, the world's sole commercial producer of heavy water.[59] A third and far more formidable challenge lay in extracting sufficient quantities of the rare isotope in which fission occurred, uranium 235. Separation of this isotope from natural uranium could be achieved—as American researchers at Berkeley had demonstrated—by accelerating atomic particles magnetically inside a cyclotron. But here Germany was critically deficient, lagging far behind the United States. Nonetheless, on February 26, 1942, Heisenberg and his collaborator in Leipzig, Robert Döpel, reported favorably to the Uranverein (Nuclear Physics Research Group) of top atomic scientists on their progress toward achieving a controlled nuclear reaction that could produce an enormous amount of energy.[60]

This news excited Hitler's minister of education, Bernhard Rust, but failed to impress other top Nazi officials such as Himmler and Martin Bormann, who, due to a secretarial blunder, stayed away from this important, four-day conference on nuclear physics held at Harnack House.[61]

It was not until the spring of 1942 that Albert Speer was fully briefed on atomic research "on the track of a weapon which could annihilate whole cities"[62] and win the war for Germany. An intrigued Speer discussed this prospect with Hitler on May 6th, and from then on the armaments minister kept himself posted on experimental developments, culminating in his attendance at a session at Harnack House on June 6th. There Heisenberg pointed out that German atomic scientists still faced several "technical prerequisites," chiefly how to enrich the uranium 235 isotope.[63] Surmounting these would take at least another two years—probably too long to have any impact on the war's outcome.[64]

Until then German and American atomic programs had run neck-and-neck. But now a fateful fork in the road was reached. Convinced a bomb could help win the war, the Americans opted to press ahead vigorously with their Manhattan Project.[65] Differently advised by their scientists, the Germans virtually abandoned any hopes of devising an atomic explosive in the fall of 1942.[66] (After being offered a few million marks by the minister for armaments to pursue bomb-related research, Heisenberg said he did not know how to spend so much money. This remark eroded Speer's backing for the project.[67]) Instead, they shifted their research focus to building nuclear reactors to power German U-boats.[68]

From his friends in the Armaments Ministry, Respondek learned about the experiments conducted by Heisenberg, Weizsäcker, and other leading nuclear physicists and about creation of the elite Uranverein to coordinate their research.[69] In the summer of 1942, about the time Sam Woods was leaving Washington for Zurich, Respondek also found out about another highly classified atomic project. Contrary to what Speer would later maintain, this information indicated that the Armaments Ministry, bankrolled by German industry, was proceeding with experiments aimed at producing an atomic bomb as rapidly as possible.

These experiments were conducted in great secrecy, without the knowledge of the Uranverein scientists, and under Speer's personal supervision. The major funding came from the AEG—Germany's General Electric Company.

Respondek's informant was none other than his longtime mentor, the chairman of the AEG's governing board, Hermann Bücher. Formerly a botanist in the German colonial service,[70] Bücher had once been a staunch backer of trade unions and Weimar democracy.[71] He had deplored the rise of the Nazi Party, and when informed of Hitler's having been appointed chancellor, he had dourly remarked, "Et maintenant, tout est fini."[72] But in wartime the industrialist had a change of heart and threw his support wholeheartedly behind Hitler and his military efforts.[73] (Later on Bücher appears to have changed his mind again. By 1942 the SS's Ernst Kaltenbrunner suspected him of harboring "defeatist" views.[74] Two years afterward he was implicated in the plot to assassinate Hitler. Bücher was freed from prison—and saved from death—only as a result of Speer's personal intervention.[75])

This onetime friend of labor became, in the words of one historian, a "cynical fascist" who exorted his factory directors to meet backbreaking production levels and threatened them with a visit from the Gestapo if they did not do so. Bücher depended heavily on slave labor from German-occupied countries to meet the AEG's wartime quotas.[76] In 1942 he joined Hitler's Rüstungsrat, a military–industry advisory board for new weapons projects. Shortly thereafter, in a conversation with Respondek, the German industrialist casually announced that he held "in the hollow of his hand the world's most secret and most dangerous invention . . . by means of which, if successful, it will be possible to destroy England, Russia and the United States."[77] Bücher based this staggering boast on the work of a Swiss physicist then being financed by the AEG. His name was Walter Dällenbach.

Dällenbach was born in Burgdorf, near the Swiss capital, and studied electrical engineering at the Eidgenössische Technische Hochschule (Polytechnic Institute) in Zurich when Albert Einstein was lecturing there on theoretical physics. Dällenbach sat in on these lectures and fell under the spell of this humble and childlike genius. Soon he became a member of the coterie of Swiss disciples gathered around Einstein.[78] (Later in his career as a technical engineer, Dällenbach would draw heavily on the insights into basic physics he had acquired from the great German scientist.) After studying relativity theory in Zurich under Hermann Weyl, Dällenbach headed a research team for a Baden firm that developed a new and more efficient way of changing alternating current into direct current. To apply this method in industry, Dällenbach then took a position with a Berlin company, Julius Pintsch AG.[79] This was in 1931.

Over the next decade the Swiss physicist patented several commercially successful devices for receiving and transmitting electromagnetic waves. By February 1942 he had finished all his projects for Pintsch.[80] Since the Berlin firm was now almost exclusively involved with armaments projects, which he, as a foreigner, was barred from undertaking,[81] Dällenbach began looking around for a new avenue of research.[82] He happened to attend a lecture of Heisenberg's on the particle accelerator constructed by Ernest O. Lawrence at Berkeley.[83] This talk inspired Dällenbach to design a new kind of cyclotron.

For financial support for this particle accelerator he first turned to his former employer in Baden, Brown, Boveri & Company, but it could not come up with the needed capital. Then Dällenbach outlined his plan to Heisenberg,[84] who in May 1942 recommended the Swiss physicist and his project to the Speer ministry.[85] Considerable interest was expressed in the proposed cyclotron, both by the armaments industry and by the AEG. In December 1942 the AEG offered Dällenbach a contract to develop various devices "for atomic energy processes" and make them available for commercial production as soon as possible.[86] For this work he was to receive 3,500 Reichsmarks a month, along with the laboratory facilities and technical assistance necessary for erecting an "extremely high-voltage installation."[87] This facility would be used to propel electrons and heavier atomic particles more effectively up to nearly the speed of light: a standing wave of electrons was to be created inside a vacuum tube and then accelerated with help from an external magnetic field.[88]

With the aid of the head of research and development at the Speer ministry, Heisenberg, and Speer himself, who took a "great interest" in Dallenbach's work,[89] the Swiss engineer struck a more attractive deal with the Kaiser Wilhelm Society. This allowed him greater freedom to construct his new circular particle accelerator, or microtron. Technical support was to be furnished by the AEG, and funding entirely by the Armaments Ministry,[90] to which Dällenbach was to report directly on his progress.[91] To achieve his objective, Dällenbach was to be made head of a new institute for "technical physics" within the Kaiser Wilhelm Society, but this plan had to be dropped when it was realized that as a Swiss citizen Dällenbach was ineligible for such a post.[92] So, instead, an autonomous "Forschungsstelle D" (for Dällenbach) was created.

At Dällenbach's request, this research laboratory was erected on the former site of a textile factory in the tiny southern German village of Bisingen. (This was so that he could be close to the Swiss border in case—as he foresaw—the tide of battle turned against Germany.[93]) In July 1943 Dällenbach brought his scientific support team to Bisingen and began to construct his new cyclotron.[94] (Worried about increasing Allied air raids, top atomic scientists soon followed him southward to rural Württemberg.) There Heisenberg, Hahn, and other colleagues kept in touch with the Swiss physicist, though they had little idea of what he was doing.[95] They would not be the last ones to wonder.

9

A SCARE FOR
THE AMERICANS

Half a century later, the wartime research of this Swiss physicist remains controversial. Dällenbach himself has vehemently and repeatedly insisted that his cyclotron project was "basic research," unrelated to the war.[1] This assertion has been backed up by his friend at the Speer ministry, Johann Sommer,[2] and by the Kaiser Wilhelm Society's secretary, Ernst Telschow, who inspected the "Forschungsstelle D" at the end of the war.[3] On the other hand, rumors have persisted about Dällenbach's working on a "secret weapon of a devastating nature."[4] One has to wonder why Minister Speer and other top Nazi officials would have shown such keen personal interest in a project that offered no concrete military "pay off."[5] One has to wonder, too, why Hermann Bücher—a person in a position to know the facts—would have told Respondek that Dällenbach was developing an atomic weapon. It is, of course, entirely possible that in order to gain their backing, the politically adroit Swiss physicist managed to convince Speer, Bücher, and others that his work was of vital importance to the war, when it actually could not have helped the Germans win.[6]

The extreme secrecy that surrounded Dällenbach's research makes it difficult to reach a fair conclusion. During a 1943 discussion with Siemens officials about the building of cyclotrons in Germany, the pro-Nazi head of the Reich's Research Council, Abraham Esau, said he could not say anything specific about Dällenbach's work because of its confidential nature.[7] He could report only that the Bisingen apparatus was "similar to the cyclotron in principle, but relied on much higher voltage"—one million volts.[8] In the fall of 1944, in response to a government query, Karl Weimer, Dällenbach's assistant, acknowledged the work at "Forschungsstelle D" was important to the war. However, when Dällenbach returned from Switzerland, he immediately set about correcting that report.[9]

Although repeatedly claiming that as a Swiss citizen and former artillery officer he wanted nothing to do with Nazi weaponry, Dällenbach was a strong admirer of Hitler and his aggressive war. Paul Rosbaud, the Austrian spy who passed along German atomic secrets to the British, considered Dällenbach worse than the Nazis.[10] In 1940 Rosbaud met the Swiss scientist several times socially in Berlin and was dismayed by Dällenbach's support for the Nazi invasion of neighboring European countries.[11] Although Dällenbach declined to acquire German citizenship in 1939 (which would have made it easier for him to pursue war-related research), he also elected to stay in Berlin, receiving special permission from the Swiss ambassador to do so.[12]

Whatever its intent, Dällenbach's laboratory did not accomplish very much before Germany's collapse. When the first Alsos team, headed by the dashing Colonel Boris Pash, passed through the Bisingen area in its hunt for German nuclear scientists, they seized Dällenbach's facility but did not find its contents particularly interesting.[13] (Dällenbach himself was then conveniently absent, safe across the border in his native Switzerland.[14]) However, when a French team of scientists reached Bisingen just a few days later in April 1945, they found the uncompleted particle accelerator more intriguing.

The French physicists were led by Colonel Frédéric Joliot, son-in-law of the famous Curies and himself a Nobel laureate for being the first to produce artificial radiation. During the war Joliot fought with the French resistance. Now he was eager to absorb whatever progress the Western Allies and the Germans had made in nuclear fission to launch an atomic energy program in his own country. Under Joliot's supervision, the French scientists in Bisingen dismantled some of Dällenbach's equipment, including a one-megavolt electrostatic generator used for producing neutrons, and had them shipped back to France.[15] The French declared Dällenbach's work "war-related." (French interest in the Swiss physicist's project continued through the late 1950s.[16] But in Germany there was a decided coolness. At the bottom of a 1949 request on Dällenbach's behalf, Werner Heisenberg scribbled, "I urgently recommend against any further association between Dällenbach and the MPG [Max Planck Gesellschaft]."[17]) If Dällenbach's accelerator was to contribute to Germany's building an atomic bomb, it was most probably by producing enough of the required enriched uranium 235, or plutonium—the major stumbling block encountered by German scientists.[18] (This microtron may also have been intended to produce neutrons, useful for investigating the properties of uranium and other fissionable materials needed for either a reactor or a bomb.) But even a contemporary analysis of his proposal does not resolve the question of whether or not his device was intended to have such a pragmatic, short-term purpose.[19]

Across the Atlantic, the Americans knew surprisingly little about German atomic-bomb research. President Roosevelt had first been warned about such a threat by Albert Einstein in two letters, dated August 2, 1939, and March 7, 1940. Similar fears, in exaggerated form, had surfaced in the *New York Times*. But these worries subsided as the war spread across Europe, and no such weapon was used. In the interim, the Allies had picked up reports only of increased shipments of heavy water out of occupied Norway and some other fragmentary information.[20] This ignorance was to end in 1943—in part due to the famous "Oslo report," compiled and slipped out of Berlin by Paul Rosbaud,[21] and in part due to what Erwin Respondek was able to pass along to the Americans.

From Hermann Bücher, Herbert Müller, and other sources, Respondek, by the middle of 1942, found out about German industry's interest in atomic research.[22] Specifically, he learned about the AEG's backing of Dällenbach, who was regarded as a "Swiss frontist... accepted by the Gestapo as trustworthy for Germany."[23] Respondek's first response to these disturbing indications that Hitler might eventually use an atomic bomb against the Allies was to attempt to sabotage these plans. Working in concert with Müller within the Kaiser Wilhelm Gesellschaft, he sought to "check the influence of the AEG in this field of highest importance and... succeeded in doing so in as much as the further treatment of this subject 'atomic bomb' was taken over by the scientists of the Kaiser Wilhelm Gesellschaft."[24] Inside the society, Müller exploited his administrative post to bog down the research in red tape. As Woods told Cordell Hull, Müller sought to "paralyze the efforts of those earnestly working on the development of the bomb, to create confusion between the Speer Ministry, the Munitions Board, the industry, the AEG, and the Kaiser Wilhelm Institute [for Physics]."[25]

Respondek realized the Americans had to be told as well. During the fall and winter of 1942 he summarized all the facts on German atomic research that he and Müller had garnered, including the names of the principal scientists involved. Because of his fear of arrest and the highly sensitive nature of this information, Respondek exercised more than his usual caution: he used numerous subterfuges, first to assemble the data he needed and then to protect these papers from falling into Gestapo hands. Documents were stashed away in separate places and worked on only late at night on the Mariannenstrasse.[26]

To inform Sam Woods, Respondek once again turned to his trusted intermediary, the Swiss attaché August Ochsenbein. Early in May of 1943, when Germans were preoccupied with the bad news trickling out of North Africa, Ochsenbein arranged for another "priest" to make his way south over the Alps through Austria into Italy—an easier route than across the now closely watched Swiss–German frontier. Crossing the beautiful Lake Maggiore by ferry to Locarno, this courier stepped ashore and inside a phone booth and rang the number for the U.S. consulate in Zurich.[27] When Woods came on the line, he was told "his friend" had a message for him. If the U.S. diplomat could arrange to be in Locarno by eight o'clock that evening, the "priest" would be waiting for him there. Woods readily agreed to make the trip. He then set out in his black 1938 Opel for the 125-mile drive south to the lakeside Swiss resort town. Arriving at the appointed hour, Woods found Respondek's messenger sitting on a park bench at the end of the pier. The consul general approached him and produced his Belgian lace collar as proof of who he was. The "priest" then handed him some papers.

This was the first news Woods had received from Respondek since late January 1943, when the German had sent word about the effectiveness of Allied air raids on the Ruhr.[28] The report in Woods's hands now was much more detailed: it described Germany's plan to mobilize two million men for the army and for armaments production,[29] and it stressed Hitler's determination to prosecute the war "without compromise" even if this meant adopting "measures resulting in destruction on [an] unprecedented scale."[30] It also spoke of Germany's success in blunting the impact of air raids on its major cities, and of High Command confidence in their troops' fighting ability vis-à-vis less-experienced Allied forces.[31]

After analyzing the Wehrmacht's new strategy of "watchful waiting" and flexible counterattack, Respondek revealed his most sensational discovery: five million Reichsmarks had been placed at the disposal of "leading professors and scientific institutions" to test the principles involved in creation of an atomic bomb. Another 30 million marks was being set aside by the government "for technical tests," to be held at an installation built at a cost of an additional two million marks. "The military authorities are anxiously awaiting [the] results of [these] tests," Respondek added.[32]

Respondek did not mention Dällenbach by name, saying only that the "inventor of the bomb" was a Swiss under contract to the AEG. Although he did not spell out the exact nature of the bomb, he did say it was probably connected with Otto Hahn's splitting of the uranium atom.[33] From what Respondek could ascertain, the idea was to "release one or two neutrons in . . . one cubic meter of uranium oxide powder."[34]

An English version of this report was prepared over the weekend and then cabled to Washington.[35] The sections describing atomic research landed on the desks of Secretaries Berle and Long on Friday, May 14th. Berle happened to be out of town, and Long, his rival now to succeed Sumner Welles,[36] wasted little time capitalizing on what struck him as a highly significant piece of intelligence. Early the following week Long had a copy of the English summary of Respondek's report forwarded to General George Strong at G-2. Strong was trusted by Long, who regarded him as a "very thorough thinking, serious minded, able officer of sound judgement."[37] His opinion of this document would be crucial.

Long met with the head of army intelligence on the morning of May 19th, in his second-floor office in the State, War, and Navy Building. By virtue of his position in the army chain of command, Strong already knew a great deal about the Manhattan Project. What he did not know was what the Germans were doing. As he sat across from Long, reading Respondek's report, the former Indian fighter grew visibly distressed.[38] He then shared some highly classified information with the assistant secretary of state: the United States was building its own atomic device. But there was concern the Nazis might develop one of their own first.[39] This would be calamitous for the Allies. To make his point, the head of G-2 proceeded to give Long a vivid description of the "staggering" explosive power of such a bomb.

Long was so taken aback by what Strong had to say that, at the general's urging, he dashed off a cable to Leland Harrison, saying Washington considered Woods's information of the "highest importance and utmost urgency" and requesting the consul general to press his Berlin source for more details. Then a still-stunned Long, who had just celebrated his sixty-second birthday amid sober thoughts of his own mortality, recorded in his diary some premonitions of the nuclear age:

If they keep up this business of developing more and more devastating explosives they will some day just blow this world out from under us. This thing is awful— or will be if actually put to "practical" use in warfare—but this will not be the end. The next may blow off another chunk to become another moon for some other kind of animal to look at—for it must be another kind of animal as this human kind as we know it will have ceased to exist—by its own smart action.[40]

To deal with this German threat, Long took steps on his own. He first briefed Vannevar Bush, the MIT computer specialist who was in charge of the government's Office of Scientific Research and Development (OSRD). A tall, gaunt New Englander with pale blue eyes, Bush had left his post across town with the Carnegie Institute to oversee an "all-out" U.S. effort to construct an atomic bomb. He was one of three people who kept President Roosevelt informed about progress in the ultrasecret Manhattan Project. Concerned for some time about Germany's building a bomb,[41] Bush felt that, given recent German U-boat successes, the war might have reached a point where "only the advent of the A-bomb could alter the trend toward world conquest by the dictatorships of Germany and Japan." Based on his knowledge of current research, Bush judged "the development of that weapon might go either way."[42]

Bush's anxiety was shared by his Germanophobic commander in chief, who could well imagine what a fanatical Hitler would do with an atomic bomb in his arsenal. On June 24, 1943, the president had lunch at the White House with his chief scientific advisor.[43] Although no record of their conversation exists, it is likely that the contents of Respondek's latest report were discussed. What steps Roosevelt may have ordered Bush to take are equally unclear. (At staff meetings of the OSRD held during the late spring and summer of 1943 Dällenbach's proposed cyclotron was apparently not mentioned. However, the OSS had one of its agents, Moe Berg, spy on the Swiss physicist later in the war.) But other top officials in Washington were intrigued by Respondek's cryptic warning.

Breckenridge Long told several of his State Department associates, notably Welles, Raymond Atherton (head of the European division), Avra Warren, and Raymond Geist.[44] His hope was to find confirmation for what Woods had cabled from Switzerland and to learn more about the German atomic project. Geist could help by verifying the support of German business for these nuclear experiments.

A stockily built career diplomat with a blunt way of speaking and a forceful personality, Geist was an old Germany hand. After studying comparative literature at Harvard, he had represented Herbert Hoover as the head of the U.S. post–First World War food relief program in Vienna; he had then served in several consulates prior to becoming consul general in Berlin in the early 1930s. (When Ambassador Wilson was called home after Kristallnacht, Geist laconically cabled Washington: "Have assumed charge."[45]) Upon his return from Berlin in 1940, the fifty-five-year-old Geist took over the new Division of Commercial Affairs within the State Department.

Because of Geist's extensive knowledge of Germany and German business affairs, Long wrote to him on May 18th, enclosing a copy of the top-secret cable from Zurich. Geist replied the same day, echoing Long's concern about the "tremendous energy of German genius" being harnessed to "outreach us scientifically and to achieve a victory by means of some *deus ex machina*."[46] From his prewar days in Berlin, Geist knew Owen Young, chairman of the board of General Electric, who had worked out a way of settling Germany's war reparations. Geist agreed to speak with Young confidentially in order to find out more about the AEG's role in atomic research and to ascertain "how far science has succeeded in releasing atomic destructive power." Although he was skeptical of Hermann Bücher's boast of a German atomic breakthrough, Geist felt this ought to be thoroughly checked out, just in case. It so happened that Geist was traveling up to New York for the National Foreign Trade Week, and he told Long he would take up the matter with Young then. But it is not clear that he actually did so.[47]

Without waiting for any confirmation on his side of the Atlantic, Secretary Long wired a message to Leland Harrison requesting more specifics.[48] Already aware of Respondek's document, Harrison raised this
matter with his military attaché, Brigadier General Barnwell R. Legge,
on May 28, 1943. Tapping their own well-informed sources inside the
Reich, the two Bern-based officials proceeded to piece together some
facts about previous German atomic research and cabled back that "experiments are now being carried out at the Kaiser Wilhelm Institute and
at a laboratory situated on the so-called Lunaburgerheide [sic] between
Bremen and Hanover."[49] These experiments were being supervised by
General Becker, head of the Army Ordnance Office. Harrison and Legge
also reported that a "Nuclear Physics Research Group"—the so-called
Uranverein—was involved in this project. Their informant had further
revealed, accurately, that the heavy water used for controlling a chain
reaction was being manufactured by IG Farben.[50] (But he mistakenly
believed a Norwegian manufacturing plant had been "dismantled and
transferred [to] England shortly before [the] invasion [of] Norway."[51])
Harrison's message to the State Department closed by pointing out the
Germans still had not managed to circumvent the requirement for an
"extremely heavy" cyclotron—a shortcoming that "would preclude use
as a practical explosive."[52]

Not all of Harrison's report was news. The British had known about
shipments of heavy water out of Norway at least as early as 1941[53] and
had attempted to knock out the Vemork plant the following summer
with an airborne commando assault.[54] Even though the British and
Americans did not share intelligence on German atomic research until
the end of 1943, General Groves had also discovered that the Norsk-
Hydro facility was producing 120 kilograms of heavy water a month.
But the Americans were still pretty much in the dark about what was
happening inside the Reich's secret laboratories. Among U.S. physicists
working on the Manhattan Project, there was in early 1943 a consensus
that the Germans knew as much or more than they themselves did about
how to construct a bomb.[55] Because they lacked the more substantial
reports obtained by the British, the Americans were more easily alarmed
by indications of recent German progress.

Intrigued by these additional facts supplied by Bern, General Strong
pressed his subordinate, General Legge, for more. How did heavy water
fit into the picture? Had the Germans managed to separate uranium
isotopes? What more could be learned about German successes in building cyclotrons?[56] While Legge and another legation official, Landreth
M. Harrison, tried to answer these technical questions through their
contacts in Poland and elsewhere,[57] an impatient General Strong sent
off another wire, this time asking for information on the location and
activities of research branches of the Kaiser Wilhelm Society, especially

any located on the Luneberger Heide.[58] Within two days General Legge was able to tell him where the Kaiser Wilhelm Institute for Physics was situated—in the Berlin suburb of Dahlem.[59] The military attaché hoped to learn more specifics, either from a German scientist named Kassner, from the British (who were already receiving useful scientific reports from the Swiss physicist Paul Scherrer[60]), or from Sam Woods's source, "Ralph," in Berlin.

Apparently the first two of these sources did not prove helpful. After waiting impatiently for over two months, Secretary of State Hull sent an urgent cable to Switzerland on August 14th: "Please ascertain whether an exact description can be furnished by Ralph of the location of manufacture, or of experiments, or of both. I shall appreciate your replying as quickly as possible. Inquire by personal contact."[61] By coincidence, Sam Woods was coming to Bern the next day, bringing with him a report from Respondek on the status of the German armaments industry.[62] After sitting down with the U.S. minister and his aide, Landreth Harrison, and listening to Washington's request, Woods promised to do all he could to obtain from "Ralph" the information desired by the secretary of state. The reason was obvious: to provide Allied bombers with the precise coordinates of one of the most important and well-concealed targets inside Germany.

The six-page document brought by Woods from Zurich was fascinating in its own right. Making use of high-level information collected from within the Speer ministry, Respondek disclosed that arms-producing factories were being dispersed around Germany to lessen the damage inflicted by Allied air strikes.[63] He also gave a breakdown of the bombing's minimal impact on war industries in the Ruhr, Berlin-Brandenburg, central Germany, and Upper Silesia. Heavy anti-aircraft fire was helping these critical factories maintain high production levels. According to Respondek, the German leadership was now worried about future raids on less-defended industrial areas of Saxony and southern Germany, with their "highly sensitive armaments centers, the weakness or widespread destruction of which would have as catastrophic consequences for the Germans' conduct of the war as [those] in the Ruhr."[64]

"Ralph" had learned that military and civilian offices were being removed from Berlin in anticipation of stepped-up air attacks.[65] Fear of Allied bombs had reached as far as Hitler's Alpine retreat: all grounds and buildings at Berchtesgaden were now camouflaged with green and yellow paint.[66]

Respondek ended his August report on an ominous note: he had heard of another German "secret weapon," capable of "decimating acts of reprisal of a militarily decisive nature." Details about this alarming threat would follow, he promised.[67]

"Ralph"'s advice to focus Allied bombing policy on vulnerable industrial targets would be ignored because the British had already decided on another strategy: to break the German people's will to fight by flattening their cities. Although Operation Pointblank, launched in March 1943, was ostensibly aimed at destroying the Luftwaffe and German aircraft production,[68] it actually carried out the wishes of British Air Marshal A. T. "Bomber" Harris to inflict indiscriminate damage on civilian targets. This strategy failed on two counts: first, it did not weaken the Germans' determination to fight on; second, it diverted Allied bombers from factories whose destruction might, as Respondek argued, have shortened the war.

The folly of Bomber Command policy was most apparent in the steady pounding of Berlin that commenced in the late fall of 1943. At the urging of Stalin, who relished news of Hitler's capital being ablaze,[69] American and British crews flew some 20,000 sorties over a five-month period. Exploding bombs reduced much of the city's stately baroque buildings to rubble and disrupted Berliners' lives, but they did not bring peace any sooner.[70]

Officials in Washington were far more interested in Respondek's scientific information. Secretaries Long and Hull, General Strong at G-2, and Vannevar Bush and his staff at the Office of Scientific Research and Development waited anxiously through the hot summer months for more facts about German atomic experiments. By now a flood of "fantastic rumors" was pouring in from OSS and British agents,[71] adding to what Respondek had already told Woods. On August 21st, for example, Hans Bethe and Edward Teller wrote to Robert Oppenheimer expressing grave fears: "Recent reports, both through the newspapers and through secret service, have given indications that the Germans may be in possession of a powerful new weapon which is expected to be ready between November and January. There seems to be a considerable probability that this new weapon is tube alloy [uranium]."[72]

The only way to determine if the Germans were actually close to producing an atomic bomb would be to send teams of knowledgeable U.S. scientists to Germany to inspect the laboratories there and interrogate German physicists. With the Allies now gearing up for an invasion of the Reich, this now appeared feasible. So, at General Groves's suggestion, an "Alsos" (Greek for "grove") mission was organized for this purpose.[73] It was to be led by Lt. Colonel Boris T. Pash, the Russian-American intelligence officer who had recently made a name for himself by his dogged questioning of Oppenheimer on security-related matters. Alsos was to see to it that the United States had—and kept—a lead in the embryonic atomic age.

Meanwhile, more disquieting news arrived from Switzerland. In late August the OSS relayed reports about a series of light earthquakes in southern Bavaria.[74] What might ordinarily have seemed innocuous took on more insidious implications in view of what U.S. intelligence now knew about German atomic experiments. Could these have been underground tests? Colonel Donovan wanted to know for sure. Could Sam Woods find out? This request was flashed back to the U.S. legation in Bern.

This was the first time Woods had initiated contact with "Ralph." Back in Berlin the two men had agreed that Wood's lace collar would be used as an identifying token if this need ever arose. But who, at this point in the war, with Switzerland surrounded by Axis troops and with Gestapo agents everywhere—who could carry the collar and Woods's vital message to Berlin? There was only one safe channel Woods knew of that still ran freely into war-besieged Germany. It ran an improbable course— from Switzerland south to Rome, and from there north again to the German capital. The guarantor of this conduit was even more improbable. He was none other than the Bishop of Rome, the Sovereign of Vatican City, the Prince of the Apostles, His Holiness, Pope Pius XII.

10

THE POPE AND OTHER
SECRET WEAPONS

The wartime Vatican was a labyrinth of shadowy intrigues and diplomatic dealings. Utmost discretion and strict secrecy obscured the pope's ties to the sundry political groups that sought to gain his blessing for their cause. Those to the German resistance were no exception. Defenseless in the midst of fascist Italy, the Vatican could ill afford to publicize any fraternizing with Hitler's enemies. Nor did Pius XII wish to expose any of his visitors to arrest or a worse fate inside a Nazi concentration camp. Accordingly, few records of a possibly compromising nature were kept, and what was written down is far from damning. Pius himself made the task of sleuthing taxing to Mussolini's police and historians alike: he made no notes of his conversations, with either friend or foe, even once the danger had passed.[1]

This papal circumspection has cut both ways, shielding the Vatican from embarrassing or dangerous revelations, but also leaving Pius open to the charge of having abandoned Europe's Jews. A scarcity of information has clouded his historical role. Some see him as the timid and aloof pontiff who could only bring himself to utter trite words of consolation for the war's millions of innocent victims—and even fewer for those who suffered persecution. To his defenders, Pius was an astute, worldly man of peace who in 1939 took great chances in mediating between the German opposition and the British—a role one scholar has placed "among the most astounding events in the modern history of the papacy."[2]

Pius's links to Erwin Respondek and his small band of anti-Nazi Catholics are equally obscured. What can be reconstructed of the pope's involvement, however, tends to make him appear to be more than simply a passive middleman for the forces opposed to Hitler.[3] Pius may have risked the Nazis' ire, and his own life, by transmitting critical intelligence to the Allies. He may even have had a hand in setting up the courier system that ran circuitously from Berlin to Sam Woods's listening post in Zurich.

The close ties between Pius XII and Germany are no secret, and it is in them that hints of his connections to Respondek and his circle can be found. Scion of a Roman family that had served the Vatican for a hundred years,[4] Eugenio Pacelli entered the priesthood around the turn of the century and at once became immersed in papal affairs of state. His first extended contact with Germany came during the waning years of the First World War, when Benedict XV appointed him nuncio to Bavaria to promote Vatican efforts to achieve a peace settlement. When the new German republic was formally recognized three years later, Pacelli took over similar duties in the German capital.

In Berlin the forty-four-year-old papal nuncio moved into a large house ringed by gardens on the Rauchstrasse, just south of the Tiergarten. There, casting off his normally ascetic manner, Pacelli entertained Weimar dignitaries and foreign ambassadors, using his "outgoing, imposing personality, . . . wit and social grace"[5] and gift for languages (he spoke six) to charm his guests and earn his reputation as doyen of Berlin's diplomatic corps.[6] Inevitably, Pacelli became embroiled in Weimar politics. Periodically he consulted with leaders of the Center Party,[7] coming to admire such personalities as Heinrich Brüning and Ludwig Kaas.[8] But the nuncio's circle of acquaintants extended beyond the Catholic political hierarchy. During his horseback rides in the city's outlying parks, he came to know Ludwig Beck, then a rapidly rising general staff officer; Wilhelm Canaris, the future head of Hitler's Abwehr; and another young army officer, Hans Oster.[9] These men would later figure prominently in the German resistance. (From his days as nuncio in Munich, Pacelli was also well acquainted with a fourth individual destined to play a crucial opposition role: the Bavarian lawyer and conservative Catholic politician Josef Müller.[10]) Of more significance to Erwin Respondek was the future pope's friendship with the Muckermann brothers, Friedrich and Hermann.

Friedrich, the Jesuit journalist and critic, was then living in Münster, following his return home from a Russian prisoner-of-war camp. He first met the papal nuncio at a Catholic congress in Magdeburg.[11] The younger Muckermann was then making a name for himself as a Catholic spokesman on cultural matters, and Pacelli would certainly have been aware of the journal, *Der Graal*, published by Muckermann after 1921. The nuncio would also have known of the Westfalian priest's lectures on modern literature and culture, which financed Muckermann's journalistic endeavors.[12]

Because of his enthusiasm for modernist trends in the arts and his hostility toward Nazi racial philosophy, Friedrich Muckermann found himself at odds with the growing nationalist movement. Although he obeyed his order's wishes and refrained from speaking out on politics,[13] Muckermann did take advantage of his popularity in Catholic circles to attack the Nazis' anti-Christian philosophy.

Hence, he was a prime target for intimidation once Hitler took over power. At least one of his speeches, in the Münsterland, was disrupted by Nazi hoodlums,[14] and another, on "Catholicism and the Nation," was banned.[15] But this harassment did not prevent the stubborn Westfalian Jesuit, convinced his faith was fighting for its very survival against Germany's new masters, from continuing to speak out and publish pamphlets that assailed the regime.[16] After fleeing arrest in 1934, Muckermann took refuge in a monastery across the border in Holland. From this base he issued newsletters and gave speeches denouncing the Nazis.[17]

The following summer, concern for Muckermann's welfare led the Jesuit general, Father Vladimir Ledochowski, and the exiled Center leader, Kaas, to summon the politically active priest to the Vatican, ostensibly to put together a documentary archive on national socialism.[18] Muckermann would remain in the Eternal City for the next two years, writing, lecturing, and doing research for the Oriental Institute. Then, with the Italian police closing in on him, he left Rome suddenly in November 1937, moving on to Vienna. There Muckermann supported the Catholic chancellor Kurt von Schuschnigg in his vain bid to thwart the Anschluss. Always one step ahead of the Gestapo, the defiant priest hopscotched from Austria to France to Switzerland. His activities did not go unnoticed by the Americans, who chose Muckermann for an advisory position in a post-Hitler government.[19] Unfortunately, Friedrich Muckermann died of a heart attack before this opportunity could materialize.[20]

His older and more cautious brother, Hermann, lived less dangerously under the Third Reich. Although kept under surveillance, he was not deemed a threat to the regime. The Nazis never learned of his spiriting Brüning and Gottfried Treviranus safely out of Germany and of his other resistance activities. The worldly priest and "Christian anthropologist" had his own entree to the Vatican. While still a Jesuit he had become friendly with the German priest and Church historian Robert Leiber, SJ, who from 1924 on served as Pacelli's private secretary, aide on German affairs, and closest advisor.[21] (Leiber belonged to a German inner circle around Pacelli, whose members included Kaas, Wilhelm Hentrich, and Augustinus Bea.[22]) As was noted earlier, Hermann Muckermann knew Pacelli personally from the latter's days as nuncio in Berlin. He was also highly regarded by the man Pacelli was to succeed, Pius XI.

Both Muckermann brothers were close to the Respondeks. Friedrich and Charlotte Respondek shared political and artistic interests, while Hermann, intellectually and temperamentally more like Erwin Respondek, became an intimate of the family's shortly after the First World War and remained on good terms until Respondek's arrest in January 1942.[23]

In addition to assisting his friend in collecting intelligence about Operation Barbarossa, Hermann Muckermann maintained sporadic contact with his emigré brother, then in Holland.[24] Friedrich's role in the anti-Hitler resistance and his presence in Rome after 1935 hint that the younger Muckermann may also have helped convey Respondek's reports to the Americans.

The facts that can be established are these: in 1936 one of Respondek's memorandums for Douglas Miller, the American commercial attaché in Berlin, fell into Nazi hands. Because of this, Respondek lost faith in the Americans' reliability.[25] He then began searching for another outlet for his high-level information. By then Friedrich Muckermann was living in Rome, attached to the Vatican's Oriental Institute. In July 1937, an unusual time for a Mediterranean holiday, Charlotte Respondek made a "sudden and unexpected" trip to Italy,[26] a country she loved and visited often. In Rome she spoke with Muckermann, who had indirect access to the pope through Monsignor Kaas and Father Leiber.[27] With the intercession of these priests Charlotte arranged a private audience with Pius XI.[28] This took place at a time when the pontiff was growing distressed about anti-Catholic measures inside the Reich.[29] His recent Palm Sunday encyclical, *mit brennender Sorge*, had plainly spelled out Pius's animosity toward the Nazis and their philosophy.[30] There was talk of his breaking openly with the Hitler government,[31] which could barely conceal its contempt for the pope. Over eighty, frail, and in poor health, Pius had little time left to oppose the Nazi regime. Did Charlotte Respondek ask him to do so by acting as a conduit between her husband and the Americans?

For obvious reasons, Charlotte Respondek made no notation in her travel diary of any papal appointments. The surviving Vatican records show no trace of her having met with Pius XI in 1937. Neither Father Leiber nor Friedrich Muckermann ever disclosed any dealings with the Respondeks. So the question remains open. Whatever help Charlotte may have solicited in 1937, little appears to have come from this sojourn in Rome. The pope's health rapidly deteriorated. Four months later Friedrich Muckermann was forced to flee Rome. And about this time in Berlin her husband first struck up an acquaintance with the jovial newcomer from Prague, Sam Woods.

But the Respondeks' Vatican connection did not end there. It was revived in 1941, shortly before Woods and his embassy colleagues were taken away by train to Bad Nauheim. In the interim Pius XI had died, and Cardinal Pacelli was elected to succeed him. At first relations between Germany and the Vatican improved, with Pius XII being considered a conciliator.[32] But then, surreptitiously, the new pope took a bold step: in the middle of October he informed Father Leiber of his willingness to facilitate a dialogue between the German opposition and the British. These negotiations, which ultimately accomplished very little, ran through February 1940. Proposals for a peace settlement were passed from the conspirators Hans von Dohnanyi, General Beck, and Hans Oster to their trusted representative in Rome, Josef Müller. Müller, in turn, conveyed these to his good friend and papal confidant, Father Leiber. A second opposition link ran through Monsignor Kaas to the British minister to the Holy See, D'Arcy Osborne.[33] These convoluted negotiations resulted in the well-known "X" report,[34] drafted by von Dohnanyi and Müller that winter. Designed to win over generals Halder and Brauchitsch to a coup, this document laid out peace terms: the Germans would not launch an offensive in the West, Hitler would be removed from power, and an "acceptable" settlement of the Reich's eastern boundaries would be worked out.[35]

But the British remained suspicious of the German opposition.[36] In spite of receiving warnings from Beck and Oster about Germany's forthcoming Blitzkrieg against the Lowlands (which the pope relayed to Osborne), London gave no encouragement to the coup concocted by the military conspirators. When this plan collapsed, in the face of Halder and Brauchitsch's hesitation,[37] a slim chance to avoid war in the west was lost. Officially, Pius was reluctant to say or do anything in the wake of this diplomatic failure. He did denounce the Nazis' invasion of Belgium, Holland, and Luxemburg but, fearing his words would do more harm than good, lowered his voice when the Nazis stepped up their persecution of Jews and Catholics. With war now raging across Europe, there was little a spiritual leader without a single division at his command could do to stop it.

But Hitler's enemies sought his help once again. This time it was Charlotte Respondek who took on the role of emissary. With Sam Woods's days in Berlin nearing an end, she had Hermann Muckermann obtain an audience for her with the German-speaking pontiff.[38] Her intention was to go to Rome and make a personal appeal to Pius—possibly to help smuggle her husband's reports out of Berlin. At first Respondek strenuously objected to this scheme: he told Charlotte it was too risky. She would be caught, arrested, put in prison. (Italian police were now keeping close tabs on all of Pius's visitors.[39])But Charlotte was firm. She would be all right. She would take "her friends" with her, and they would protect her.[40] Finally, Respondek consented to her going to Rome.

Financing this trip presented another problem. The Respondeks had already sold off most of their valuable art and furnishings, and virtually no money had come into the household on the Mariannenstrasse for several years. Swallowing his pride, Respondek turned to his collaborator, Sam Woods. Could he or the embassy possibly pay for his wife's expenses for a trip to see the pope? The well-paid commercial attaché agreed to give Respondek the money out of his own pocket.[41] With this tucked in her purse, an agenda that remains a secret to this day, and a veil she had made especially for her papal audience,[42] Charlotte Respondek then set out by train for the Eternal City.

When and how she reached Rome, and with whom, is not known. Charlotte concealed the true purpose of her visit even from her close friend Agnes Dreimann, saying she was simply attending to "personal matters."[43] In the Italian capital it is highly likely the door to the pope was partially opened for her by Father Leiber. Charlotte had another friend in Rome at that time—Josef Müller, the blunt-speaking Bavarian of peasant stock who still went by his boyhood nickname, "Ochsensepp." After the failure of his liaison work, Müller had kept his ties to the Vatican intact. (He was also in touch with President Roosevelt's personal representative to the Holy See, Myron C. Taylor.)

Previously the Bavarian attorney had belonged to the Respondeks' circle of conspirators.[44] Charlotte and Erwin had visited him while on their art-collecting excursions to Munich, and he had often come to dine at their home in Berlin. During 1940 the peripatetic Müller had traveled from his hotel on the Via Veneto to Germany and back several times, including two visits to Berlin within a single week in January.[45] In Rome, Müller was close to Father Leiber—whom he met secretly at the Universita Gregoriana to pass along word from General Beck—and to Monsignor Kaas.[46] As administrator of St. Peter's, the German prelate was one of the few persons Pius had taken completely into his confidence.[47] Kaas, who had a set of keys to the pope's personal apartments,[48] was also one of very few Church officials who knew exactly why Müller was in Rome.[49] The onetime Center leader had for many years worked closely with his party's chancellor, Heinrich Brüning.[50] Together with Müller and Johannes Bell (a former minister of justice), he had attended prewar parties at the Respondeks' home.[51] Consequently, in 1941 Charlotte Respondek could count on a wealth of Catholic connections leading directly to the pope.[52]

What use did she make of these? She may have sought Pius's assistance in relaying her husband's reports to Sam Woods. Or she may have asked the pope to help set up, or at least condone, a courier service of Catholic priests. (Friedrich Muckermann had devised such an "intelligence apparatus" for distributing his own anti-Nazi leaflets back in 1934, and this may have inspired the Respondeks.) It is even possible Charlotte briefed the pope on the imminent Nazi invasion of the Soviet Union.

Whatever Pius may have agreed to do, he had to conceal very carefully. The Vatican had already angered the Germans by handing over some military intelligence to the British. And the pope had allowed the British ambassador Osborne to use the papal pouch for communicating with London.[53] The Nazis were not likely to condone further such transgressions on his part.

It is equally possible Pius declined to do anything. All that is definitely known is that Charlotte Respondek returned safely to Berlin and that then, in the fall of the following year, a series of persons purporting to be priests began carrying her husband's secret documents to Switzerland.

Pius XII figures in the Woods–Respondek story on one further occasion. This came when the OSS was receiving reports about earthquakes in southern Germany. After being asked by the State Department in September 1943 to have "Ralph" verify these,[54] Woods approached an American woman residing in Zurich, the brewery heiress Wilhelmina Busch.[55] A Catholic convert exiled from her home south of Munich, she arranged for the consul general to contact Respondek "through a high Church dignitary in Germany."[56] (Respondek's daughter, Valeska, says her mother told her it was Pius himself who acted as go-between.[57])

Eventually Woods's request was received by Respondek, who checked into several explosions near Ulm during July and September and confirmed that they were, indeed, minor earthquakes. He then relayed this good news back to Woods.[58] Unfortunately, he had some bad news, too.

It had to do with more "secret weapons." Not all of them, it seemed, were figments of a hyperactive Nazi imagination. After Robert Goddard's successes with liquid-fuel propellants in the 1920s, German rocketry had made impressive strides forward. London and other English cities would feel the deadly impact of that pioneering research when the first V-1 "buzz bombs" began raining down out of the skies in 1944. There are some indications that Respondek learned of these awesome "reprisal weapons" and warned Woods.[59] He also tipped off his American friend about another, potentially more devastating weapon being developed to bring the British to their knees.

After the Allies learned from Swiss sources of a secret rocket-launching site at Peenemünde and confirmed this by photo reconnaisance on June 18th,[60] Allied Bomber Command ordered 596 bombers across the Channel on the moonlit night of August 17th to knock out this facility. The celebrated Peenemünde raid killed some 180 German scientists and technical personnel (as well as, inadvertently, over 500 Polish laborers) and severely damaged the testing and launch sites, setting back the German rocket program by at least two months.[61] Hitler, who had counted on the V-2 (or "A-4," as it was then known in Germany) to reverse his sagging fortunes on the battlefield, now turned to a weapon just in its experimental stage.

This was a long-range gun, built in gigantic underground barrels and trained on the heart of London. Known to only a very few top Nazis, this weapon could fire a projectile that was a cross between an artillery shell and a rocket—a 300-pound, nine-foot-long, finned missile carrying an incendiary warhead. It was to be accelerated out of its concrete-lined shaft, at speeds of more than 4,000 feet per second, by a series of explosive "kicks." The "shells" would race in a flat arc toward their targets in a continuous barrage of 600 an hour.[62]

Construction for the barrels for this "high-pressure pump" was proceeding deep inside a hill near Mimoyecques, southwest of Calais, at a point just 95 miles from the tower of Big Ben. Given a green light by Hitler in August, work on two separate sites, housing a total of 25 gun barrels, picked up pace during the fall, promising to give Germany a highly accurate and virtually unstoppable weapon of mass destruction. But refinement of the pump and its high-resiliency shell ran afoul of technical snags and bureaucratic squabbling between the engineer in charge and the army's weapons office. As a result, the "V-3" was nowhere near completion by June 1944, and then, with the Allies storming ashore at Normandy, it was too late. The fabled long-range guns at Mimoyecques never fired a shot.[63] Although they had detected these sites by aerial reconnaisance and bombed them in November 1943, the British never guessed the true nature of this threat.[64] But Erwin Respondek did.

The second half of 1943 was marked by wild rumors in London and Washington, amplified by the Nazi propaganda machinery, about Germany's widely anticipated "miracle weapon." In September Allied intelligence circles still disagreed about whether this danger consisted of "rockets," "pilotless aircraft," "aerial torpedos," or "long-range guns."[65] The truth was that Hitler was pushing ahead with several such projects— the "buzz bomb," the V-2, and the long-range "high-pressure pump"— all at once. But tight security and Nazi hyperbole frustrated American and British efforts to identify and destroy these experimental sites.

Respondek, too, was prevented from verifying any "secret weapon" rumors by the death, retirement, and transfer of several of his key informants.[66] But he still managed to acquire classified information on armaments from civilian scientists working on weapons projects and from an unnamed industrialist who maintained "relations with army staffs and experts of [the] Reichs Ministry for Armaments and War Production in charge [of] development of and research work in arms."[67]

This was probably the AEG's Hermann Bücher, then a member of the advisory Armaments Council.[68] In September, a month after Hitler reactivated the "V-3" project, Respondek discovered that the Germans were perfecting, as Harrison cabled Secretary Hull, a "new long range gun independent of weather condition[s,] curvature of earth[,] with [a] low angle [of] elevation [and] great accuracy."[69] Respondek reported that this gun had been successfully tested and that it was now being manufactured at Ruhr factories and at the SS-run Skoda works in Czechoslovakia. He could not confirm that the first of the long-range guns had been installed in Holland, as he had been told second-hand.[70]

Since Respondek's news came without a "reasonable confirmation," it may not have sounded definitive to Breckenridge Long—or the others who learned of it, Vannevar Bush and General Strong at G-2. They probably treated this as another disconcerting sign of German progress with "secret weapons," but not as a cause for taking military action. Where, after all, could Allied bombers find this alleged new gun? Respondek gave no location, and the German ordnance experts had already taken great pains to conceal under French soil all but six inches of muzzle. In spite of the imprecision of his description, Respondek's brief reference to the experimental "high-pressure pump" shows how well-informed he remained at this late stage in the war.

By sources inside the Ministry of Armaments "Ralph" was told about other "secret weapons." One of these was a heavier dive bomber, whose "capabilities exceed all other types."[71] By the end of October 3,000 of these new planes were to be fully operational, and some 10,000 pilots and crew had allegedly completed training to fly them. (Respondek may have been describing one of several aircraft: a variant of the modified Junkers 87-D, the dive bomber that replaced the once-feared "Stuka"; the Junkers 88C-4, adapted for a night fighter mission from its original bomber role; the Messerschmidt Bf 110G, a three-seat night fighter; or the Heinkel 219. Of these, the Heinkel 219 comes the closest to Respondek's specifications, but it was not produced in the quantities he indicated. Either he was misinformed about this new fighter plane, or else his production figures represented projections that were not fulfilled. It is unlikely Respondek was referring to Germany's greatest aircraft advance: the Messerschmidt 262, the world's first jet fighter. This plane was only in the prototype stage by November 1943, when Hitler gave it top-priority status.[72])

Respondek's September memorandum also stated that "magnetic-optical" instruments were being installed in a new type of night fighter— an added hazard to Allied bombers attacking Germany.

"Ralph" also had some comforting news for the Americans: Germany had not made any spectacular breakthroughs in armaments research. "Feverish" efforts to produce a decisive "miracle weapon" had thus far failed.[73] In his report Respondek recounted the gist of conversations he had had with staff officers at the Army High Command: Hitler was still committed to pulling back his forces into a tight defensive ring. In the east he would rapidly withdraw his battered and badly mauled armies to erect a "final line" stretching from the Baltic, through the marshes around Minsk and the Polish high plateau, to the Carpathian Mountains and the Black Sea. (This closely matches the Wehrmacht's actual retreat from Russia during the second half of 1943.[74])

On the western front, the Germans intended to dig in along the foothills of the Pyrenees, the fortified French coastline, and the Alps. Their defensive perimeter would reach as far as Norway and Finland.[75] The German forces had to speed up these measures because the situation in Italy was deteriorating, and because the High Command realized Germany would have to fight on by itself.[76] The outlook was made more unsettling for Hitler and his warlords, Respondek pointed out, by the turmoil along Germany's southern flank and by the expected Allied invasion of France. (Entrenched Wehrmacht troops on the Atlantic Wall were being kept at the highest state of alarm.[77]) If the Allies attacked in the east and in the west before the Germans could consolidate their positions, the war would be lost for the Nazis within a few months.[78] Thus a golden opportunity presented itself to the British and Americans.

Within the Reich, Heinrich Himmler, head of the SS, now reigned supreme. He and his cohorts were brutally crushing any opposition or defeatist sentiments as Germany braced for invasion: "Any sort of personal, even intellectual resistance that might threaten the determination to fight on or the war effort, even comments reflecting the general mood, is being eliminated without trial, by the public and secret agents of the Reichsführer." In the face of such drastic repressive measures and incessant Allied air raids, the German people were still not ready—or able—to rise up against the Nazis. (As Respondek explained: "The German people are in the position of a victim who is compelled to bear the brunt of each defeat. Resistance would be savagely put down as if it had occurred on enemy territory."[79])

Woods had a paraphrase of this wide-ranging report encoded and then wired on to Washington on October 16, 1943. There it was handed to Breckenridge Long. He shared the document with Raymond Geist, who distributed copies to Vannevar Bush and General Strong. Overall, this latest message from Berlin was reassuring. Bush and his fellow scientists were relieved to hear the Nazis had not perfected any "new revolutionary weapons or materials, including poison gas and explosives."[80] Military planners at G-2 were heartened to find out the Germans had no hidden threat that could "guarantee absolutely [the] failure of [a] landing against [the] Atlantic Wall."[81] Respondek's belief that there was "complete ignorance of Allied invasion plans" at Hitler's headquarters[82] must have pleased the Combined Chiefs of Staffs, who were then weighing General Dwight Eisenhower's proposal for a Normandy landing. The new dive bomber and long-range gun were somewhat disturbing developments, but "Ralph" pointed out that neither of these represented "any extraordinary improvements or changes."[83]

His talks with "high officers in the OKU [sic] whose knowledge and reliability is above question"[84] indicated that Hitler was not contemplating an immediate counterattack on any front and that his forces were already retreating in Russia. Although Respondek's advice about pressing ahead on both fronts made good sense militarily, it was not so easy for the Allies to follow. In Italy, for example, the Wehrmacht might be defeated if Mark Clark's troops pushed vigorously up the peninsula, but they were already stymied by stubborn German resistance. With local field commanders now determining the pace and direction of the fighting, Respondek's strategic intelligence was of little value. This could be also be said of his latest statistics on German livestock and crop production.[85] Similarly of limited importance was a six-page document summarizing a recent pastoral letter issued by German Catholic bishops, who firmly rejected the principles of national socialism and reminded their flocks that ultimate loyalty was owed not to the Führer, but to God.[86]

Of more long-range significance was Respondek's blueprint of a book-length plan for postwar German reconstruction, passed on to Woods in the spring of 1943.[87] In the course of this exhaustive analysis Respondek offered several major recommendations: a defeated Germany should be placed under Allied military control for a transitional period leading to the formation of a liberal parliamentary democracy; all vestiges of Nazism should be eliminated through a war crimes tribunal; "the leading and responsible persons" in private industry should be purged; a free-market economy should be created to respect "private capital and its valid principles"; and a unified, federalist German state should be established.[88]

Respondek's proposals came to Secretary Hull's attention coincidentally at a time when State Department advisors were in the midst of drafting a plan for postwar Germany. Two moderate-minded scholars, Philip E. Mosely of Columbia and David Harris of Stanford, proposed a solution to the "German problem" that closely corresponded to Respondek's. This outline was submitted to Hull on August 17, 1943, and was taken by the president to his Quebec conference that same month.[89] With Sumner Welles (who favored dismembering Germany) out of power, the two professors subsequently argued more forcefully against partitioning the Reich and for a federalist arrangement and restoration of the German economy. Hull brought a modified version of this plan with him to Moscow in October, but Roosevelt eventually rejected it, arguing that dividing up Germany was the only way to prevent a future war.[90]

Highly valued as his information was in Washington, Respondek's postwar plan may have influenced government thinking, as Leland Harrison thought it might.[91] Or it may have only reiterated views on German occupation and reconstruction that were already jelling at the State Department.

With Germany now losing the war, "Ralph" was to sound one final warning about a German "secret weapon." Unfortunately, only hints about the contents of this message remain. It is another loose thread in the Woods–Respondek espionage story.

In 1944, New Year's Day fell on a Saturday. All over the United States it was a muted holiday, with hundreds of thousands of GIs still far from home in this, the fifth winter of the war—bogged down in the Italian peninsula and holding precarious footholds on the Gilbert Islands and the Solomons.

For Breckenridge Long, New Year's was not a day to celebrate or even to spend quietly with his family. Matters were weighing heavily on his mind, and he came downtown to his office near the White House to give them some thought. The Palestine question was troubling him. Long, the Southern patrician, was uncomfortable dealing with "Jewish demands,"[92] which now consisted of pressure on the U.S. government to back creation of a Jewish state. Long wanted Roosevelt to stay out of this tangle and leave it to the British to sort out.[93] But no easy resolution was in sight. Upheaval in South America was also spoiling the assistant secretary's brief holiday respite. A Nazi-inspired coup in Bolivia had just taken place, and Long feared similar trouble was brewing in Paraguay, Chile, and Peru. If there was a single bright spot on this otherwise raw and gloomy New Year's Day, it was the bit of news Long recorded in his diary before leaving for home:

Sam Woods and I got in one good lick in Germany the other night when the bombers flattened out one industry. But that cannot be written now. There is involved a German "prisoner of war," a message through OSS and a bomber activity—of which more can be written in safety some time later. It is a fascinating story.[94]

It is a story that remains untold to this day. What was this target? What "industry" did Long have in mind? Why was it so secret he could not divulge its nature? What impact did its destruction have on the war? The questions proliferate without satisfactory answers. What is known about the Allied air war at this point can be summarized as follows. In late December 1943 Bomber Command was focusing its attention on Berlin, sending sortie after sortie on the nearly 600-mile flight over German territory, dodging ever more effective fighter planes and anti-aircraft batteries in a bid to end the war by spring. The German capital was hit heavily on Christmas Eve and again on December 26th—around the time indicated by Long—but the only "industry" that may have warranted a special strike was the uranium reactor of Werner Heisenberg and Walther Gerlach, housed in an air raid shelter in Dahlem. This facility survived the Battle of Berlin intact.[95]

The heavy-water plant at Vemork in Norway suggests itself as another objective of the December raid, but, in fact, it was not bombed around this time.[96] The only other known German "secret weapon" targets bombed during December 1943 were the V–1 "ski sites" then nearing completion in the Cherbourg peninsula and in the Pas de Calais.[97] However, these rocket launch sites hardly qualify for Long's term "industry." Nor were they so veiled in secrecy.

Nonetheless, there is evidence a raid against the site of some German "secret weapon" did occur. Sam Woods believed that an end-of-the-year raid took place—and that it was aimed at German atomic research facilities. In an August 5, 1948, sworn statement Woods declared it was a report of Respondek's giving the location of atomic-research experiments that resulted in "the destruction of the laboratories."[98] Woods repeated this assertion on several occasions after the war, once telling a reporter for the New Orleans *Times-Picayune* his German contact had "told him the location of Germany's atomic bomb experiments [and] that Britain promptly bombed them to smithereens, killing 800 scientists in 20 minutes during one raid."[99]

In a posthumous biographical profile the story is further embellished:

[Woods] supplied information that led to the destruction of a heavy-water experimental plant at Peenemünde, Germany. Following receipt of his report, the British royal air force responded with one of the greatest bombings in its history and obliterated this closely guarded secret plant, thus preventing Germany from continuing with its researches in atomic science and halting the German A-bomb project.[100]

This matches the recollection of Long's daughter, who has stated, "The only thing that we can remember his [Long's] speaking about at that time was a successful bombing attack on a plant, possibly at Peenemünde, that was manufacturing heavy water."[101]

As far as is generally known, there never was any "atomic research laboratory" at Peenemünde, and the Baltic test site was not attacked by British and U.S. bombers in December 1943. (However, it is intriguing to note that Allen Dulles told William Donovan he had learned, in May

1943, about a "German experimental laboratory at Peenemünde for the testing of a secret bomb."[102]) Some important experimental work did continue there, chiefly the manufacturing of liquid-oxygen fuel for German rockets. Allied intelligence on this brought back Flying Fortresses in July and August of 1944. Did they also go back in December 1943? Top U.S. and British officials connected with the wartime Air Ministry (namely, Walt Rostow, Charles Kindleberger, Charles Hitch, and Lord Zuckerman) do not recall any December raid on a heavy-water or atomic-research installation.[103] The only other plant known to be involved with heavy-water production was IG Farben's Leuna chemical works at Merseburg. And it was not attacked until May 12, 1944.[104]

So the mystery persists. If Peenemünde was not the target, and neither was Leuna, what was?[105] Was there ever a massive RAF raid on a German atomic research site? Does this suggest that German scientists were making greater progress in perfecting a bomb than is generally believed?

Such lingering questions overshadow the value of what Respondek and Woods did accomplish: alerting American scientists and military leaders to major developments in German atomic research. Despite the inaccuracies and exaggerations in their reports, this was one of their greatest contributions to the Allied cause. The two amateur spies sounded an alarm when one was badly needed, if only to lay great doubts to rest: in the race to build the world's first atomic bomb the Americans had no one to fear.

11

ANOTHER BRUSH WITH THE GESTAPO

Time was quickly running out for Adolf Hitler. It was also running out for the Germans who were trying to kill him. In late 1943 German forces held the Allies at bay in Italy, but on other fronts the Thousand-Year Reich was starting to crack. Mile by mile, remnants of the mighty Wehrmacht that had once swept like a wind across the Russian steppe were now being driven back—out of Smolensk on September 25th, out of Kiev in November. The German defensive line was too undermanned, too thinly spread out to take a firm stand against a rejuvenated Red Army.[1] In the North Atlantic, with the "Enigma" code finally broken,[2] Allied radar was zeroing in on German U-boats, ending that threat to shipping. Inside the Reich, a steady pounding by U.S. and British bombers—200,000 tons that year, twice the amount in 1942—was disrupting some war production and bringing the war home to the German people. It was becoming unmistakably clear that they were losing it. Overshadowing these trends lay concern about an Allied invasion on the coast of France—the two-front war Hitler and his generals had dreaded all along.[3]

Germany's mounting losses on the battlefield presented new opportunities to the anti-Hitler resistance. Long dormant, the military conspirators now found events playing into their hands. Quick action was required to topple Hitler in a coup before onrushing Allied armies would "once more, and forever, rob them of their chance to act."[4] Yet key conspirators hung back. The field marshals who could turn Hitler's armies against him did not act. Even the generals—Beck, Halder, and Witzleben—who had vowed to oust the Führer harbored doubts: their sense of military propriety was still strong. The eclectic, idealistic band of intellectuals centered around Count Moltke was too preoccupied with plans for a post-Hitler Germany to help pave the way for it.[5] Arguments between the Kreisau Circle and the older, more conservative politicians around Carl Goerdeler kept any coordinated strategy from emerging. Something had to be done, and soon, but who would take the crucial steps—and how? Peace feelers to the British and to the Americans via Allen Dulles had been rebuffed: with victory at hand, the Allies were not going to budge from their policy of "unconditional surrender." If the German opposition was going to eliminate Hitler, it would have to do so without making any deals first.

But the Führer was no easy target. Half a dozen plots were hatched against him in 1943, but each time sheer luck, a sudden change of plans, or Hitler's uncanny instinct for danger saved his life. The most notable mishap occurred in March when a detonator triggering a bomb on board the Führer's plane inexplicably failed to go off. And when Hitler's conference barracks in East Prussia was torn apart by a tremendous blast in July 1944, the German dictator escaped death once again.

In the meantime, leaders of the resistance sought other ways to end the war. One of these plots involved Erwin Respondek. Up until now he had shied away from other anti-Nazi circles, distrusting their motives and fearing he might be compromised. In the past he had rejected overtures from Schacht, a field marshal, and two former members of the Reichstag to join the plotters.[6] Schacht, once Hitler's economics minister and financial "wizard," had soured on the regime early on and forged bonds both to the U.S. embassy and to the conspirators.[7] In 1943, through a mutual friend at the Reichsbank, Schacht tried to enlist Respondek's help but was bluntly told the professor of economics had no use for him: if Respondek survived the war, he would "stigmatize him [Schacht] and his accomplices as the guilty men, who . . . have done all to bring Hitler into power since 1930, and who did it . . . with heart and hand, money and connections, lies and treachery, who prepared, with their joyful help, egoism, and arrogance, the way for complete dictatorship and war."[8]

But Respondek's circle of professional acquaintances did contain several resistance figures. In this hour of shifting allegiances, both within and outside the Nazi hierarchy, and of renewed desire to make peace with the Western Allies, these individuals would draw him into a perilous intrigue.

One of them was the Berlin industrialist Paul Lejeune-Jung. A native of Cologne, Lejeune-Jung came from a French Huguenot family that had emigrated to the Rhineland during the French Revolution. He thus shared an ancestral home with Erwin Respondek.[9] The two men came to know each other well during the 1920s, when they had offices in the same building, at Grolmannstrasse 5, in Charlottenburg.[10] Lejeune-Jung was then, in his early forties, a leading spokesman for the cellulose industry, a specialist in trade and tariff matters, and a German National People's Party representative in the Reichstag. He held a doctorate in economics and was keenly interested in history and environmental matters. He was, in short, a well-rounded Weimar *Weltbürger*.

During their years together on the Grolmannstrasse the two men often discussed German industrial and political matters. Respondek appreciated Lejeune-Jung's knowledge in these fields,[11] and after moving his offices to the more centrally located Pariser Platz in 1930, he kept up this professional friendship. An early nationalist, Lejeune-Jung soon rejected Nazi ideology and drifted into the orb of the resistance. Early in 1943, while taking the waters at a Silesian spa, he was approached by an old political comrade-in-arms, Max Habermann, former secretary of the German National Association of Clerical Workers. Habermann wondered if Lejeune-Jung would be willing to explain his views on Germany's economic future to Carl Goerdeler and a small group of his friends.[12] The industrialist agreed to do so, first meeting privately with the former Leipzig mayor in February[13] and then elaborating his economic proposals with other conspirators.[14] Increasingly, Lejeune-Jung had become convinced the German economy was nearing collapse under the strain of greater war demands (including expenditures for "atomic weapons"[15]). Looking beyond the Nazi era he argued for nationalizing key industries and reforming trade policies.[16] These opinions impressed Goerdeler, who proposed Lejeune-Jung as his economics minister in a post-Nazi cabinet.[17]

Respondek also had access to Goerdeler's circle through Max Planck's son, Erwin. A career civil servant, first appointed state secretary in the Reich chancellory in 1932, the younger Planck had first had some illusions about "taming" the Nazis in a coalition government,[18] but after Hitler took over power, he gravitated toward defiant if concealed opposition. Later Planck joined forces with Oster, Beck, Goerdeler, Ulrich von Hassell, and Gisevius, convinced that an attempt on Hitler's life had to be made, "if only for the moral rehabilitation of Germany."[19] Respondek, a year his junior, had known Planck from the days when he was living in the renowned physicist's home in Grunewald.[20] During the prewar years they had conferred on the fluid political situation and found a good deal of common ground. (Although Respondek knew of Planck's ties to General Beck and other conspirators, he did not divulge his own to Brüning and Secretary of State Hull.[21]) Planck was closely allied with another key resistance figure, who also happened to be a friend of Respondek's. This was Johannes Popitz. It was he who drew Respondek into the 1943 intrigue.

Popitz was the son of a Leipzig pharmacist. He had grown up poor, but he quickly distinguished himself intellectually, publishing his *summa cum laude* dissertation at the age of twenty-three. An authority on financial matters, he had held positions in the Prussian bureaucracy for many years before being appointed minister of finance in 1933. Politically astute, loyal to Prussia but suspicious of the Nazis, Popitz made up his mind to oppose the regime from within, from his base of power.[22] The pogrom of Kristallnacht had shaken him to the core, and he had offered Goering his resignation, declaring that the persons responsible for this outrage ought to be punished. (Replied the Prussian prime minister wryly, "My dear Popitz, do you wish to punish the Führer?")[23] Afterward Popitz's hostility toward the Nazis intensified, and he entered into the conspiracy against them.

His administrative skills and financial know-how earned him a pivotal role (with Hassell and Erwin Planck) in drafting a constitution for postwar Germany. But this document called for a strong central government, and Goerdeler opposed it. So, eventually the plan was discarded.[24] While stigmatized in the eyes of the younger conspirators for his continuing association with Goering and other top Nazis, as well as for his "outmoded" thinking, Popitz was also the architect of an abortive coup in December 1939. This was a last-ditch, ill-conceived bid to stop Hitler from going to war in the west by having him arrested in Berlin.[25] At that time Popitz considered drawing Goering into the plot, but he wisely did not approach him.[26]

As the war worsened for Germany, and even Goebbels began to think about negotiating a peace settlement,[27] the fifty-nine-year-old Popitz concocted his most daring strategem: he would speak privately to the Reichsführer of the SS, Heinrich Himmler, and win his support for a putsch. Popitz was joined in this scheme by a Berlin attorney named Carl Langbehn. A former neighbor of Himmler's on the Bavarian Tegernsee,[28] Langbehn had acted as the SS leader's lawyer before the war.[29] Langbehn knew that Himmler now felt, after the failure of a German Panzer offensive at Kursk, that the war was lost. Buoyed by this knowledge, Popitz arranged a meeting with Himmler at the Interior Ministry, on August 26th.[30] In that conversation the Prussian bureaucrat slyly suggested that Germany was floundering on the battlefield and, accordingly, that a stronger, steadier hand was needed to take charge. But Himmler declined to accept this implicit invitation. Later Bormann got wind of this conspiratorial meeting and had his agents keep an eye on both Popitz and Langbehn.

Two days later, on the 28th, Langbehn left Berlin bound for Switzerland in another bid to "feel out...the reactions of the Allies to a change of regime."[31] In the Swiss capital he spoke with both British and U.S. intelligence officers, but he made no headway. A cable sent by the French resistance describing Langbehn's mission was intercepted by German agents, and when he and his wife attempted to return home, they were arrested on the border. Escorted back to Berlin, Langbehn was interrogated, summarily tried, and convicted of treason. Before the sentence of death was carried out, in October 1944, he was handed over to SS thugs, who tortured him, tearing off his genitals.[32] Because of Langbehn's exposure, Popitz himself came under a cloud of suspicion.[33] Himmler's ambitious young protégé, Walter Schellenberg, knew of the Prussian minister's tie to Langbehn's Swiss mission. He placed Popitz under Gestapo surveillance to see if he would tip his hand. Around this time Popitz sought out Erwin Respondek.

The two men were old friends. Respondek had first met Popitz during the First World War when, fresh back from the front, he was working at the treasury office.[34] Popitz was then serving as Prussian interior minister. The two officials had similar interests and personalities. They were both well educated, professorial by nature, and highly knowledgeable about political economy and finance. They shared misgivings about developments in Weimar Germany, notably the rise of the Nazis. Once Popitz assumed the finance minister's portfolio, in 1933, he regularly discussed Hitler's domestic and foreign policies with Respondek.[35] These conversations took place without Respondek revealing his ties to Washington.[36]

Popitz kept Respondek informed about opposition proposals for Germany's future political and economic order.[37] In October 1943 he began to talk specifics. By now, shaken by the arrest of his friend Langbehn and worried about his own fate, the physically frail finance minister was growing desperate in his desire to topple the Nazis and shorten the war. A central figure in his plans was the young, handsome, Oxford-educated aristocrat Adam von Trott zu Solz.

Trott made use of his Anglo-Saxon background (he was a descendant of John Jay) and academic friends in England to establish resistance ties to the West. In March 1937, en route to China, he had stopped off in the United States and visited an old Oxford acquaintance, the Vienna-born Felix Frankfurter, who was then teaching law at Harvard.[38] But Frankfurter was somewhat distrustful of his visitor's motives. Returning to Europe from the Far East, the thirty-year-old Trott next traveled to England, in June 1939, to brief Prime Minister Chamberlain on the status of the German opposition. He was given an icy reception.[39] Having been outfoxed by Hitler, the British leader was in no mood to be taken in by another emissary of peace and good will—even an Anglophile like Trott.[40] The German official returned across the Channel without having been given the slightest encouragement. Undaunted, the German aristocrat now looked again to the United States.

As Hitler's armies were subduing the Poles, Trott boarded a steamer for the United States, ostensibly to attend a conference of the Institute of Pacific Relations. In fact, he was casting out lines for the opposition and for a new plan for postwar Germany. But the Americans proved just as wary of him as the British. A second meeting with Frankfurter was a disaster.[41] The State Department's George Messersmith at first liked both Trott's memorandum and Trott himself when he encountered the opposition emissary in Washington. But the FBI was tailing the young German visitor and compiling a dossier on him that suggested Trott was covertly seeking U.S. help in overthrowing Hitler.[42] Messersmith and other officials were frightened off by this allegation, and even though Trott did manage to have tea with Eleanor Roosevelt at the White House, he came away with no promises.[43]

To prove his opposition credentials, Trott sought out the best-known German émigré politician living in the United States—Heinrich Brüning.[44] During a three-day stay in Cambridge Trott succeeded in convincing the former chancellor of his sincerity and in obtaining a written recommendation.[45] The two men conferred again in the middle of December,[46] and this time Brüning consented to speak with the president personally on Trott's behalf.[47] But even this did not dispel all doubts about Trott's mission, and he went back to Germany a disappointed man.

Introduced to the Kreisau Circle by his good friend Hans Bernd von Haeften,[48] Trott persisted in seeking Allied backing for the German opposition. From 1942 up to the July 20, 1944, attempt on Hitler's life, he traveled abroad some 16 times—chiefly to Sweden and Switzerland, where he cautioned Allen Dulles about a defeated Germany's succumbing to communism.[49] Bound by the "unconditional surrender" terms of the Allies, Dulles could offer him no consoling words.

If he were going to make any headway with the Americans, Trott concluded he would have to speak directly with President Roosevelt. This, in the fall of 1943, was certainly an audacious idea for a German Foreign Ministry official, but Trott was still sanguine enough to believe he could pull it off. In his optimism he was apparently encouraged by Hitler's predecessor in the chancellory, Franz von Papen.

Then German ambassador to Turkey, Papen had already decided to convince the U.S. president to change his mind about the precondition of unconditional surrender. In April 1943 he had found out about plans for a coup during a Berlin dinner with Count Helldorf and Gottfried von Bismarck. Papen had promised to get in touch with the U.S. president after returning to Ankara. He also agreed that "Herr Trott zu Solz, who often came to Ankara on behalf of the Foreign Office, should act as our courier."[50] Back in Turkey, Papen sent off a message to Roosevelt's personal representative, former Pennsylvania governor George H. Earle. In July Trott visited Papen in the Turkish capital and was told no reply had yet been received from Washington.[51] This talk may have induced Trott to pursue his own peace efforts more vigorously. During subsequent official trips to Italy and Sweden, he attempted to establish a link of his own to the White House.[52]

This goal Trott shared with Johannes Popitz in October. Eager to help out, Popitz approached Respondek late the following month: could he possibly open a door to Roosevelt through Heinrich Brüning? Respondek did not commit himself:

I informed Popitz about Dr. Brüning's position regarding the Third Reich. There was no need to point out that he was one hundred percent opposed to Hitler. Still, at our last meeting in London in 1938 he had explained to me that, living abroad, he did not want to take any position against the Third Reich. The present situation, namely Hitler's certain defeat in the war, did not mean any change in this position.[53]

Dubious about the president's interest in any overtures from the German opposition, Respondek was still willing to do what he could. He proposed to Popitz that Trott be given a token testifying to his "absolute trustworthiness," which the German diplomat could, in turn, present to Brüning—if and when he managed to reach the United States. Respondek suggested a slip of paper bearing the ex-chancellor's Cambridge address and the typed words "Freundliche Grüsse." This note he would sign with his codename, "Ralph."[54] With this in hand, Trott could easily gain entree to Secretary of State Hull, Respondek said. But under no circumstances was his own name to be used. Trott was simply to be told the piece of paper came from Popitz.[55]

Popitz did not immediately take Respondek up on this offer. Some time elapsed before they met again, during an intermission of a late December performance of *Der Rosenkavalier*. Huddled unobtrusively in a corner with Respondek, Popitz whispered that Trott was still attempting to contact the U.S. government, now by way of the Allied invasion forces in Italy.[56] Respondek again offered to vouch for Trott, but it is not certain that he actually handed Popitz the promised note. In any event, Trott never had a chance to make use of it.[57]

During this conversation Respondek urged that Popitz and other resistance leaders take steps to safeguard themselves against the Gestapo in case their coup should fail.[58] Although he doubted this would happen, Popitz agreed to discuss arrangements for concealing the conspirators and then report back to Respondek.

Respondek did not wait for an answer. Accompanied by Hermann Muckermann,[59] he went to see the diminutive bishop of Berlin, Konrad Count von Preysing. A member of an aristocratic Bavarian family, Preysing was a leading Catholic critic of Hitler's.[60] He was in touch with several members of the Kreisau and Goerdeler circles, including Moltke and Stauffenberg.[61] He knew exactly what was being planned against the

Führer. After listening to Respondek's concerns, Bishop Preysing offered sanctuary to the plotters in several southern German monasteries. His younger brother and alter ego, Albert, dean of St. Martin's in Landshut, would make the arrangements.[62] Shortly afterward, Respondek made a slight detour during a trip to Regensburg and spoke with the bishop's brother. The younger Preysing said it would be possible to hide between four and six of the conspirators in each of five monasteries scattered between Passau, Landshut, and Regensburg if this was done quietly, over a period of time. The Domprobst himself would oversee their concealment.[63]

When Respondek talked to Popitz again, probably in January of 1944, the older man related that the plotters were afraid of taking any self-protective measures:

Seeking a haven too early would mean that the participants would be withdrawing from their spheres of activity, which would naturally awaken suspicion and, in this case, be sufficient grounds to arrest members of their families.... None of the conspirators could bear to see their relatives in the *Sippenhaft* of agencies of the Third Reich if only for a single hour.[64]

So Respondek's escape plan was stillborn. The conspirators would stay by their posts, waiting nervously for Count Stauffenberg to make his move.

Stauffenberg, driven by the "impulsive passions of the disillusioned military man,"[65] was eager to strike, and this fact may have accounted for the urgency of Respondek's midwinter discussion with Popitz. Indeed, the war-crippled staff officer was set to carry out Operation Valkyrie on December 26, 1943, when he arrived at Hitler's East Prussian field headquarters with a timebomb hidden in his suitcase. Unfortunately for the conspirators, the Führer suddenly cancelled this conference to begin his Christmas holiday, and a dejected Stauffenberg had to head back to Berlin biting his lip.

By now the Nazis were closing in on their enemies. A Gestapo agent infiltrated an anti-Nazi circle in Berlin, and in the ensuing investigation Moltke and his Kreisau Circle were implicated. Their arrests, coupled with the exposure of Admiral Canaris and his Abwehr resistance group, dealt the anti-Hitler forces inside Germany a major blow. The remaining opponents of the regime would have to finish off the Nazi leader soon, before they, too, were found out.

Aside from helping to arrange a hiding place for its leaders, Respondek did not participate in the Attentat of July 20th. Clearly he had ambivalent feelings about the conspirators. Few—certainly not Stauffenberg—were German democrats. Many had initially sided, albeit passively, with the Nazis. Respondek probably also wondered if the coup would succeed. If it did, what would come afterward? If it did not, he was obviously better off keeping his distance.

In the end, this reasoning saved Respondek's life. When Adolf Hitler stumbled out of the wrecked conference barracks at Rastenburg on July 20th—stunned, partially paralyzed, singed, but still very much alive—the coup was doomed. In Berlin troops loyal to the Führer held the conspirators at bay. Confused and hesitant, rebel officers were arrested and shot on the spot, Beck, Stauffenberg, Werner von Haeften, and Olbricht among them. In other German cities the long-awaited revolt never came off. By one o'clock in the morning of the 21st, when a raspy Hitler spoke on German radio to dispel any doubts about who was in charge of the Third Reich and to vow revenge ("We will settle accounts the way the National Socialists are accustomed to settle them"[66]), the surviving conspirators were already being hunted down. A few tried to flee: Hans Bernd Gisevius eluded arrest in Berlin and found a haven in the countryside before escaping to Switzerland.[67] Goerdeler set out with a knapsack on his back but was spotted in a restaurant and apprehended.[68] But most of the plotters simply waited helplessly for Himmler's men to come banging on their doors.

And they came. The same night Hitler told the nation of his miraculous escape from death, the arrests began. In the Gestapo's sweeping net were snared all the principal conspirators, including three persons close to Respondek—Joseph Wirmer, the Paderborn-born attorney slated to become minister of justice, Paul Lejeune-Jung, and Johannes Popitz. Erwin Planck was also picked up. They were all taken away in handcuffs to the Gestapo's nefarious Prinz Albrechtstrasse prison, where teams of Gestapo investigators dragged incriminating information out of them. And still the arrests went on and on.[69] As the plotters had feared, Hitler's wrath extended to their relatives. They were rounded up by the hundreds, with Himmler vowing entire families would "be wiped out down to the last member."[70]

This massive retaliation paralyzed Respondek. What should he do? Flight would only tip his hand—and where could he go? For weeks he lived with the growing anxiety that he might be next. Members of the Kreisau and Goerdeler circles might have blurted out his name.[71] Popitz, for one, knew of Respondek's offer to find a safe haven for the conspirators. In the Gestapo's merciless hands he might give this away.

But Popitz kept quiet. The hot, midsummer days passed agonizingly slowly on the Mariannenstrasse, and still the Gestapo did not appear. Then, toward the end of August, Himmler and Kaltenbrunner ordered a second wave of arrests, encompassing all known remaining foes of the regime, including former members of opposition parties. Respondek's name was on this list. Around the 24th of the month, Gestapo agents came without fanfare and took him away, along with a Communist by the name of Hoffmann, a Dr. Vockel, and Heinrich Krone, former deputy general secretary of the Center Party.[72]

Respondek was put in an overcrowded cell at the Alexanderplatz police prison. Shaken, he was confident he would eventually be let go because only a few of the detainees knew his name. None knew of his association with Cordell Hull. And there was no proof he had taken part in the Attentat.[73] Hardened by his previous Gestapo interrogations, Respondek now braced himself for more long "conversations" in his small, uncomfortable cell.[74] Off and on over the next six weeks he was questioned again and again about his friendships, his professional work, and his political activities.[75] Mainly the Gestapo suspected him of having been a "significant political link between ... Goerdeler and ... Brüning in the preparation of the assassination attempt."[76] Respondek endured all kinds of threats. Even though his wife managed to bring him extra food, hidden within bundles of fresh clothes,[77] Respondek lost considerable weight on the scarcely edible prison rations—over 30 pounds—and was so mentally and physically weakened by his ordeal that the prison doctor was called in to treat him.[78] Finally, in the last week of September, Kaltenbrunner informed Charlotte that her husband's "name did not appear on any of the lists of persons associated with the attempt on Hitler's life, but that his case had, nevertheless, to be brought before the Führer's Hauptquartier for further investigation."[79]

Herbert Müller may have influenced Kaltenbrunner's decision to let Respondek go. According to Agnes Dreimann, Müller pleaded Respondek's case to his superior at the Kaiser Wilhelm Society, Ernst Telschow. Telschow's brother ran a café frequented by Kaltenbrunner, and this tie was exploited on Respondek's behalf.[80] But before releasing him, the Gestapo had one last gambit to play with their prisoner. Out of the blue one day, Respondek was asked if he could get in touch with Sam Woods![81]

Respondek was told Papen wanted to extend a peace feeler to the Americans. Since Respondek had close ties to Woods, he was the logical go-between for such an offer.[82] Feigning ignorance about his American friend, Respondek innocently asked about Woods's whereabouts and was told he was living in a "neutral country."[83] He surmised the Gestapo was setting a trap: if he took Papen's message to Zurich, his family in Berlin would be held hostage until he returned. Charlotte agreed with him. To avoid this mission Respondek would have to stall for time. He deliberately made himself ill, sleeping without blankets to worsen his rheumatism, and weakening himself further by refusing to eat his meals. After several weeks he was in such poor health that he could not possibly go abroad. At the end of October 1944 the Gestapo released Respondek with a warning that he would remain under surveillance, subject to weekly interrogation and liable to be arrested at any time.[84]

What was Papen trying to do? His earlier overture to Roosevelt had failed.[85] After the July 20th fiasco Papen had left Turkey for the Reich, expecting to be arrested as soon as he set foot on German soil.[86] When this did not happen, he resolved to redouble his efforts to end the war, this time audaciously proposing directly to Hitler that peace terms be conveyed to the Western Allies. But the Führer burst into a rage and would hear nothing of this. Although chastized, Papen persisted:

In view of the hopeless situation on the Western front.... I decided to make one last attempt to stop the conflict. I thought that if we could come to some agreement with the Western Powers it would be possible to halt the Russians on our eastern frontiers.... I decided to make another appeal, through Baron Steengracht, the Secretary of State at the Foreign Office."[87]

Papen declared himself ready to go to Madrid to speak to Allied representatives there, but Foreign Minister Ribbentrop refused to authorize this, saying such a trip would only "weaken Germany's power of resistance."[88]

How did Papen learn about Respondek's ties to the Americans? How would he have had the leverage to send out a peace feeler through Kaltenbrunner? Most likely there was some collusion between Papen and the notorious head of the Reichssicherheitshauptamt. Kaltenbrunner did attempt to replace Himmler as a liaison with the International Red Cross and to contact Dulles toward the end of 1944. And during his interrogation at Nuremberg, the chief of Hitler's security police claimed he had sought to shorten the conflict as early as February 1943, using the Vatican as an intermediary.[89] His alleged efforts to strike a bargain with Dulles involved several emissaries to Switzerland. This suggests that Kaltenbrunner may have conferred with Papen first and then come up with the idea of employing Respondek in this capacity.

Respondek left prison at the end of September physically and emotionally broken. Most of his friends in the conspiracy were already dead. Wirmer and Lejeune-Jung had been hanged at the Plötzensee prison on September 8th. Erwin Planck, after being beaten and tortured to extract more information,[90] was still alive, as was Popitz, but not for long.[91] The scattered surviving remnants of the opposition could not conceivably mount another coup. Alone once again, thrown back on his own resources, Respondek could only hope somehow to stay alive until the end came—the hour of Germany's defeat, the hour of his liberation.[92]

Sam Woods was tipped off about the July 20th attempt on Hitler's life a week ahead of time. While having dinner at the Zurich home of Joe

Basler, a Swiss importer, he had received a phone call from another Swiss acquaintance, Dr. Walter Keller-Staub. A lawyer with offices just down the street from the U.S. consulate, Keller-Staub had previously been blacklisted for alleged dealings with the Nazis, but Woods had found no proof of this and had his name removed.[93] Keller-Staub happened to be the attorney for Eduard Waetjen and was thus indirectly involved in the conspiracy.

Related to the Rockefellers by his sister's marriage, Waetjen was a contact person for the resistance in Switzerland. Through his duties at the German consulate he had access to valuable intelligence from Germany, Japan, and countries under their dominance.[94] Under the codename "Homer" (Waetjen was working on a translation of *The Odyssey* during the war[95]), he conveyed several peace offers from the Oster and Kreisau circles to Allen Dulles.[96] (Waetjen also knew Sam Woods, but only socially.[97]) In June, the Ascona-based attorney told Dulles that Beck and Goerdeler would launch a coup on condition that the Allies dealt with them as Germany's legitimate rulers once the Nazis had been defeated.[98] But the OSS spymaster was not prepared to make any such concession. Not long afterward, Waetjen met with his fellow conspirator Gisevius and discussed the coup's chances of succeeding.[99] Two days later, on July 11th, Gisevius quietly left the apartment he shared with his mother at the Pension Muralto and boarded a train headed for Berlin to join the plotters at this fateful hour.[100] What Keller-Staub, eager to show his anti-Nazi colors, had to tell Woods on the telephone that night came from Gisevius: the Germans planning to kill Hitler had just left Zurich.[101]

This news did not surprise the U.S. consul general. He already knew about Gisevius's role in the conspiracy from a Jewish refugee then living in the same Zurich boarding house. And, as was noted earlier, Woods also knew about the existence of the Goerdeler circle and its intent to assassinate the Führer. From interviews of refugees, anti-Nazi Swiss, and cooperative German business travelers to Switzerland, Woods had pieced together an outline of the German resistance and shared this with the State Department. Much of what he found out was duplicated in Dulles's cables to OSS headquarters.[102] Such was the state of State–OSS cooperation in wartime Switzerland.

In the coup's aftermath, information out of Germany was scarce. With Gisevius in hiding, Dulles's line to "Breakers" (the Hitler opposition) was cut. Now he and Woods would have to rely on press and radio bulletins emanating from Berlin. The consul general followed these with intense interest. He had known at least one of the resistance figures now under arrest, the Berlin chief of police, Count von Helldorf.[103] But far more important to him personally was the fate of Erwin Respondek.

Woods had not heard from "Ralph" in over half a year. Now he had every reason to fear for Respondek's life. It was impossible for him to find out what had happened to his German confidant. And, even if he could, there was nothing Woods could do to help.

Meanwhile, the Mississippian was doing his best to help others in need, writing another colorful chapter in his already improbable wartime career. Starting in the midsummer of 1943, B-17 Flying Fortresses and B-24 Liberators of the U.S. Eighth Air Force struck German industrial targets in Frankfurt, Mannheim, Kassel, and Hannover. Returning bombers crippled by anti-aircraft fire, disoriented, or short on fuel periodically made emergency landings on Swiss territory. Some were forced down for violating Switzerland's air space. Many of these aircraft landed at the Dübendorff military airbase outside Zurich.[104] The planes, their valuable bomb sites and navigational equipment, and even the crews' personal clothing were confiscated by Swiss authorities, and the airmen were placed in detention camps, held under armed guard.[105] These actions were taken largely to avoid antagonizing the Germans and were justified by the 1907 Hague convention governing treatment of belligerents in neutral countries.[106]

All told, over 1,500 U.S. flyers were interned in Switzerland during the Second World War, together with 13,500 soldiers and airmen from various warring nations.[107] The Swiss policy particularly galled the Americans, who resented having their valuable equipment taken away and their even more irreplaceable bomber pilots put out of action. At Cordell Hull's behest the U.S. legation vehemently protested to the Swiss government, but without much success.[108] Leland Harrison and General Legge could do very little to help these flyers. Indeed, the U.S. military attaché warned the airmen they would be courtmartialed and put in Swiss jails if they tried to escape.[109] By the summer of 1944 the U.S. government changed its policy: the OSS was asked to evacuate 1,000 of the internees.[110] Furthermore, Hull instructed his representatives in Bern to assist the interned flyers in escaping from Switzerland. After this directive, some were hidden at the legation and then transported in sealed boxcars to the border with liberated France, from where they made their way back to England.[111]

The secretary of state also asked Woods to help out,[112] and the consul general, himself a former Marine Corps aviator, responded with his usual panache and penchant for the cloak-and-dagger. Soon he was singlehandedly running his own twentieth-century version of the underground railroad. It worked like this: Woods would procure forged passes allowing a group of airmen out of their detention camp.[113] Then the commanding officer of the internees in Davos would telephone Woods at his home and arrange for five flyers to meet the diplomat inside a Catholic church near Lucerne.[114] In the church, while pretending to pray on his knees, Woods would cough and discreetly drop a handkerchief as a signal. When the flyers came forward, he would utter the words "I am an alumnus of Washington University" to identify himself.[115] (Mary Bancroft says Woods and his fellow consul, Robert Cowan, would wear green ties because they had noticed no Swiss men did.[116]) Then they would follow Woods outside, squeeze into his large black Opel, and drive the short distance to the frontier.[117] En route, the escapees would slip into the French peasant garb obtained by Woods, sometimes disguising themselves as women.[118] On the border they would leap out of the car and enter a tavern that was connected to the French side by an underground sewer tunnel.[119] A telephone line ran through the sewer, and Woods would use it to alert a French pub at the other end that the American detainees were coming. Once across the border the flyers would be met by members of the French underground and escorted safely back to England.[120]

Bribes were needed to gain the cooperation of the two innkeepers. To pay them, Woods found some help from an unlikely quarter. For some time the millionaire president and founder of IBM, Thomas J. Watson, had been concerned about the plight of U.S. airmen interned in Switzerland. He had donated $10,000 to buy them recreational equipment.[121] In August 1944 the acting head of the European office of International Business Machines (IBM), Werner C. Lier, proposed putting this money at Woods's disposal. The consul general and General Legge readily accepted this offer, and the bulk of these funds was entrusted to them, in part to pay for "services rendered in acting as guides."[122]

With this cash in hand, Woods stepped up his daring escape operations. At times he drove airmen across the border into German-occupied France, concealed inside hearses or under the false bottoms of apple carts.[123] Obliging clergy slipped escape kits into prison cells, and one cooperative Swiss soldier obtained the required travel documents. Woods also got some help from an Italian waiter and a Swiss waitress, who collected civilian clothes for the airmen and escorted them to the border near Lucerne.[124]

Many a cold night during the winter of 1944–45 Woods, or "General Sam," as the airmen affectionately called him,[125] would leave his warm, comfortable home on the Toblerstrasse, climb inside his car, and drive off in the dark to keep another rendezvous with a band of tired, gaunt-faced, and frightened American airmen. In the early hours of the morning, he would return, chilled and exhausted, to catch a few hours' sleep before starting another day at the consulate.[126]

All together, Woods personally brought at least 200 airmen to safety in France,[127] and he helped arranged the escape of as many as a thousand more. Several years after the war he was awarded the Medal of Freedom for "patriotic services of unusual value to the American Army."[128] Along with this official tribute came dozens of grateful letters from the men he had helped, as well as a watch they had bought for him, inscribed "To the Best Friend an American Ever Had."[129] He treasured that most of all.

12

BITTER FRUITS
OF VICTORY

For Erwin Respondek, trapped inside the Third Reich, each passing day brought closer the war's end and his release from twelve nightmarish years of Nazi tyranny. But there were still dangers, Even as Allied armies pierced the Reich's frontiers and sped toward Berlin, the Nazis were rounding up and executing their opponents. And the skies over Respondek's head held another threat: day after day the U.S. and British planes returned. Their tumbling, whistling bombs did not discriminate between diehard Nazis and Germans who had longed for Hitler's defeat.

Luckily, Respondek and his family were spared. His old office on the Pariser Platz was destroyed during one raid,[1] but the Mariannenstrasse home, located several miles from the city's center, escaped major damage. Two bombs struck it but only burned part of the roof and garage,[2] and no one was hurt.

As winter gave way reluctantly to spring in the rubble-strewn, charred capital, other dangers loomed closer. On March 22nd, Patton's troops breached the Rhine en masse, while the Red Army, having already conquered Silesia and East Prussia, paused along the banks of the Oder, barely an hour's drive from the Brandenburger Tor. Respondek was more alarmed by this menace from the east. As a Catholic and German democrat he had no liking for Soviet-style communism.[3] Certainly he could expect no comradely embrace from Stalin's marauding soldiers, even if it was he who had sought to save them from Nazi perfidy four years before. Respondek saw a final perverse irony in Hitler's yielding to the Russians in the east: in his version of *Götterdämmerung*, the maniacal Führer was bent on opening the floodgates to his worst enemies, allowing the communists to "enter into the heart of Europe...as a final means of destruction."[4]

Already the Nazi propaganda mills were gearing up for the Red Army with placards all over the city depicting the horrors that lay in store if Berlin should fall.[5] Practical-minded Berliners took advantage of lulls in the air raids to climb out of their cellars and bury their silver. Now they listened openly to the British Broadcasting Corporations's *Feind-sender*,[6] which told of a steady Allied advance. Darting down empty, bomb-cratered streets, Respondek's neighbors scoured for scraps of food, wondering how much longer their ordeal would last.

Like a human tidal wave, the Russians, two-and-a-half million strong, swept toward Berlin. On the night of April 15th and into the early morning of the 16th, five days before Hitler's fifty-sixth—and last—birthday, Allied bombers pounded the city as a prelude to the Russian onslaught. As shells from Soviet artillery guns exploded, combat units took up positions inside the northern and southern suburbs. By the 25th the Reichshauptstadt was completely surrounded. Five days later, with the Russians scant yards from his bunker, Adolf Hitler shot himself in the head. The news was solemnly broadcast at one o'clock in the morning.[7] After little over a dozen years, the Thousand-Year Reich was finished.

Its surviving citizens—waving white sheets, cowering in their basements—had to make their own separate peace with its conquerors. In Lichterfelde, pillaging Russians[8] moved in, accompanied by commando units on the lookout for German atomic scientists. The large garden and intact Respondek home at Mariannenstrasse 3 caught the eye of a Soviet signal outfit:

The commander inspected it with his female interpreter and asked why there were so many books. I replied that I was a university docent and had myself written many scholarly works. At that he removed his military cap, withdrew to his trailer, and ordered that no soldier should enter the house, except after knocking to obtain water or other such items. He celebrated the 1st of May with six other officers in my house.[9]

Cordial relations were thus established between the Russians and their professorial host. The commanding officer's adjutant spoke passable German, and through him Respondek secured permission to visit the Soviet officer in charge of Dahlem and to inspect the grounds of the Kaiser Wilhelm Society, now in the hands of Soviet troops. From the Soviet commandant Respondek could learn nothing about what had happened to the German scientists there, but he was permitted to go looking for friends and family members elsewhere in the city.[10]

The Respondek's younger daughter, Dorothea, and her physician husband were safe in another Berlin neighborhood. But twenty-five-year-old Valeska and her family were missing in Würzburg. Unbeknownst to her parents, she had survived a devastating air raid and then fled with her husband and young son, Joachim, to a farm in Württemberg, close to the Swiss border. Realizing her best hope of returning to Berlin safely lay with Sam Woods, Valeska mailed off four identical letters to his consular offices in Zurich.[11] Not long afterward a huge black sedan with diplomatic plates pulled into the courtyard, bearing Woods, his driver, and a mound of soap, silk stockings, and shoes. Along with those provisions, Woods left behind an official letter, typed in both English and French, proclaiming Valeska the "daughter of Dr. Erwin Respondek, a well-known German professor and economist of Berlin, who...rendered extremely valuable services to the Allied war effort."[12] The letter requested that she and her family be rendered "every courtesy and help."

In late July, [13] a U.S. Army jeep arrived at the south German farm, driven by a Major Louis Putze. A friend of Woods, he took the Hoffmanns to Frankfurt, where, disguised as GIs, they boarded a special "Eisenhower Train" for Berlin. Seeing them off at the station was an old friend, Jacob Beam.[14]

One of the few U.S. government officials who knew the Respondeks, Beam had left his wartime post in the London embassy to join the occupation forces as a political advisor, working under Robert Murphy. He was among the first American civilians to enter occupied Berlin. He moved into a large house in Dahlem, sharing these quarters with another Berlin veteran, Donald Heath,[15] who was now director of the State Department's political affairs division. The city once so thoroughly enjoyed by these two diplomats was now barely recognizable. It was full of desolation and death. Corpses lay half buried under mounds of debris. The subways were flooded, the trains at a standstill, the trees in the once-elegant Tiergarten chopped down.[16] Berlin's remaining three million inhabitants lived from day to day on the edge of starvation.

Acting on orders from the now-retired Cordell Hull, Heath and Beam set out to locate the Respondeks in Lichterfelde to see if they were all right. Accompanied by a former military attaché in Berlin, Colonel William D. Hohenthal, the two State Department officials rode in an army jeep over to the Mariannenstrasse on July 10th.[17] It was a poignant reunion of old friends who had feared they might never see one another again. Beam was glad to find the Respondeks in generally good physical health, but he was distressed that they looked "shaken," "numbed," and "disoriented."[18] Respondek also seemed a bit too fond of the recently departed Russians.[19]

Respondek experienced a rush of conflicting emotions. This visit from his American friends revived his faith in the United States and in the cause of democracy. Still, he felt let down. During their conversation neither Beam nor Heath brought up the promise made to him by Woods back in 1942: that he would be invited to Washington to assume a high-ranking post. Respondek did not feel it was appropriate for him to remind his visitors, and so he did not.[20] He suffered his disappointment in stoic silence. After waiting so long for this, his hour of triumph, he now had to resign himself to waiting some more. His American friends left with only a handshake and an offer to put him in touch with other officials.[21]

In the coming months and years, Respondek's feelings of betrayal would only intensify. His dreams of recognition and of a new life in the United States would be dashed by official indifference and the ironic twists and turns of postwar U.S. policy toward Germany. Slowly Respondek's idealistic, naive hopes would turn to bitter anger.[22]

The American most eager to help the impoverished Respondeks[23] was Sam Woods. On top of asking the secretary of state to locate his Berlin friends, Woods attempted to land Respondek a job with the U.S. occupation. In October he drafted an official statement addressed to "all military and civilian authorities in Germany" stating that Respondek had "opposed the Nazis in every way possible from the beginning" and recommending him for a "position of importance, trust, and confidence" with the military government.[24] In a telegram he urged Hull to "repay [the] debt [of] gratitude owed by our country to [a] loyal friend who without thought of compensation risked [his] life for our cause."[25] This came on the heels of a letter asking that Respondek and his son-in-law, Friedrich Hoffmann, be found positions in the United States.[26] Now out of office, Hull could not handle this request himself and turned it over to State Department officials. A cable concerning Respondek was sent to Robert Murphy in Berlin, but, inexplicably, no action was taken on it for ten months.[27]

A determined Woods even offered to come to Washington to set the record straight about what Respondek had accomplished for the U.S. government (and to disprove Sumner Welles's version of the Barbarossa warning to the Soviets[28]). Unfortunately for Respondek, the ailing Hull was no longer in a position to help his onetime spy in Berlin. After Roosevelt's re-election in November 1944, the seventy-three-year-old Hull, exhausted after 12 demanding years in harness, had gone straight from his State Department office to the Bethesda Naval Medical Center, where he spent seven months resting and recuperating. Now back in his suite at the Wardman Park Hotel, the former secretary of state was hard at work on his memoirs. The best he could do for Respondek would be to set the record straight on paper.[29] Could Woods help him reconstruct the facts?

The consul general obligingly agreed to do so. He first had Respondek prepare a 12-page "personal confidential report" summarizing their wartime collaboration, and then he presented this, together with his own somewhat different account, to Hull.[30] These documents formed the basis for the description of the State Department warning in the chapter entitled "We Help Russia" in Hull's memoirs. However, at Heinrich Brüning's urging, and with Respondek's concurrence, the retired secretary of state did not refer to Respondek by name to protect him against possible recrimination in Germany.[31] When the memoirs were serialized in the *New York Times* in 1948, Sam Woods was prominently featured but Respondek was described only as a "German friend" of his.[32] This well-intentioned omission would keep the identity of America's spy in Berlin a secret for years to come.[33]

In Europe, Woods kept up his dogged efforts on Respondek's behalf. With Hull's backing, he first tried to have the penniless German sent funds by way of General Lucius Clay, the U.S. military commander.[34] Then, during a May 1946 meeting in Munich, he introduced Respondek to a visiting congressman, Daniel R. McGehee of Mississippi,[35] who promised to ask General Clay about a position for Respondek with the U.S. military government and to find the German a "special task" on a congressional committee.[36] But that November the six-term Democrat was not renominated by his party, and so nothing came of this promise.

In September 1947 Woods set up a Zurich meeting between Respondek and several influential members of the House Committee on Foreign Affairs. Sitting in the consul general's office, Respondek could not help but be impressed by the framed, autographed photographs of President Roosevelt, President Truman, and other top U.S. officials[37] and feel gratified by the interest expressed in his own work.[38] After drafting several memorandums for the visiting legislators on postwar Germany and its participation in the proposed Marshall Plan, Respondek returned to Berlin convinced he could now count on help from Washington.[39]

But this promise, too, went unfulfilled. So did another from Woods's close friend in the Congress, Karl Stefan, a key Republican member of the House Appropriations Committee.[40] Undaunted, Woods also introduced Respondek to occupation officials in Frankfurt and Berlin.[41] As a result of these meetings, attended by Donald Heath, Jacob Beam, and Robert Murphy, the basis for a close working relationship with the Americans was developed. Indeed, four days after Heath and Beam stopped by his home on July 10, 1945, Respondek submitted a wide-ranging memorandum on Allied postwar policies in regard to industry, agriculture, and politics.[42] This was intended for Murphy, the only U.S. occupation official invited to attend the upcoming Potsdam conference.

A career diplomat, Murphy had been named to the top civilian post in occupied Germany that March with little guidance from an ill and distracted Franklin Roosevelt on how to carry out his duties.[43] Although he had spent considerable time in Bavaria during the 1920s, the tall, genial Murphy had little grasp of current conditions and of how to treat a defeated Germany. Now immersed in drafting position papers for the U.S. delegation on reparations, German production levels, living standards, and other economic matters,[44] he welcomed Respondek's unsolicited advice.[45]

On the strength of these policy recommendations, Respondek was "immediately requisitioned to work further with the State Department ... naturally on an informal basis."[46] Over the next several years, eager to curry favor with the Americans and to help solidify the West's foothold in Germany, the former professor of economics churned out a flood of reports and position papers for Murphy and his staff. These covered topics as diverse as reconstruction of the Reichsbank, the work of German atomic scientists now in Soviet hands, Russian progress toward building an atomic bomb, Soviet policies toward Germany, denazification, and a new German constitution.[47] As the cold war intensified, State Department officials paid more attention to what Respondek had to say.[48] Murphy was particularly appreciative of his views: Respondek was one of the "half dozen people" who convinced the U.S. political advisor that Germany needed to recover its Polish-occupied territories in the east if it were going to attain economic stability.[49] Murphy also made use of Respondek's proposals for organizing a postwar German government at the December 1947 London conference of foreign ministers.[50] The Americans further benefited from his April 1947 tip-off about a Soviet explosive device more powerful than the atomic bomb[51] and from his thoughts on fixing Germany's eastern frontier.[52]

All this research and writing the now-destitute Respondek did gratis for the U.S. government,[53] living on the hope that Sam Woods would eventually honor his 1942 pledge of a top-level Washington post.[54] But it appeared that the consul general had made this promise entirely on his own, without ever consulting his superiors in the State Department. With both Hull and Breckenridge Long now out of office[55] and a new administration in charge, Respondek had even fewer allies willing—or able—to speak up for him.[56] And some of the State Department officials who had stayed in office did not particularly care for the upstart Woods[57] and were not inclined to do him any favors.

In occupied Berlin an ever-hopeful Respondek cultivated friendships with several Americans. One of the them was Thomas B. Stauffer. A somewhat unconventional, bespectacled, well-educated army lieutenant, Stauffer was chief of the evaluation section in the Division of Civil Affairs, tasked with checking out anti-Nazi Germans who might be of help to the occupying powers. Stauffer had first learned about Respondek in July 1945, when the German's name surfaced on a "white list" then being compiled by the OSS and the army.[58] The next month he met Respondek ("a tiny sly-looking man") when he hand-delivered Sam Woods's statement of gratitude for their wartime collaboration.[59] Of Pennsylvania Dutch origins, conversant in German, and knowledgeable about economics and international affairs from his graduate-school days, Stauffer quickly took a liking to the unemployed professor on the Mariannenstrasse. Respondek offered his opinion on the anti-Nazi credentials of Germans under review by civil affairs,[60] and Stauffer gave the seasoned German politician pointers on the U.S. system of government.[61] (Respondek was then, with Herbert Müller,[52] drafting a new constitution for the revived Center Party.[63])

His friendship with the twenty-eight-year-old Stauffer also gave Respondek some measure of official protection. One day a pair of U.S. airmen showed up on the doorstep of his Lichterfelde home and announced they were confiscating the property. They said that the older Respondeks would have to clear out, but that their daughter Valeska could stay on as a "maid." Respondek at once telephoned Stauffer, who ran over and straightened things out by telling the servicemen they were harassing a German with "top connections in Military Government."[64]

But even Stauffer could not find his new friend a job. As a mere lieutenant he lacked the requisite authority and political clout. And when he had a chance to evaluate Respondek for an advisory post with the U.S. delegation to the United Nations, Stauffer was less than wholly supportive: he described Respondek's Weimar-shaped way of thinking as "unsuited to the present time" and characterized by "unreality."[65] Why, Stauffer asked, did the State Department not help Respondek emigrate to Switzerland or find him a teaching post in the U.S. zone?[66] This equivocal assessment may have scuttled Respondek's chances for any further State Department assistance.[67]

No one else in the military chain of command in Berlin knew who Respondek was or what he had done for the United States. Army officers who ran across him found the ex-professor too clever and demanding for their liking,[68] and they did little to help him.[69] No influential German, or group of Germans, came forward to vouch for Respondek. As Stauffer later summed up, "He was a lone wolf and had no resonance, no constituency, represented nothing."[70]

Respondek was the victim of a sad, tragic irony. Whereas the Americans had once shielded his identity from the Nazi regime so he could continue his intelligence gathering, they were now loath to divulge the nature of his work for fear that Respondek would be condemned as a "collaborator" or traitor in a post-Hitler Germany. Furthermore, the United States was trying to reestablish a working democracy in its occupation zone, and dispensing favors to old friends was not considered conducive to that process.

Without a champion inside Germany Respondek could only bank on Sam Woods. But the American was not having any luck either. When

Woods tried to raise Respondek's plight with Hull during a 1947 home leave, he found the retired secretary of state "so ill it was impossible to talk to him about anything."[71] Whatever further exertions the Mississippian might have been willing to make for Respondek were now derailed by a momentous event in Woods's personal life.[72] He was about to become a very rich man.

Among the prominent personages who had found a wartime haven in Switzerland was the German-American heiress Wilhelmina Busch-Borchard, the ninth child and youngest daughter of the brewer Adolphus Busch, the fabulously wealthy cofounder of Anheuser-Busch in St. Louis.[73] At his death in October 1913 Busch had left his wife and seven children an estate estimated at $50 million.[74] A large, red-headed woman with dark eyes and a passion for big floppy hats, blonde wigs, and undistinguished works of art, Wilhelmina and her first husband, Eduard Scharrer, owned a huge estate and villa situated on the shores of Lake Starnberg. To this Wagnerian kitsch paradise came, in the fall of 1930, a rabblerouser by the name of Adolf Hitler, seeking a contribution for his nascent cause.[75] He left not a pfennig richer and, perhaps to settle this old grudge, had the Bavarian estate confiscated and turned into a sanitarium when he came to power a decade later.[76]

When Eduard Scharrer died in 1933, Wilhelmina married Carl Borchard, a physician from Garmisch. They were divorced in November 1941, and shortly thereafter, allegedly because the Nazis were making life unpleasant for her,[77] the American heiress left for Switzerland. Together with her recently widowed sister,[78] Claire von Gontard, and her niece, Lilly Claire Berghaus, Wilhelmina Borchard took a suite at the posh Hotel Baur au Lac, located in the heart of Zurich and right around the corner from Sam Woods's consular offices. Frau Berghaus was married to one of Goering's secretaries, a Nazi with business interests in the armaments industry in Switzerland and Germany,[79] and she herself was suspected of being a Gestapo agent.[80]

These dubious connections caused the two Busch sisters some difficulties in 1944, as the State Department was cracking down on firms and individuals doing business with the Axis powers. Worldwide some 15,000 persons and companies were either blacklisted or threatened with economic sanctions once the war was over. All future trading with Britain and the United States was to be proscribed, no new export licenses issued, and all assets in the United States frozen.[81] In Zurich, the U.S. consulate compiled a list of over 1,000 such violators of Swiss neutrality.[82] Wilhelmina Busch and her sister were two of the persons whose dubious Nazi ties earned them a place on this blacklist.[83] This action meant that Wilhelmina's monthly allotment of 10,000 Swiss francs from the St. Louis Union Trust Company[84] stopped coming and, furthermore, that the sisters' reported assets of between $50 and $80 million might be confiscated.[85]

The person in the best position to affirm their loyalty and have them taken off the blacklist was Sam Woods. He had met the Busch heiresses when he was also staying at the Baur au Lac. (This probably occurred during a period of strain in Woods's marriage.[86]) The consul general readily seized this opportunity to play knight-errant. He did so largely out of gratitude for Wilhelmina's earlier help contacting Respondek about feared German atomic tests. Soon he was exerting his considerable influence in the nation's capital to have the St. Louis–born heiress removed from the State Department's blacklist.[87] Having succeeding at this, he let it be known, after the war, that Mrs. Borchard was prepared to donate her Bavarian estate, valued at over $11 million, to the U.S. government, along with eight apartment buildings, the 220-room Park Hotel in Munich, and an annual gift of $150,000 toward construction of a Foreign Service officers' club in Washington.[88]

Although he arranged with his old friend James Byrnes to have American troops vacate Mrs. Borchard's Bernried property,[89] Woods ran into "political obstacles" to this real-estate offer, and the deal was never consummated.[90] Worse for Woods, his zeal on Mrs. Borchard's behalf alienated many of his fellow Foreign Service officers[91] and dealt a severe blow to his chances of further State Department promotion.

So that he might better personally oversee the Busch heiress's affairs, Woods requested in 1947 that he be reassigned to Munich as consul general.[92] Because of the notoriety of his clandestine exploits during the war, this transfer was granted.[93] Woods did not tell Respondek his real reasons for wanting to go to Munich, however. Instead, he promised his former collaborator he was planning to "build up a new political position" so that they could continue to work together.[94] When he learned this, Respondek felt renewed hope. But it was misplaced. Woods never followed through. Outside the Bavarian capital the American was busy with more private affairs.

In October Milada Woods, his wife of nearly 24 years, traveled across the Atlantic and the United States to Reno, where she obtained a divorce. Woods sheepishly told his friends the Stefans this was "all my fault."[95] The truth was he had made up his mind to marry Wilhelmina Busch-Borchard, and Milada, a younger and shrewder woman, had agreed to allow him to do so—for a million dollars.[96] This news came as quite a shock to the Woodses' circle of friends in Switzerland and back in the States.[97] People simply did not get divorced in those days, and wives were not cast aside for the sake of a fortune, even a stupendous one like Minnie Busch's. Many of his long-time friends would never forgive Woods for abandoning Milada.[98]

After spending Christmas in the "snowcovered fairyland of Höhen-ried,"[99] the newly appointed consul general was married to Wilhelmina Busch-Borchard, eight years his senior, on February 22, 1948, in a private, thousand-year-old stone chapel on the Lake Starnberg estate.[100] The bride wore a dazzling diamond tiara. (Woods gave her a 50-karat diamond the size of a quarter as a wedding present.[101]) Among the 30 guests attending were the military governor of Bavaria, the pretender to the Bavarian throne, and a neighbor, the former Hungarian regent, Admiral Nicholas Horthy.[102] The correspondent for the *New York Times* described the occasion as "one of the most elaborate ceremonies in the postwar history of the Bavarian capital."[103] For Sam Woods, who had once worked barefoot for a few dollars a day in a Mississippi sawmill, it marked the end of a long road out of poverty and obscurity.

Like some perverse medieval Wheel of Fortune, Woods's rise to incredible wealth came as Erwin Respondek plummeted to depths of despair.[104] Impoverished and embittered by discovering why the American had really come to Munich, Respondek resolved to make a final dramatic plea over Woods's head, directly to Cordell Hull.[105] On April 4, 1948, he wrote, plaintively, that

the time has come that forces me to let you know quite frankly that the work done by me during these last years has called for such immense sacrifices of property that at present I am at a point where it is difficult for me to continue without support from the outside.[106]

In this letter Respondek complained about his shabby treatment by U.S. military officials and about his deteriorating financial situation. Having previously refused to seek compensation for his wartime services, he now implored Hull for a post with the State Department ("according to my abilities and suitable conditions") or the Economic Cooperation Administration (ECA) overseeing Marshall Plan aid to Europe.[107]

The aging Hull responded to this plea by forwarding a copy of his recently published *Memoirs* and by turning over the letter to colleagues still in government. Fortunately for Respondek, it reached Jacob Beam, who was now back in Washington as head of the Central European desk.[108] With Hull's personal approval, Beam took it upon himself to obtain $500 worth of CARE packages for his onetime host in prewar Berlin,[109] but beyond this "token of appreciation" (which Respondek understandably resented), Beam saw little that the U.S. government could do for its former German informant.[110] No documents in the State Department files corroborated Respondek's claim of a promised government post. Although he remained personally concerned, Beam reluctantly had to conclude, in his reply to Respondek, that "our

Government cannot carry the matter further forward on the present basis."[111]

What Beam did not convey in his letter to Respondek was his opinion that the fifty-four-year-old German was "not in a balanced state of mind" due to his wartime ordeal and the Soviet occupation of Berlin.[112] Although Respondek was a "fine German" and once "of considerable use to us," Beam believed his country's "moral obligation" was "in large part fulfilled" by the attention Respondek was receiving from U.S. military officers.

For all practical purposes, Respondek's case was now closed.[113] To make matters worse, Sam Woods got wind of the appeal over his head to Hull and became furious, particularly at Respondek's account of his involvement with Minnie Busch.[114] For his part, Respondek was now thoroughly disgusted with Woods. ("He deliberately disappointed me and cast me aside after his marriage for millions," Respondek brooded to Heinrich Brüning.) His faith in Washington's word and fairness, sustained so steadfastly through the long, dark Nazi era, had suffered "a heavy blow."[115]

Down but not out, Respondek now asked his former political mentor, Brüning, to approach American firms that did business in Europe to ascertain whether they might need a German representative.[116] Brüning did what he could. Not finding any business or academic positions open, he tried to land a job for Respondek in the embryonic West German government, urging Konrad Adenauer[117] to appoint this loyal friend of the United States ambassador to Washington.[118] This was exactly the position Respondek felt he deserved and secretly wanted.[119] It would fulfill President Roosevelt's "promise" to invite him to the United States as the "first German" after the war.[120] But building his own team to run the Bundesrepublik, Adenauer chose another ambassador.[121] Brüning also asked former political associates[122] about having Respondek ("an extremely conscientious observer of the whole financial and economic evolution in Germany in the past twenty years"[123]) designated head of Germany's delegation to the Economic Recovery Program (ERP). Even though Respondek was formally proposed for this job, in the ensuing jockeying for political patronage he lost out.[124]

What offers did come his way Respondek turned down. There was talk of his going to Washington to work for an international bank,[125] but he dismissed this as too lowly an offer. Old Center Party friends urged Respondek to follow them to Bonn and join the federal government.[126] This, too, he rejected, believing "the abandonment of Berlin as capital of the Federal Republic to be a great mistake."[127] Respondek's abiding commitment to the former German capital and to German unity likewise kept him from accepting a post with the Christian Democratic Union.[128]

Too often Respondek was his own worst enemy, making too many demands on his friends, alienating persons he needed to befriend.[129] Humbly ingratiating himself was not his forte, and whatever patience Respondek had once possessed was now depleted by waiting so long to gain his due. No longer would he trust so blindly in the future.[130]

Amid this professional frustration came personal hardship and grief. During the bitterly cold winter of 1947–48 Charlotte fell gravely ill and nearly died following a major operation.[131] As she was recovering, the couple experienced a period of intense joy over the birth, in June, of a grandson ("a beautiful boy, with long black hair and dark eyes!"[132]) But this happy mood did not last long. The young, self-effacing mother, Dorothea—Respondek's favorite daughter and source of his "inner, silent happiness"—was stricken with pleurisy some five months after giving birth and then contracted tuberculosis. Unable to afford a sanitarium, the Respondeks could only stand helplessly by Dorothea's bedside as her condition rapidly worsened. Barely twenty-two years old, "Dore" died on November 22, 1949.[133] Now all the Respondek children were gone— lost to premature death or to the United States. (Valeska had already followed her husband to Maryland.) The pain of this loss brought out old, simmering tensions in the Respondek marriage. Not long after Dorothea was laid to rest, Charlotte left her husband and moved into an apartment with Herbert Müller, who was then separated from his wife. In the early 1950s the Respondeks were divorced.[134]

Throughout all these travails Respondek continued to lend his expertise to the U.S. government. As a former financial advisor to German Jews he counseled U.S. lawyers preparing for the "Aryanization" trial at Nuremberg, which sought to redress the Nazis' illegal seizure of Jewish property.[135] He drafted a proposal for restoring a "functioning economy and currency" in Germany.[136] Respondek also kept Robert Murphy abreast of developments in the east, including the Soviets' plans to blockade West Berlin.[137]

At the same time, he became a spokesman for German reunification, helping Gustav Heinemann, Helene Wessel, Erhard Eppler, and others to found the Gesamtdeutsche Volkspartei (United German People's Party). In the polarized cold war climate of the Adenauer era, this party did not gain popularity. United States officials suspected it of "neutralist" tendencies and spurned it.[138] So did most West Germans, who were content to grow prosperous in a divided land. When the new party ran candidates in the 1953 Bundestag election, it failed to pick up the 5 percent of the votes required to gain any seats. When the United German People's Party was dissolved in 1957, Respondek found himself saddled with many of its debts and had to sell his Lichterfelde home to pay them off.[139] Financially, politically, and personally he was now a broken man.

Sam Woods was faring much better. Down in Bavaria the avuncular, fifty-six-year-old career diplomat was once again turning his attention to helping others in distress. For impoverished refugees from the east he procured U.S. visas.[140] To Germans employed by the Bavarian government he gave generous Christmas presents.[141] To local employees of the consulate on the Ludwigstrasse he furnished monthly CARE packages, paid for out of his own deep pockets.[142] To all who met him he displayed a disarming, irresistible charm.

For his generous deeds and easy-going manner Woods was enormously well liked. An old friend visiting from Mississippi pronounced him "the most popular American in Germany, Austria, or Switzerland."[143] Most of Woods's free time was divided between a 13-room apartment in Munich's Park Hotel (filled from baseboard to ceiling with hundreds of valuable paintings[144]) and Minnie's luxurious *Schloss* in the foothills of the Bavarian Alps. At Bernried he led the storybook life of a twentieth-century duke. The 1,000-acre estate included the village of Bernried, an 800-year-old castle, the massive, onion-turreted castle Minnie had had built in the 1930s, her Catholic chapel, and an elaborate guest house. The grounds were covered with thousands of dahlias, azaleas, and camellias, as well as lakes, greenhouses, truck gardens, a dairy, a sawmill, a twelfth-century monastery stable, wild deer, and a large garden a somewhat homesick Woods dubbed "little Mississippi."[145] A staff of 120 tended the property.

The sprawling, three-story Höhenried castle contained 76 rooms, including seven dining rooms, priceless paintings, Ming vases, Louis XVI furniture once owned by Napoleon, a sleigh that had belonged to "mad" King Ludwig II of Bavaria,[146] and a 10,000-bottle wine cellar. Within these walls the couple entertained in an appropriately ostentatious manner, with Minnie invariably arrayed in a "long flowing gown, huge picture hat atop a massive blonde wig, and decorated with a string of pearls."[147] Each Fourth of July the newlyweds invited several hundred guests for an afternoon carnival of outdoor band music, opera, arias, sausages, ice cream, and freely flowing beer, flown in from the Anheuser-Busch brewery in the United States.[148] Friends and relatives who came to stay at Höhenried were likely to find themselves sitting down to dinner with princes and princesses.[149]

Back in Mississippi, Woods had formed a bank with his brother Clarence and built up other business interests in anticipation of his retirement and return to the States with Minnie. In 1951 he became a member of the board of directors of Anheuser-Busch.[150] The new multimillionaire also kept himself busy lobbying his Washington friends—in vain—to obtain the more prestigious post of U.S. minister.[151]

But there was not to be any peaceful retirement for either Woods or his third wife. After several bouts of illness, Minnie died suddenly of a heart attack on November 23, 1952. She was sixty-eight years old. She was buried on the grounds of her beloved Bernried, where she had spent most of her life. In her will she left her husband all of her estate, estimated to be worth $5 million.[152]

A retired, widowed Woods found himself burdened with the responsibility of looking after Minnie's properties in Germany—a task that weighed heavily on his broad but tired shoulders.[153] To lighten this load, he emptied his Munich apartment of its art treasures, sending several boxcars of Renaissance furniture, books, paintings, and maps[154] back to his relatives in Mississippi and to his alma mater, Southern Mississippi College.[155] He intended to follow them back home to the South.

But ten months after Minnie died, returning from a trip to Zurich, Woods was involved in a bad automobile accident.[156] During his convalescence at the U.S. Army hospital in Munich, he made up his mind to go back to Switzerland and ask Milada to marry him again, perhaps to ease his conscience for having left her.[157] He was still not a well man. Throughout his life he had been afflicted with gout, diabetes, and other ailments. Now he was badly overweight and suffered from high blood pressure. For some reason, after his discharge Woods decided to walk all the way back to the hospital from downtown Munich. Climbing the steep steps to his room, he suffered a cerebral hemorrhage. He died the same day, May 22, 1953. He was buried on the shores of Lake Starnberg, in a grave next to Minnie's that he had prepared for himself.[158]

In Berlin, Erwin Respondek was starting a new life. The year after Woods died he met a young nurse from Pomerania named Elsbeth Lange.[159] Unhappy and alone for the first time in his life, Respondek was eager to start a new family. The couple was soon married and had a daughter, Henriette. Now sixty-two, out of step in his appearance and views with what he derided as West Germany's "clever mercenary business spirit,"[160] and virtually without any hope of finding a full-time job (he could only find occasional business consulting and legal work for West Berlin and West Germany firms[161]), Respondek had to depend financially on his new wife's income.

Politically he was still very much involved. In 1959, he sent Robert Murphy, then deputy secretary of state, a memorandum about the Soviet ultimatum on Berlin.[162] Many parts of this report adumbrated in both tone and substance the official U.S. white paper—the so-called "Herter Plan"—on this international crisis.[163]

Resolved to improve his "rather miserable situation,"[164] Respondek turned to Thomas Stauffer—now out of the army, living in Chicago—for help in selling articles of his on assorted aspects of the German situation.[165] But nothing came of this: editor after editor politely declined to publish these long, journalistically unwieldy pieces.[166] Just as unsuccessful was a scheme to represent U.S. exporters in West Germany.[167]

Even when Respondek did find a consulting job, it turned out to be more of a bane than a boom: his claim for compensation against a Geneva tobacco firm dragged on in the Swiss courts for years without his ever receiving any payment.[168]

Chronically in bad health, but as feisty and stubborn as ever, Respondek spent his final years in a small Berlin apartment. His passion for current affairs remained undiminished. Each day he read the newspapers religiously, filing away clippings as he had done habitually for years.[169] In his small family circle Respondek took a special interest in young Henriette—the child of his old age, his hope for the future.

He made one last bid for government compensation as a victim of Nazi persecution. His petition for a pension was routinely submitted to the appropriate authorities in Berlin. They wrote back, asking if he could prove his claim. A quarter century after the fact, the only documentation Respondek could produce of his wartime exploits consisted of a yellowed testimonial statement from Sam Woods, another from his Center Party colleague Heinrich Krone, some photocopied pages from Cordell Hull's memoirs, and a couple of related letters. He did not have any other records. What had not perished in the air raids or the Gestapo had not burned, he had destroyed himself. Respondek's remarkable success in eluding detection now came back to haunt him: he was the spy who never was.[170]

In the summer of 1970, in a letter to Stauffer ("the only person from the time of the Third Reich and after 1945 with whom I am still in touch"), the seventy-six-year-old Respondek mentioned he was finally going to write down the full story of his anti-Nazi activities "so that at least one American will know" what he had done—and how he had been undone after the war.[171] On the mend after an illness that had hospitalized him the year before, he sounded full of vigor: "At my age all of my forefathers worked very sprightly without doctors or medication and lived to be 90!"[172] But he was sadly wrong. Life would disappoint him one last time. The final report he had promised Stauffer would still be unwritten the next winter, when his heart stopped beating.

AFTERWORD

After the war and her former husband's death, Milada Woods stayed on in Zurich. She went to California for a while in the 1950s but then returned again to Europe. Still physically active in her late eighties, she now divides her time between Hattiesburg, Mississippi (where her stepdaughter and family live), Switzerland, Austria, and Bernried, Germany, where Sam Woods and Wilhelmina Busch once dwelt in great splendor.

In Germany, Charlotte Respondek managed to survive her exhusband by a dozen years. She and her companion Herbert Müller explored various money-making schemes to regain assets lost during the Nazi years, but they were largely unsuccessful. Charlotte published a few Silesian cookbooks, and she and Müller briefly attempted to promote the then-novel idea of disposable diapers. Müller taught political science at an adult night school in Berlin before resuming private law practice and his legal scholarship. But his career never really got going again before his death in 1972. Respondek's oldest daughter, Valeska, remained in Maryland, and after her husband died in 1967 of pancreatic cancer, she resumed her nursing career. She is now retired and lives with her daughter, Gabriella, director of personnel for a Baltimore law firm.

Respondek's second wife, Elsbeth, remarried and moved with her new husband to a small north German village near the Baltic. Their daughter, Henriette Respondek, lives outside Hannover with her young son. Respondek's other grandson, Peter, still lives in Berlin.

In 1948, at the age of seventy-one, Hermann Muckermann resumed his academic career of blending science with Christian humanism. He taught applied anthropology at the Technische Hochschule in West Berlin and published numerous popular articles and books. He returned to the pulpit as well, giving well-attended sermons every Sunday at a Catholic hospital in a northern suburb of Berlin. Muckermann spoke out forcefully against collectivist tendencies in Eastern Europe. In 1952 he was awarded the Grosse Bundesverdienstkreuz—West Germany's highest civilian honor—for his efforts to reconcile science and ethics. During these years his friendships with the Respondeks lapsed, a victim of postwar strains and conflicts. Muckermann died in Berlin, at age eighty-five, on October 30, 1962.

Most of the other characters in the Woods–Respondek espionage story have either died or faded into obscurity. Thomas Stauffer, his closest American friend after the war, loaned Respondek some money in the 1950s but never succeeded in finding a publisher for his articles. After spending the postwar years in the State Department, Stauffer taught at a Chicago college before moving to California in 1973. There he was active in politics and worked for an art and Oriental-rug dealer. He died of a heart attack in 1987.

H. Walter Dällenbach, the Swiss physicist who had worked on a cyclotron during the war, reestablished himself as an engineering consultant in his native country. His work focused on electrical processes. As this book was nearing completion he died in Bern at the age of ninety-seven.

Jacob Beam left his State Department desk in Washington for posts in Indonesia, Yugoslavia, and the Soviet Union, where he served as acting head of the embassy after the recall of George Kennan. During the Eisenhower administration he was named U.S. ambassador to Poland. Subsequently, Beam negotiated with the Chinese over the islands of Quemoy and Matsu. Before retiring he held the post of ambassador in Prague and Moscow, under President Nixon. Now in his eighties, he lives with his wife in the Georgetown section of Washington.

Toshikazu Kase, Respondek's purported contact in the Japanese Foreign Ministry, retired from public life after having served as his country's first ambassador to the United Nations. Now eighty-nine, he lives in Tokyo.

In Berlin, until recently, lived two persons who knew the Respondeks well during the Nazi years: Agnes Dreimann, longtime friend and tutor to their children, and Herta Chojnacki, Hermann Muckermann's housekeeper. (Frau Dreimann died in 1990, at the age of eighty-five.) Otherwise, in the city that was his home for so long, Erwin Respondek's name is little known.

ABBREVIATIONS

The following abbreviations are used for major sources for materials cited in the notes:

AIP	Niels Bohr Library, American Institute of Physics, New York
BA	Bundesarchiv, Koblenz
ETH	Eidgenössische Technische Hochschule, Zurich
FDRL	Franklin D. Roosevelt Library, Hyde Park, N.Y.
IZG	Institut für Zeitgeschichte, Munich
KAS	Konrad-Adenauer-Stiftung, Sankt Augustin bei Bonn
KZG	Kommission für Zeitgeschichte, Bonn
LVA	Landesverwaltungsamt, Berlin
LC	Manuscript Division, Library of Congress, Washington, D.C.
MPG	Archives & Library, Max Planck Gesellschaft, Berlin
NA	National Archives, Washington, D.C.
NDP	Archives of the Norddeutschen Provinz, SJ, Cologne
NRC	National Records Center, Suitland, Md.
NSHS	Nebraska State Historical Society, Lincoln
NRWHSA	Nordrhein-Westfälisches Hauptstaatsarchiv, Düsseldorf
SHSW	Mass Communications History Center, State Historical Society of Wisconsin, Madison
USAWC	U.S. Army Military History Institute, U.S. Army War College, Carlisle Barracks, Pa.

NOTES

PREFACE

1. Walter Laqueur, *The Terrible Secret: An Investigation into the Suppression of Information about Hitler's "Final Solution"* (New York: Simon and Schuster, 1986), p. 96.

2. This has been denied by Wouk's literary agent (letter of Suzanne Stein to author, 1 November 1985).

3. Sam E. Woods, undated memorandum, p. 11, folder 184, Cordell Hull Papers, LC (hereafter cited as Hull Papers).

4. Ibid., p. 24.

CHAPTER 1. THE MAKING OF A SPY

1. Erwin Respondek, enclosure, reparations claim, 21 May 1970, p. 4, LVA.

2. Interview with Valeska Hoffmann, 18 April 1987.

3. Wilhelm Respondek became the owner of the Adler Hotel in Berlin, Max a teacher in Turkey, and Georg, the oldest, studied physics and later went on to teach as well. Interview with Agnes Dreimann, 26 July 1986, and letter of Elsbeth Schukat to the author, 22 November 1986.

4. Erwin Respondek, report on the Kaiser Wilhelm Gesellschaft, 12 November 1970, p. 4, II. Abt., Rep. 1A Gründung, Nr. 1/1-4, Files of the General Administration, MPG.

5. Respondek, *Lebenslauf*, Valeska R. Hoffmann Papers, private collection, Bel Air, Md. (hereafter cited as Hoffmann Papers).

6. Letter of Erwin Respondek to Friedrich Dessauer, 5 April 1932, Dessauer Papers, FD 12, KZG.

7. After forming the Kriegsrohstoffabteilung with permission of the War

Ministry on 13 August 1914, Rathenau headed it until April 1915. See Walther Rathenau, *Tagebücher, 1907–1922* (Düsseldorf: Droste Verlag, 1967), p. 187.

8. Interview with Agnes Dreimann, 26 July 1986.

9. Interview with Valeska Hoffmann, 22 March 1986. See also letter of Maria Schachtner to the author, 8 October 1986, and Dreimann interview.

10. Schachtner letter to the author.

11. Respondek received his degree for a dissertation on "Steuer und Anleihe-politik im Frankreich im Krieg."

12. Erwin Respondek, *Frankreichs Bank und Finanzwirtschaft im Kriege (August 1914 bis 1916)* (Berlin: G. Fischer Verlag, 1917).

13. Erwin Respondek, *Kriegsentschädigung: Förderungen unserer Gegner* (Berlin: Verlag von Julius Springer, 1919).

14. Wrote Respondek: "They cannot force Germany to accept this power of theirs as rightful." Ibid., p. 31. Author's translation.

15. See *Führer durch Gross-Lichterfelde bei Berlin* (Berlin: Geschäftstelle des Ver-kehrsausschusses, 1910).

16. Valeska Hoffmann believes the residence was built around 1924. See letter of Gabriella Hoffmann to the author, 1 February 1988.

17. See Respondek's *Lebenslauf,* 6 January 1953, Diether Koch Papers, private collection, Bremen. (Hereafter cited as Koch Papers.)

18. See letter of Respondek to Friedrich Dessauer, 14 June 1932, Dessauer Papers, KZG.

19. Bücher served as Geschäftsführende Präsidialmitglied from 1921 to 1924. Respondek did consulting and freelance articles for the Reichsverband during these years and subsequently. See his articles published by the association in Jan. 1925 and Sept. 1927. See also Respondek letter to Carl Duisberg, 12 February 1925 (written on Reichsverband stationery), Duisberg Papers, Bayer Archives, Leverkusen.

In 1924 the American journalist Edgar Ansel Mowrer interviewed Respondek, whom he described as Bücher's "gifted assistant." See Mowrer, *Triumph and Turmoil: A Personal History of Our Time* (New York: Weybright and Talley, 1968), p. 165.

20. Respondek's links to these top industrialists are outlined in his corre-spondence with Friedrich Dessauer during the period when Respondek was building a base of financial support for his campaign for the Reichstag in 1932. See his letter of 14 June 1932, Dessauer Papers, KZG.

21. *Verlauf und Ergebnis der Internationalen Wirtschaftskonferenz d. Völkerbundes zu Genf (vom 4–23.5.1927), Wiedergabe der Plenar-Kommissionensitzungen: Zusam-mengestellt von E. Respondek* (Berlin: Carl Heymann, 1927).

22. In 1948 Brüning told the U.S. diplomat Jacob D. Beam that he had known Respondek for nearly 20 years and had brought him into the Reichstag. Letter of Brüning to Beam, 5 November 1948, Folder 34, Box 792, POLAD (Political Advisor for Germany) Files, RG 84, IZG.

23. Respondek actually joined the Center Party in 1916. See his *Lebenslauf,* Koch Papers, private collection, Bremen.

24. In 1924 it captured the votes of 76 percent of German Catholics through-out the country. See Konrad Repgen, *Hitlers Machtergreifung und der deutsche Katholizismus* (Saarbrücken: Verlag des Saarlandes, 1967), p. 19.

25. Franz von Papen, *Memoirs* (New York: Dutton, 1953), p. 133.

26. For Brüning's assessment of Respondek I am indebted to Miss Claire Nix, interview of 26 February 1987.

27. For details of Respondek's affiliation with Popitz and Lejeune-Jung, see enclosure with his reparations claim, 21 May 1970, LVA.

28. According to Agnes Dreimann, these individuals, Adenauer excepted, occasionally visited the Respondek's Lichterfelde home. The Lübkes were on a "per Du" basis with the Respondeks, and Mrs. Lübke stayed with the Respondeks during visits to her husband when he was arrested by the Nazis. Interview with Agnes Dreimann.

29. Wirmer, a native of Paderborn, was expelled from the National Socialist Lawyers' Association because of his hostility to the regime and work on behalf of German Jews. See Eberhard Zeller, *The Flame of Freedom: The German Struggle against Hitler* (Coral Gables, Fla.: University of Miami Press, 1969), p. 228.

30. Dreimann interview. This association is confirmed by Wirmer's daughter. See letter of Maria (Wirmer) Hermes to the author, 15 May 1987. For Wirmer's ties to Semnonia, see *20. Juli: Portraits des Widerstands* (Düsseldorf: Econ Verlag, 1984), p. 339.

31. In 1913 Muckermann also became editor of the Jesuit journal *Stimmen der Zeit*.

32. For more particulars, see Hermann Muckermann's autobiographical essay "Aus meinem Leben," Muckermann Papers, *Hochschularchiv*, Technische Universität, Berlin.

33. So relates Muckermann's brother, Friedrich, in his memoir, *Kampf zwischen zwei Epochen: Lebenserinnerungen* (Mainz: Matthias Grünewald Verlag, 1973), pp. 240–41. Here it is suggested that other priests, out of spite, circulated stories about Hermann's relationship with his sister. This led to Muckermann's being summarily ousted from the Jesuit order. Friedrich Muckermann insists there was no basis to these charges. This allegation has also not been substantiated by Muckermann's longtime housekeeper, Herta Chojnacki, or by other persons who knew him well. See interview with Herta Chojnacki, 23 July 1986; and with Fr. H. Kugelmeier, SJ, 29 July 1986.

34. Cf. Friedrich Glum, *Zwischen Wissenschaft, Wirtschaft und Politik: Erlebtes und Erdachtes in vier Reichen* (Bonn: H. Bouvier, 1964), p. 371.

35. In December 1936 Fischer, Erwin Bauer, and Fritz Lenz, leading German authorities in the field of race, published *Menschliche Erblehre und Rassenhygiene* [*Human Genetics and Racial Hygiene*], in which they conceded that the average Jew was more intelligent than the average German.

36. Muckermann once called Hitler an "idiot," a damning indictment of a Führer who believed the mentally incompetent ought to be put to death.

37. Glum, *Zwischen Wissenschaft*, p. 372. See also Hoffmann interview, 22 March 1986.

38. Chojnacki interview, 23 July 1986.

39. For these details of Muckermann's association with the Respondek family I am indebted to Valeska Hoffmann. Interview of 21 January 1986.

40. According to Muckermann's housekeeper, Pacelli visited his home in Schlachtensee at least twice. Chojnacki interview, 23 July 1986.

41. Ibid.

42. Herta Chojnacki reports Muckermann had a special soutane made for this visit.

43. Letter of Brüning to Beam, 5 November 1948, POLAD Files, IZG.

44. See Respondek, *Lebenslauf*, Koch Papers.

45. For these recollections of the Respondeks' social life, see interviews with Valeska Hoffman, Herta Chojnacki, and Agnes Dreimann.

46. Letter of Respondek to Thomas B. Stauffer, 19 January 1961, Stauffer Papers, private collection, Berkeley, Calif. (hereafter cited as Stauffer Papers).

47. Miller was appointed trade commissioner in Berlin in May 1924, assistant commercial attaché in January 1925, and acting commercial attaché in 1933. He became commercial attaché in 1937.

48. William L. Shirer, *20th Century Journey: The Nightmare Years, 1930–1940* (Boston: Little, Brown, 1984), p. 232. Martha Dodd, in her memoir, *Through Embassy Eyes* (New York: Harcourt, Brace & World, 1939), p. 322, calls Miller "one of the most painstakingly accurate and objective men in Berlin."

49. So state Valeska Hoffmann, interview of 22 March 1986, and Respondek, in his "Personal Confidential Report" for Cordell Hull, May 1946, p. 2, Stauffer Papers.

50. By coincidence, Hitler's press chief, Ernst "Putzi" Hanfstaengl moved into an apartment at the same address, Pariser Platz 3, in the fall of 1933. Although Hanfstaengl and Respondek shared an interest in the fine arts and politics, it is not known whether the two men had any personal contact during the Nazi era.

51. Interviews with Agnes Dreimann, 26 July 1986, and Valeska Hoffmann, 22 March 1986.

52. Otto Friedrich, *Before the Deluge: A Portrait of Berlin in the 1920's* (New York: Fromm International Publishing Corp., 1986), p. 205.

53. Between 1924 and 1928 the military budget nearly doubled, from 490 million marks to 827 million. See Friedrich, *Before the Deluge*, p. 236.

54. Respondek note on General Thomas, 17 October 1945, p. 2, Stauffer Papers.

55. Friedrich, *Before the Deluge*, p. 201.

56. A. P. Young, *The "X" Documents* (London: Andre Deutsch, 1974), p. 16.

57. Three weeks before, the Reichstag had ratified the controversial Young Plan, greatly reducing, but not ending, Germany's reparations payments. See Hans Luther, *Vor dem Abgrund, 1930–1933: Reichsbankpräsident im Krisenzeiten* (Berlin: Propylaen Verlag, 1964), pp. 141–42.

58. Papen, *Memoirs*, p. 132.

59. Ibid., p. 136.

60. See interview with Claire Nix, 12 February 1987.

61. Letter of Respondek to Friedrich Dessauer, 14 June 1932, Dessauer Papers, KZG.

62. See letter of Brüning to Beam, 5 November 1948, POLAD Files, RG 84, IZG.

63. See letter of William Patch to the author, 15 December 1986, referring to letters in Dessauer Papers, KZG.

64. See Respondek's speech describing the "historical lies of national socialism" before a Center Party gathering in Oppeln, 2 July 1932. A newspaper

article containing the text of this address is attached to Respondek's letter of Friedrich Dessauer, 11 July 1932, Dessauer Papers, KZG.

65. Respondek's friend Wilhelm Kalle, a Reichstag delegate of the German People's Party since 1919, was severely beaten by Nazi thugs and as a result was unable to run for election in November. Letter of Prof. Larry E. Jones to the author, 23 October 1987.

66. Heinrich Brüning, *Memoiren, 1918–1934* (Stuttgart: Deutsche Verlags-Anstalt, 1970), p. 670.

67. Letter of Respondek to Friedrich Dessauer, 8 April 1933, Dessauer Papers, KZG.

68. Respondek statement on the Enabling Act, April 1947, Schwertfeger Papers, 255, BA.

69. Aside from some private financial consulting, the only position he was allowed to keep was the presidency of the Professional Association for Health Services and Social Work (Berufsgenossenschaft für Gesundheitsdienst und Wohlfahrtspflege). He held this post from 27 January 1931 to 31 December 1934. See letter of Hans Josef Wollasch to the author, 19 January 1988.

70. Respondek had held the post of secretary but was not a member of the party's executive committee.

71. Letter of Respondek to Wilhelm Frick, 22 October 1933, NS 46/25, BA.

72. Many Catholic politicians and newspapers came out in favor of the new regime at this point. See Ernst W. Böckenförde, "Der deutsche Katholizismus im Jahre 1933," *Vom Weimar zu Hitler, 1930–1933* (Köln/Berlin: Kiepenheuer & Witsch, 1968), pp. 322–25.

73. Gottfried B. Treviranus, *Das Ende vom Weimar: Heinrich Brüning und seine Zeit* (Düsseldorf: Econ-Verlag, 1968), p. 398.

74. Louis P. Lochner, *Always the Expected: A Book of Reminiscences* (New York: MacMillan, 1956), p. 245.

75. Interview with Agnes Dreimann, 26 July 1986. See also Dreimann letter to the author, 26 July 1986.

76. F. Muckermann, *Kampf*, p. 113.

77. Muckermann subsequently escorted the Center politician Treviranus and his wife to safety in Holland.

78. Brüning, *Briefe, 1934–1945* (Stuttgart: Deutsche Verlags-Anstalt, 1965), p. 344.

79. He was assisted by the Dutch prelate Pools. See Respondek's "Personal Confidential Report," May 1946, p. 1, Stauffer Papers.

80. Letter of Brüning to Otto A. Friedrich, 8 July 1949. For calling this correspondence to my attention I am grateful to Prof. Rudolf Morsey.

81. After Brüning moved to the United States, Miller brought him Respondek's reports there.

82. These were subsequently published under the title *Via Diplomatic Pouch* (New York: Didier, 1944).

83. William E. Dodd, *Ambassador Dodd's Diary* (New York: Harcourt, Brace & World, 1941), xiii.

84. Respondek, "Personal Confidential Report," May 1946, p. 2, Stauffer Papers.

85. Unsigned memorandum, 10 April 1941, Welles folder, Box 1208, RG 165, NRC.

86. Respondek report of May 1946, p. 2, Stauffer Papers.

87. Interview with Valeska Hoffmann, 22 March 1986.

88. Interview with Agnes Dreimann, 26 July 1986.

89. Interview with Valeska Hoffmann, 22 March 1986.

90. Letter of Respondek to Thomas B. Stauffer, 2 May 1961, Stauffer Papers. Respondek had patronized the Bernheimer establishment for many years, and he did so again after the war. He also helped liquidate the business under the Nazis.

91. Respondek's undated report for Heinrich Brüning, Brüning Papers, private collection, Hartland, Vt. (hereafter cited as Brüning Papers).

92. Interview with Agnes Dreimann, 26 July 1986.

93. Ibid. See also Respondek's confidential report of May 1946, Stauffer Papers.

94. Letter of Respondek to Thomas B. Stauffer, 3 February 1961, Stauffer Papers.

95. Undated Woods memorandum, p. 2, Hull Papers, LC. This startling assertion is difficult to confirm, as Respondek's office files have all been destroyed.

CHAPTER 2. THE FLOWERING OF A CONSPIRACY

1. In 1932 Hermann Muckermann had drafted for the Prussian Ministry of Health a bill allowing for sterilization. Later, following issuance of the papal *Encyclia casti conubii*, he disavowed such measures. See his letter to Father Koffler, 12 June 1947, Muckermann Papers, NDP.

2. Interview with Herta Chojnacki, 23 July 1986.

3. See his article in *Katholische Correspondenz*, 8 February 1934, quoted in Heinz Boberach, ed., *Berichte der SD und der Gestapo über Kirchen und Kirchenvolk in Deutschland, 1934–1944* (Mainz: Matthias Grünewald Verlag, 1971), p. 42.

4. See Nazi flyer, 12 May 1938, Muckermann Papers, NDP.

5. For the names of these individuals, see Dreimann interview. See also Dreimann letter to the author, 26 July 1987. (Dr. Ursula Schornstein, daughter of Johannes Schornstein, confirmed a tie between him and the Respondeks in her letter to the author, 12 November 1988.) Of these, Dr. Schornstein went on, after the war, to hold various government posts. Respondek found Fetzer a job as secretary to Friedrich Dessauer.

6. Interview with Herta Chojnacki.

7. Frau Chojnacki recalls the number 7 being used in conjunction with the group, possibly because of Hermann Muckermann's name's day, April 7. He was also born in 1877. See Chojnacki interview.

8. So assume Valeska Hoffmann and Agnes Dreimann. Since these gatherings were held at night, it may have been difficult for the Gestapo to identify the individuals entering and leaving the Respondek home. See interviews with Valeska Hoffmann, 22 March 1986 and 4 April 1987. See also Dreimann interview.

9. Interview with Claire Nix, 12 February 1987. See also letter of D. N. Heinemann to Brüning, 14 July 1939, Brüning Papers.

10. Brüning, *Briefe, 1934–1945*, p. 184.

11. Ibid., p. 210.

12. The date of their meeting is unclear. In a 1946 letter to Wilhelm Hamacher, Respondek gives the date as October, whereas in an undated letter to Brüning sometime after the war he says it took place in September. See letter to Hamacher, 3 July 1946, Muckermann Papers, KAS, and undated Respondek manuscript, Brüning Papers. In a third document, attached to a letter to Thomas B. Stauffer, 4 August 1970, Stauffer Papers, he puts the time as August 1938.

13. During this meeting, or on an earlier occasion, Brüning urged Respondek to come to the United States to accept a teaching post at Harvard. See undated manuscript of Respondek's, Brüning Papers.

14. David Kahn, *Hitler's Spies: German Military Intelligence in World War II* (New York: MacMillan, 1978), p. 179.

15. Telford Taylor, *Munich: The Price of Peace* (Garden City, N.Y.: Doubleday, 1979), p. 804. See also Kahn, *Hitler's Spies*, p. 182.

16. Kahn, *Hitler's Spies*, p. 185.

17. Letter of Respondek to Brüning, 12 July 1939, Brüning Papers.

18. Ibid.

19. William Shirer, *The Rise and Fall of the Third Reich: A History of Nazi Germany* (New York: Simon and Schuster, 1960), p. 562.

20. David Irving, *The War Path: Hitler's Germany, 1933–1939* (New York: Viking, 1978), p. 231. See also Shirer, *Rise and Fall*, p. 564.

21. Irving, *War Path*, p. 249. In a statement written after the war Respondek claimed he gave Brüning the exact date of the war's beginning. See his statement attached to letter to Thomas B. Stauffer, 4 August 1970, Stauffer Papers.

22. Interview with Claire Nix, 12 February 1987.

23. Interview with Agnes Dreimann, 26 July 1986.

24. Interview with Jacob D. Beam, 4 December 1985. See also Beam letter to the author, 4 April 1987. Cf. remarks about Miller's activities, Morgenthau Diary, group meeting of 10 July 1941, No. 355, Vol. 419, FDRL.

25. Beam recalls this took place in the spring of 1938, but Miller did not depart the German capital until early 1939. See Beam letter to the author, 26 January 1988.

26. Interview with Jacob D. Beam, 4 December 1985.

27. Ibid.

28. Interview with Valeska Hoffmann, 22 March 1986.

29. Interview with Jacob D. Beam, 4 December 1985.

30. For these details see the unpublished memoir of Jacob D. Beam, private collection, Washington, D.C., pp. 160–62 (hereafter cited as J. D. Beam Papers).

31. Interview with Katharine A. H. Smith, 13 September 1986.

32. Smith was on such cordial terms with these officers that he had only to invite them over to his home on the Corneliastrasse, offer them some whiskey, and "they would tell him everything." Interview with Amelie Riddleberger, 28 June 1985.

33. Interview with Katherine Smith, 13 September 1986. Columnists Walter Lippmann and Walter Winchell publicly lambasted Smith for his "exaggerated"

reporting. See Truman Smith, *Berlin Alert: The Memoirs and Reports of Truman Smith* (Stanford, Calif.: Stanford University Press, 1984), xvi.

34. Beam, unpublished memoir, p. 161. Cf. Beam interview, 4 June 1985. Beam apparently went ahead and informed Ambassador Wilson, who promised to send a cable back to James Dunn, political advisor on European affairs for Secretary of State Hull. But it appears Beam's news was not relayed to Washington.

35. For example, he brought the "X" report to Halder in April 1940.

36. See Respondek's note on Thomas, 17 October 1945, Stauffer Papers.

37. Respondek confidential report, May 1946, Stauffer Papers.

38. Respondek letter to Brüning, 21 February 1940, Brüning Papers.

39. Letter of Freya von Moltke to the author, 16 March 1987.

40. The only exception was Friedrich Muckermann. Since he had gone into exile in 1934, this tie could not be significantly cultivated.

CHAPTER 3. ENTER THE MAN FROM MISSISSIPPI

1. Woods's Marine Corps records and a 1910 Mississippi census, NA, list him as "Samuel," but throughout his life he referred to himself officially as "Sam."

2. See remarks of Rep. William W. Colmer on Woods's career, *Congressional Record*, Appendix, August 1952, A4795.

3. Interview with Milada Woods, 19 October 1986. Mrs. Woods stated there was also a family connection to Lincoln's secretary of state, William H. Seward.

4. Robert Cecil Cook, *McGowan Place and Other Memoirs* (Hattiesburg, Miss.: Educators' Biographical Press, 1973), p. 273.

5. Book K, Lamar County Land Records, p. 304. For this information I am indebted to Leonard L. Slade, Sr.

6. Interview with Milada Woods, 12 February 1987. Damon Palmer, another relative of Woods, says Woods was cleaning a .22 rifle when it accidentally discharged. See letter of Leonard L. Slade, Sr., to the author, 4 December 1986.

7. Interview with Milada Woods, 12 February 1987. Cf. letter of Leonard L. Slade, Sr., to the author, 4 December 1986.

8. During the Second World War Woods confessed to the American heiress Mary Bancroft that all the good he was seeking to accomplish in his life was to make up for this one tragic mistake. Interview with Mary Bancroft, 25 February 1986.

9. Interview with Milada Woods, 12 February 1987.

10. See Woods obituary, *Hattiesburg Commercial Appeal*, 23 May 1953, Woods File, Mississippi Department of Archives and History.

11. Alumni records, Valparaiso University.

12. Cook, *McGowan Place*, pp. 274–75.

13. Interview with Mary Bancroft, 25 February 1986.

14. See article by Dennis Murphree, *Clarion-Ledger*, 28 June 1942, Woods File, Mississippi Department of Archives and History.

15. Interview with Milada Woods, 12 February 1987.

16. Cook, *McGowan Place*, p. 275.

17. Woods liked to say he had been sent to "teach the Czechs to play." Interview with Mary Bancroft.

18. See speech of Felix J. Underwood, "Public Health Activities in Mississippi," 20 December 1926, RG 51, Mississippi Department of Archives and History.

19. William D. McCain, "The Life and Labor of Dennis Murphree," *Journal of Mississippi History*, 12, 4 (October 1950): 185.

20. Clayton Rand, "Spinal Column," *Dixie Guide*, September 1949, Rand Papers, Mitchell Memorial Library, Mississippi State University, Mississippi State.

21. Interview with Mary Bancroft, 25 February 1986.

22. Interview with Milada Woods, 12 February 1987.

23. Letter of Sam E. Woods to Mrs. Joseph T. Robinson, 15 July 1937, Robinson Papers, private collection of H. Grady Miller, Jr., Little Rock, Ark. (hereafter cited as Robinson Papers).

24. See photograph taken at Slovenky Meder, 1934, Robinson Papers. Long was also a good friend of Robinson's. See letter of Mrs. Joseph T. Robinson to Sam and Milada Woods, 5 March 1941, Robinson Papers.

25. These included Sen. James F. Byrnes of South Carolina, Sen. McKellar, Sen. John H. Bankhead of Alabama, and Henry A. Wallace, then Roosevelt's secretary of agriculture, in addition to Sen. Robinson.

26. See memorandum of President Franklin D. Roosevelt to Secretary of Commerce Daniel W. Roper, 2 June 1937, Official File, 2725, FDRL: "Sam Woods—comm. attache in Poland or Prague. Joe Robinson says good man, married." See also letter of Daniel W. Roper, Secretary of Commerce, to Sen. Joseph T. Robinson, 5 June 1937, Robinson Papers.

27. There is no documentation in the Roosevelt Library to indicate that the president took a personal interest in the diplomat's reassignment to Berlin, only that Sen. Robinson informally recommended it. Nor are there any papers, either at the Roosevelt Library or at the National Archives, suggesting that Woods reported to the president or even ever met with him. This lack of personal contact is confirmed by Milada Woods, letter to the author, 10 June 1988.

For Secretary Roper's recommendation that Woods be assigned to the post of commercial attaché at-large, based in Berlin, see his letters of 2 July 1937 and 13 August 1937 to Secretary of State Cordell Hull, 70801/11 Pt. 7, RG 40, General Records of the Department of Commerce, General Correspondence, NA.

28. Interview with Milada Woods, 12 February 1987. An article in the *Jackson Daily News*, 24 March 1939, states that the Woodses were living in a mansion once owned by the famed Warburg family. In what must be taken as sheer coincidence, Erwin Respondek was using this same address as an office several years before. See his letter of 23 March 1932 to Friedrich Dessauer, Dessauer Papers, KZG.

29. Interview with Milada Woods, 12 February 1987. Their friendships included Prince Konstantin Karadjin of Rumania, who later made use of his tie to Woods to convey back to Washington word of U.S. flyers wounded during the raid on the German oil refineries at Ploesti.

30. Before he left Berlin in December 1941, Woods sold his car to Helldorf. In 1944 he received a report from Helldorf asking that the British and Americans try to keep the Russians out of Berlin. See Woods memorandum to Leland Harrison, 25 July 1944, Box 13, Bern Confidential File, RG 84, NRC.

31. Interview with Rev. Stewart Herman, 20 May 1985.

32. Interview with Patrick E. Nieburg, 6 December 1985. Nieburg worked for Woods during this time and recalls his keen interest in current affairs.

33. Nieburg interview. The term was a rough translation of the German word *Vollkornbrot.*

34. See Woods report, 26 September 1939, Reports of the Commercial Attaché, Berlin, 1937–1941, RG 151, NA.

35. Interview with Mrs. John Lovell, 27 January 1987.

36. Apparently Kirk, something of a misogynist, wanted all the embassy wives to leave after war broke out but was thwarted in this wish. Jacob D. Beam, unpublished memoir, p. 230, J. D. Beam Papers.

37. Interview with Angus Thuermer, 28 June 1985.

38. William Russell, *Berlin Embassy* (New York: Dutton, 1941), pp. 71–72.

39. Interview with Carl F. Norden, 6 January 1986. See also letter of Ralph Izzard to the author, 27 November 1985.

40. Letter of Sam Woods to Mrs. Joseph T. Robinson, 7 March 1939; letter of Sam Woods to Mrs. Joseph T. Robinson, 8 November 1939, Robinson Papers.

41. Woods's correspondents included Sen. McKellar and congressmen Karl Stefan of Nebraska and Louis Rabaut of Michigan. He also tried to win favor with the president himself, sending him stamps for his collection. See Woods letter to Miss M. E. LeHand, 9 September 1941, President's Personal File, 7785, FDRL.

42. Letter of Sam Woods to Mrs. Joseph T. Robinson, 2 July 1939, Robinson Papers. In this letter he thanks her for speaking to George Messersmith about his promotion. Woods was one of five of the one hundred and five eligible for this promotion to receive it. The higher rank carried with it a considerable increase in salary—and the resentment of other State Department officials. See interview with Jacob D. Beam, Washington, 4 December 1985. Woods may have played a role in lobbying the State Department to absorb the Bureau of Foreign Commerce. See interview with Carl Norden, 6 January 1986.

43. Norden interview. Woods told his companions how he would travel all over Germany and then file his expense account in U.S. currency amounts. Compensated in dollars, he would then convert these into marks on the black market, for a tidy profit.

44. Interview with Patrick E. Nieburg, 6 December 1985. See also interview with Mary Bancroft, 25 February 1986.

45. Interview with Milada Woods, 12 February 1987. She claims both men disliked each other and that she had to keep Woods away from Kennan, especially when they were interned together after Pearl Harbor.

46. Interview with Jacob D. Beam, 4 June 1985.

47. William Shirer was one of the Americans in Berlin fooled by Woods's manner. In *Rise and Fall*, p. 843, Shirer describes the commercial attaché as "a genial extrovert whose grasp of world politics and history was not striking" and "the last man in the American Embassy in Berlin likely to have come by such crucial intelligence [about Barbarossa]."

48. Shirer, *Nightmare Years*, p. 183.

49. Martha Dodd, *Through Embassy Eyes*, p. 21.

50. Shirer, *Nightmare Years*, p. 164.

51. Interview with Amelie Riddleberger, 28 June 1985.

52. Interview with Katharine Smith, 13 September 1986.

53. Dodd may have been eased out of his post by German displeasure at his openly anti-Nazi sentiments. See Shlomo Shafir, "American Diplomats in Berlin," *Yad Vashem Studies*, 9 (1973): 92.

54. Wilson had served as counselor to the U.S. mission after the First World War.

55. Smith interview.

56. Ibid. See also Truman Smith, *Berlin Alert*, p. 126.

57. See unpublished memoir of Jacob D. Beam, p. 230.

58. Interview with Amelie Riddleberger. See also Beam memoir, p. 230.

59. Interview with C. Brooks Peters, 22 November 1985.

60. Interviews with Amelie Riddleberger and Jacob D. Beam, Cf. Beam's unpublished memoir, p. 230.

61. Letter of Joseph C. Harsch to the author, 4 December 1985. Kirk once told George Kennan that "the only thing worth living for is good form." Kennan, *Memoirs, 1925–1950* (Boston: Little, Brown, 1967), p. 114.

62. In his memoir, Jacob Beam recalls having had a glimpse of Kirk's Gestapo dossier, in which the Germans concluded he was not a person "to be trifled with." Unpublished memoir of Jacob Beam, p. 231.

63. Letter of George F. Kennan to the author, 18 October 1985.

64. Interview with Mary Bancroft, 25 February 1986.

65. Interviews with Mary Bancroft and Valeska Hoffman. Milada Woods disputes this, however. Interview of 19 October 1986.

66. The exact date remains unclear. In a 20 January 1949 letter to Jacob Beam (Stauffer Papers), he says his reporting to Woods commenced in 1938; Woods himself stated he met Respondek soon after he arrived in Berlin, in the fall of 1937 (Woods memorandum, p. 1, Hull Papers). Long after the war Respondek made the startling claim that Woods had been "designated as my contact, by Washington, from 1936 on" (Respondek letter to Stauffer, 3 February 1961, Stauffer Papers). In another letter, to the journalist Edgar Ansel Mowrer, Respondek stated that he dealt with Woods "by order of your highest governmental agency" from 1937 on. Letter of 26 May 1961, Mowrer Papers, LC.

67. Interview with Jacob D. Beam, 17 April 1987.

68. Interview with Valeska Hoffmann, 21 January 1986.

69. Author's translation. Letter of Respondek to Brüning, mid-March 1939, Brüning Papers.

70. Woods memorandum, p. 2, Hull Papers, LC.

71. Woods's prior knowledge of the date of the invasion of Poland may have come from Respondek. According to Woods's daughter, the American cancelled a sailing date because he knew war was coming. Interview with Mrs. Hardin (Woods) McClendon, 6 June 1985.

CHAPTER 4. THE GREATEST MILITARY OPERATION IN HISTORY

1. Cf. Adolf Hitler, *Mein Kampf*, Abbots Langley, trans. (New York: Hurst Blackett, 1981), p. 363: "The Russia of today...is not a possible ally in the

struggle for German liberty"; p. 364: "The present rulers of Russia are blood-stained criminals.... Only a bourgeois simpleton could imagine that Bolshevism can be tamed.... Today Germany is the next battlefield for Russian Bolshevism."

2. Franz Halder, *Kriegstagebuch*, Vol. 1 (Stuttgart: W. Kohlhammer Verlag, 1963), entry for 18 October 1939, p. 107. On 23 May 1939, in the presence of his top generals, Hitler had remarked, "If fate forces us into a conflict with the West, it would be desirable that we possess more extensive space in the East." This was primarily to secure the needed food supplies for the German army.

3. Peter Fleming, *Operation Sea Lion* (New York: Simon and Schuster, 1957), p. 239. This was in June 1940.

4. Shirer, *Rise and Fall*, pp. 796–97.

5. Bryan Fugate, *Operation Barbarossa: Strategy and Tactics on the Eastern Front, 1941* (Novato, Calif.: Presidio Press, 1984), p. 63. Halder had been ordered by Gen. Brauchitsch, fresh from his victories in the West, to draw up a plan for an invasion. According to Halder, Brauchitsch had first mentioned Hitler's thoughts about attacking the U.S.S.R. toward the end of July, in Fontainebleau, France. Halder's first discussion with Hitler of military strategy for an invasion of the Soviet Union occurred on 21 July 1940. See Halder, *Kriegstagebuch*, Vol. 2, p. 41 (note 2).

Gen. Jodl informed four of Hitler's officers of the Führer's plan in a railroad car outside Berchtesgaden on 29 July 1941. See Walter Warlimont, *Inside Hitler's Headquarters, 1939–1945* (London: Weidenfeld & Nicolson, 1964), p. 111.

6. Gen. Brauchitsch issued his directive laying the groundwork for Sea Lion on 16 July 1940 in the wake of a British rejection of Hitler's peace overtures. Peter Bor, *Gespräche mit Halder* (Wiesbaden: Limes Verlag, 1950), p. 176.

7. Frederick W. Winterbottam, *The Ultra Secret* (New York: Harper & Row, 1974), p. 56.

8. Fleming, *Sea Lion*, pp. 54–55.

9. Ibid., p. 63.

10. Ibid., p. 297. Gen. Jodl felt Hitler was never fully committed to invading England and finally "decided to abandon Sea Lion completely" by 13 September 1940. See Shirer, *Rise and Fall*, pp. 761, 770. In mid-October Halder noted in his diary that the invasion of Britain had been "postponed." See Halder, *Kriegstagebuch*, Vol. 2, entries for 12–14 October 1940, pp. 133–34. Hitler's chief military reason for shelving Sea Lion may have been a reluctance to strike by sea without air superiority over the Royal Air Force.

11. Barton Whaley, *Codeword BARBAROSSA* (Cambridge: MIT Press, 1977), p. 267.

12. Ibid., pp. 268, 270–71.

13. Some recent commentators have cast doubt on the definitiveness and even existence of this State Department warning. Ruth R. Harris, in her dissertation "The Shifting Winds: The American-Soviet Rapprochement from the Fall of France to the Attack on Pearl Harbor" (George Washington University, 1975), was one of the first to point out that earlier claims about this Barbarossa tip-off are not substantiated by extant historical records—namely, that Respondek knew Operation Sea Lion was only a ruse.

This critical position has been taken further by Richard C. Koloian, who argues in his unpublished master's thesis ("A Myth of History: The American State

Department Warning of Operation Barbarossa," Defense Intelligence College, 1988) that the warning did not occur and was a myth fabricated after the fact by various government officials. Koloian's conclusion is based on a thorough examination of existing documents, but it fails to account for the undisputed fact that the U.S. government did notify the Soviets about an attack as a result of Woods's messages.

14. Woods memorandum, p. 2, Hull Papers.

15. Whaley, *BARBAROSSA*, p. 267. See also Max Domarus, *Hitlers Reden und Proklamationen, 1932–1945*, Vol. 2 (Neustadt: Auslieferung Verlagsdruckerei, 1963), p. 1565. Hitler met with Halder, Raeder, and other staff officers on 31 July 1940. The invasion was slated for the coming spring and was to aim at the cities of Kiev and Moscow. This strike, Hitler argued, would destroy England's last hope in the war.

16. Hans Herwarth von Bittenfeld, *Against Two Evils* (New York: Rawson, Wade, 1981), p. 182. This occurred on a special army train at the Grunewald station, Berlin. The date was 1 August 1940. See *Der Spiegel*, 36, 31 (2 August 1982): 38.

17. Herwarth, *Against Two Evils*, p. 177. Cf. Herwarth letter to the author, 31 May 1985.

18. See, for example, Whaley, *BARBAROSSA*, pp. 81–82. For Harold Deutsch's clarification of Whaley's assertion, see his affidavit of 6 December 1982.

19. Herwarth, *Against Two Evils*, p. 183.

20. Ibid., pp. 177–78. In a letter to the author, 31 May 1985, Herwarth further emphasized this point: "I certainly did not speak to my American friends about Barbarossa. I did not know the plan."

21. See Respondek's May 1946 report, p. 4, Stauffer Papers. See also Woods memorandum, p. 4, Hull Papers.

22. Woods memorandum, p. 5.

23. Ibid., p. 3.

24. Ibid.

25. Ibid., p. 2. See also cable of Leland Harrison to Hull, No. 6516, 16 October 1943, Diplomatic Cables, Decimal File 7400.0011 European War 1939/ 3 1596, State Department Central File, RG 59, NA.

26. Dietrich Orlow, *The History of the Nazi Party*, Vol. 1 (Pittsburgh: Univ. of Pittsburgh Press, 1969), p. 290.

27. Adolf Hitler, *Table Talk, 1941–1944* (London: Weidenfeld & Nicolson, 1953), p. 127.

28. Respondek's confidential report of May 1946, p. 1, Stauffer Papers.

29. Letter of Respondek to Brüning, 8 July 1939, Brüning Papers.

30. Undated *curriculum vitae* of Respondek's, Brüning Papers.

31. Ronald Smelser, author of a recent biography of Ley, points out that he was "one of the last Nazi bigwigs to hear about Barbarossa," chiefly because of Ley's drinking habits. See letter of Smelser to the author, 23 May 1989.

32. Trained as a chemist, Ley had worked with IG Farben in Leverkusen in the 1920s. But his deep hostility toward the Center Party once he joined the NSDAP in 1924 makes it highly unlikely Ley and Respondek would have been on speaking terms.

33. Woods memorandum, p. 3, Hull Papers.

34. Ibid. However, Woods's account is not consistent with Respondek's report of 3 January 1941, now in the National Archives. See "Report on German Military Plans," Military Intelligence Report (hereafter cited as MI Report) No. 17,875, 17 January 1941, 2016–1326 7, Military Intelligence Reports, Berlin. Records of the Office of the Assistant Chief of Staff, G-2, Intelligence, 1939–55. Records of the Army Staff, RG 319, NRC. In this latter document an invasion of England is still seen as scheduled to take place before an attack on the Soviet Union.

35. Woods memorandum, pp. 3–4, Hull Papers.

36. Ibid., p. 4.

37. Ibid., p. 7.

38. Interview with Alex Dreier, 8 June 1987. Dreier's source for this information was Paul Pearson, who worked under Woods.

39. Letter of Richard C. Hottelet to the author, 20 June 1985.

40. Interview with Alex Dreier.

41. Woods memorandum, p. 8. See also account in the *Hattiesburg American*, 30 January 1954, p. 8, Woods File, McCain Library and Archives, University of Southern Mississippi. According to Alex Dreier, the usherettes in the theater were actually nuns involved in Respondek's Catholic resistance group. See Dreier interview.

42. See cable of Alexander Kirk to Cordell Hull, 11 October 1940, No. 5981, 862.00, 740.00114 EW 1939/3441, RG 59, NA. See also Kirk to Hull, 24 July 1940, No. 4823, and Kirk to Hull, 10 August 1940, No. 5064.

43. So pledged the Reichsmarschall on 9 September 1939. See Frederick Oechsner, *This Is the Enemy* (Boston: Little, Brown, 1942), p. 206.

44. Jefferson Patterson, *Diplomatic Duty and Diversion* (Cambridge, Mass.: Riverside Press, 1956), p. 256.

45. Interview with Russell Hill, 2 January 1986.

46. One landed in the courtyard of the U.S. chancery. Interview with Mrs. Jefferson Patterson, 6 December 1985.

47. William L. Shirer, *Berlin Diary: The Journal of a Foreign Correspondent, 1934–1941* (New York: Knopf, 1943), p. 521. See also interview with Amelie Riddleberger, 28 June 1985.

48. Letter of Milada Woods to Mrs. Joseph T. Robinson, 11 January 1940, Robinson Papers.

49. Letter of Clinton B. Conger to the author, 24 September 1985.

50. Letter of Milada Woods to Mrs. Joseph T. Robinson, 18 November 1939, Robinson Papers.

51. Interview with Valeska Hoffmann, 22 March 1986.

52. Woods memorandum, p. 4, Hull Papers.

53. Ibid., p. 4.

54. Kennan cannot recall any involvement in this incident, however. See letter of Constance Goodman to the author, 18 November 1986.

55. See letter of Kennan to the author, 18 October 1985, for comments on his administrative duties. The *Christian Science Monitor*'s Joseph C. Harsch recalls Kennan outlining a chart of the Nazis' "pattern of conquest" in Europe and believes the diplomat was occupied with more than paperwork at the time. See Harsch letter to the author, 25 November 1985.

56. William E. Griffith, who knew Respondek after the war when Griffith was head of the denazification program in Bavaria, says Respondek told him Woods did send the "invasion ruble" back to Washington. See interview with Griffith, 30 April 1985.

57. Bor, *Gespräche mit Halder*, pp. 127–30. Halder was prepared to occupy the chancellery and place Hitler under arrest.

58. Hans Bernd Gisevius, *To the Bitter End* (Boston: Houghton, Mifflin, 1947), p. 288.

59. John Wheeler-Bennett, *The Nemesis of Power: The German Army in Politics, 1918–1945*, 2nd ed. (New York: St. Martin's Press, 1964), p. 428.

60. Peter Hoffmann, *History of the German Resistance, 1933–1945* (Boston: MIT Press, 1977), p. 102.

61. Ibid., p. 286.

62. Ibid.

63. Ibid., p. 479.

64. Harold C. Deutsch, *The Conspiracy against Hitler during the Twilight War* (Minneapolis: Univ. of Minnesota Press, 1968), p. 197.

65. Gen. Brauchitsch briefed him on that date. See Halder, *Kriegstagebuch*, Vol. 2, entry for 3 July 1940, p. 6.

66. So confided Halder to Brauchitsch in January 1941. See letter of Gerd R. Überschar to the author, 30 September 1986.

67. In the view of the British military historian Basil Liddell Hart, Halder and Brauchitsch were compelled to do so as loyal, professional officers and because the "immensity of their own successes hitherto made it more difficult for them to impose a policy of moderation." See Liddell Hart, *The German Generals Talk: Startling Revelations from Hitler's High Command* (New York: Quill, 1979), p. 40.

68. Letter of Gen. Curt von Hobe to the author, 4 September 1986.

69. Cf. Jacob D. Beam, unpublished memoir, p. 161, J. D. Beam Papers.

70. Muckermann was first barred from speaking in public in August 1936. Bishop Berning of Osnabrück intervened to have this lifted in December, but the ban was reinstated on 23 March 1937. See Ulrich von Hehl, ed., *Priester unter Hitlers Terror: Eine biographische und statistische Erhebung* (Mainz: Matthias Grünewald Verlag), p. 858.

71. Interview with Agnes Dreimann, 26 July 1986.

72. Woods memorandum, p. 5, Hull Papers.

73. Alfred Rothe, SJ, "Pater Georg von Sachsen," *Mitteilungen aus den deutschen Provinzen der Gesellschaft Jesu*, vol. 17, issue 1, no. 113, p. 201.

74. Interview with Fr. H. P. Kugelmeier, SJ, 30 July 1986.

75. Henriette Schall-Riaucour, *Aufstand und Gehorsam: Offiziertum und Generalstab im Umbruch* (Wiesbaden: Limes Verlag, 1972), p. 313.

76. Woods memorandum, p. 5, Hull Papers.

77. Rothe, "Pater Georg," p. 34.

78. Interview with Fr. Kugelmeier, 30 July 1986.

79. Rothe, "Pater Georg," p. 90.

80. Elisabeth Schonau, *Vom Thron zum Altar: Georg Kronprinz von Sachsen* (Paderborn: F. Schoningh, 1955), pp. 64–65. Author's translation. Cf. Rothe, "Pater Georg," p. 88.

81. Letter of Gen. Hobe to the author, 12 November 1986.

82. Rothe, "Pater Georg," p. 89. In his diary, Halder cites conversations with Georg as taking place on 23 February 1941 and 23 March 1941. See Halder, *Kriegstagebuch*, Vol. 2, entries for these dates, pp. 291, 325. Interestingly enough, the March meeting with the former crown prince occurred barely a week after Hitler declared to his generals that the Soviet Union must be "smashed."

83. As Halder later admitted, he did not record meetings of a sensitive nature in his diary because it was available for others to read and "discretion on his part was therefore imperative." See Franz Halder, *The Halder Diaries*, Vol. 2 (Boulder, Colo.: Westview, 1976), Appendix B, p. 1592.

84. Sam Woods, for example, affirmed in a postwar sworn statement that "late in 1941 [sic] . . . Respondek . . . made a report available to me giving detailed plans for the German attack on Russia during the following spring." Statement of Woods, 5 August 1948, Stauffer Papers.

85. See Woods memorandum, p. 6, Hull Papers, LC. This is disputed by Halder's son-in-law, Curt von Hobe, who maintains the general "certainly would not have revealed details or a time for an attack on Russia." Letter to the author, 12 November 1986.

86. Respondek stated this also occurred in November, but from what Halder reveals in his diary, it seems unlikely he would have known at that time what Hitler's timetable was. It was not until 17 March 1941 that Halder recorded the date of 16 May 1941 as the time when Barbarossa was to be launched. See Halder, *Kriegstagebuch*, Vol. 2, p. 315. It should also be noted that as late as December 1940 Halder still felt that an invasion of the Soviet Union was only a contingency, to occur only if circumstances so dictated. See Bor, *Gespräche mit Halder*, p. 194. At that point the general believed Operation Sea Lion was merely being "postponed."

87. Fugate, *Operation Barbarossa*, p. 64.

88. Ibid.

89. Trumbull Higgins, *Hitler and Russia: The Third Reich in a Two-Front War, 1937–1943* (New York: MacMillan, 1966), p. 94.

90. According to Woods, neither "suspected that he [Respondek] was seeking information to be used against the Nazi regime." Woods memorandum, p. 5, Hull Papers.

91. Basil Liddell Hart, *History of the Second World War* (New York: Putnam, 1970), pp. 154–155.

92. See letter of Gerd R. Überschar to the author, 30 September 1986.

93. Karl Balzer, *Verschwörung gegen Deutschand: So verloren wir den Krieg* (Preussisch Oldendorf: R. W. Schutz, 1978), p. 176.

94. Schall-Riaucour, *Aufstand*, p. 298.

95. Balzer, *Verschwörung*, p. 204.

96. *Command and Commanders in Modern Warfare*, Proceedings of the Second Military History Symposium (Colorado Springs, Colo.: USAF Academy, 1971), p. 191.

97. See "Affidavit of Franz Halder," 22 November 1945, Halder Folder, Box 66B, Donovan Papers, USAWC.

98. Cable of Woods to Hull, No. 288, Section 7, 7 January 1943, 740.0011 EW 1939/26912, RG 59, NA.

99. Hitler did not make clear to Halder his intention to abandon the idea of invading Great Britain until 3 February 1941. At a conference attended by Halder, Jodl, Brauchitsch, and other military leaders, Hitler agreed that Operation Sea Lion was no longer feasible. See *Trial of the Major War Criminals before the International Military Tribunal*, Vol. 11 (Nuremberg: International Military Tribunal, 1947), p. 338.

100. Hitler informed Halder on 17 March 1941 that he wanted to launch the invasion on 16 May 1941. Halder, *Kriegstagebuch*, Vol. 2, entry for 17 March 1941, p. 315. In his April memorandum for Woods, Respondek cited May as the time when all preparations for Operation Barbarossa were to have been completed. See untitled memorandum 5a, dated "April 1941," "Germany" Folder, Safe File, Box 4, President's Secretary's File, FDRL.

101. Rothe, "Pater Georg," p. 208.

102. After the war, Woods put this around Thanksgiving. See Woods memorandum, p. 6, Hull Papers, LC. However, the earliest of Respondek's extant reports touching on this subject is dated early January 1941.

103. For these details I am indebted to Milada Woods, interview of 12 February 1987.

104. Ibid.

105. Woods apparently confided in at least one colleague about his espionage. This was his assistant, Paul Pearson. Interview with Alex Dreier, 8 June 1987.

106. Woods memorandum, p. 6, Hull Papers, LC. Kirk had left in October for the States, eager to warn the American people about the threat of a Nazi-dominated Europe.

107. Woods memorandum, p. 6.

108. Ibid., p. 7.

109. Interview with Lloyd Yates, 4 August 1987. Since Yates was interviewed some 46 years after the fact, and at the advanced age of eighty-four, his memory on these details may not be completely reliable. There is no mention of Yates's having traveled to the United States in early 1941 in the State Department files relating to his personal affairs (Decimal File 123, Y 2, RG 59).

110. A memorandum of Col. Peyton to the Assistant Chief of Staff, G-2, dated 10 February 1941 (2655-B–390 21, RG 165, NA), suggests Yates left Berlin during the first week in that month. The long delay between when Respondek wrote his report and when it was brought out of Berlin may be due to the time required to prepare a complete translation and then fully evaluate its contents. Doubts about the report's value on the part of U.S. military attachés may also have contributed to this time lag.

CHAPTER 5. A WARNING UNHEEDED

1. Chargé d'affaires Leland Morris was to remain skeptical about reports of a German strike against the Soviet Union, and this may also have accounted for this delay. As late as May 1941, Morris would discount rumors about likely "German military actions against Russia." See his cable to the State Department, 27 May 1941, Box 27, Binder No. 4, Dispatches, 1939–41, Safe File, President's Secretary's File, FDRL.

2. Breckenridge Long, *The War Diary of Breckenridge Long: Selections from the Years 1939–1944* (Lincoln: Univ. of Nebraska Press, 1966), p. 119.

3. Ibid., pp. 175–76.

4. Neither Woods's cover letter nor the original German document can be located in the National Archives or the Roosevelt Library at Hyde Park, N.Y.

5. In an introduction to his edition of Long's diary, Fred L. Israel says Long was eager to serve Roosevelt in "almost any capacity." Long, *War Diary*, xxiv.

6. Long had touted Mussolini's government as one of "the most interesting experiments in government to come above the horizon since the formulation of our Constitution," Long, *War Diary*, xviii.

7. Ibid., entry for 20 November 1940, p. 156.

8. It is not clear how much attention Hull gave these papers.

9. Long, Diary, entry for 21 February 1941, p. 30, Box 15, 1941, Long Papers, LC.

10. Quoted in ibid. As noted, this does not jibe with Respondek, Woods, and Hull's postwar claim that they knew plans for an invasion of England were only a "blind." In Respondek's original, German-language report of 3 January 1941, he stated that military action against the Soviet Union would come only after a defeat of the United Kingdom and pressure on the Soviets to increase shipments of raw materials to Germany. See MI Report No. 17,875, 17 January 1941, pp. 4–5, 2016–1326 7, RG 165, NRC, and Respondek's accompanying report, pp. 5–6.

But Long had not seen that report by February 21st. Furthermore, the sections of Respondek's memorandums dealing with German labor, finance, and raw materials now in the National Archives and Roosevelt Library do not refer to a planned attack on the Soviet Union. This fact has led some commentators to conclude that Long misinterpreted the summary translation prepared for him on the 21st, or exaggerated its contents. See Brüning, *Briefe*, p. 345, note 6. According to Brüning's editors, Long reached this conclusion before he read the complete report in an English version. Since Respondek did know about Barbarossa in early January and referred to the likelihood of a German offensive in a separate document, dated January 3rd, but which did not reach the State Department until some time after February 21st, it appears more probable that the crucial economic section from which Long quoted (and which referred to the January 3rd report) was, at some point, separated from the other parts. What happened to these pages cannot be determined.

11. Long, Diary, entry for 10 February 1941, p. 17.

12. Long noted that an invasion of England was expected "in April at the latest." Ibid. British intelligence did not finally accept that Hitler was going to move eastward, instead of across the Channel, until only three weeks before Operation Barbarossa was launched. See F. H. Hinsley, *British Intelligence in the Second World War: Its Influence on Strategy and Operations*, Vol. 1 (London: Her Majesty's Stationery Office, 1979), p. 429.

13. Long, Diary, entry for 21 February 1941, p. 28.

14. Ibid., p. 30.

15. See Respondek's "Memorandum II: Status of War Raw Materials," 24 January 1941, Box 1208, RG 165, NRC. Col. General Fromm, chief of army equipment and commander of the Replacement Army, had reported on these

shortages to Gen. Halder on 23 December 1940. See Barry A. Leach, *German Strategy against Russia, 1939–1941* (Oxford: Clarendon Press, 1973), p. 146.

16. Woods memorandum, pp. 8–9, Hull Papers.

17. Fresh back from his tour of Paris over Christmas, Hitler met with the heads of the Army High Command on January 8–9. See Leach, *German Strategy*, p. 146.

18. Woods memorandum, p. 9, Hull Papers.

19. Respondek's "Memorandum II: Status of War Materials," 24 January 1941, p. 9, Box 1208, RG 165, NRC. In his report Respondek indicated the German army had sufficient supplies to conduct war through 1941 but that growing shortages would "limit considerably the war preparations" if the conflict were prolonged.

20. Long, Diary, entry for 21 February 1941, p. 28.

21. Ibid., p. 34. Cf. memorandum of E. M. Watson to President Roosevelt, 5 March 1941, "Germany" Folder, Safe File, FDRL.

22. Long, Diary, entry for 21 February 1941, p. 29.

23. Hinsley, *British Intelligence*, p. 444.

24. Ibid., p. 432. Churchill expressed this view before his military commanders, 31 October 1940.

25. But Churchill continued to expect the Germans would strike across the Channel first. See Robert Sherwood, *Roosevelt and Hopkins: An Intimate History* (New York: Harper, 1948), p. 257. The British leader did not finally agree that Operation Sea Lion had been scrapped until March 1941.

26. Hinsley, *British Intelligence*, pp. 441–42.

27. Hinsley says only the Respondek documents transmitted in April still exist in foreign office files. These did not go beyond "very generalised accounts of German intentions and strategic objectives." One British intelligence expert commented, "The Book of Revelations read backwards would be more helpful." See FO 371/26521, C6928/C7205/78/38. Quoted in Hinsley, *British Intelligence*, p. 444.

28. Lt. Col. H. E. Maguire, project officer at G-2 and military intelligence liaison with the State Department, evaluated Respondek's raw materials summary on March 1, 1941, finding it of "exceptional interest." Maguire did have reservations about the document's authenticity, fearing it could be a plant and feeling that "a certain reserve [should] be maintained until more is known as to how it originated and the reliability of the person who secured the document." See Maguire's "Status of War Raw Materials in Germany," 1 March 1941, Box 1208, RG 165, NRC.

29. Brüning, *Briefe*, p. 344. Long, however, indicates that Brüning was coming to Washington in any case, and he simply "arranged to have a conversation with him." Long, Diary, entry for 21 February 1941, p. 34.

30. Brüning said the raw materials summary reflected the somewhat pessimistic views of Gen. Fromm regarding Germany's existing supplies. See Brüning, *Briefe*, p. 344, note 5.

31. Ibid., p. 344.

32. See Long's memorandum, "Concerning Certain Secret Documents in the German Language," 4 April 1941, Box 1208, RG 165, NRC.

33. Long noted Brüning's disagreement with some of Respondek's conclusions regarding German raw materials, finance, and labor, but he also observed

that previous Respondek reports had in general proven accurate. See Long's memorandums of 4 April 1941 and 7 March 1941, Box 1208, RG 165, NRC.

34. Long memorandum of 4 April 1941.

35. MI Report No. 17,875, 17 January 1941, p. 1, 2016–1326–7, RG 165, NRC.

36. Ibid.

37. Ibid., p. 16.

38. It appears that because of its military nature, this document was not sent along directly to the State Department. When Long finally received this report, he showed it to Gen. Miles, of military intelligence, who commented that this was "the most important document that had been received by the Army [from the State Department] in his recollection." Long, Diary, entry for 24 March 1941, p. 40.

39. Ibid.

40. Ibid.

41. MI Report No. 17,875, p. 3, RG 165, NRC.

42. Ibid., p. 4.

43. Ibid.

44. Ibid., pp. 5, 10.

45. He correctly reported that German amphibious units were slated to be launched from the French ports of Cherbourg, Le Havre, Dieppe, Boulogne, Calais, and Dunkirk.

46. Morgenthau, Diary, entry for 3 March 1941, Book IV, March-December 1941, FDRL.

47. Cordell Hull, *The Memoirs of Cordell Hull*, Vol. 2 (New York: MacMillan, 1948), p. 968. Here Hull also erroneously reports he received this information in January, instead of February.

48. Sumner Welles, *The Time for Decision* (New York, London: Harper, 1944), p. 170.

49. Adolf Berle, Diary, January-April 1941, entry for 5 March 1941, Box 217, Berle Papers, FDRL.

50. This assessment is based upon a review of documents known to exist in government archives. As noted earlier, parts of the January economic report, including Respondek's original version, are missing from these files.

51. Roosevelt was distrustful of the Soviets and resented their increasing demands on the U.S. government. He may have wanted to nudge them into the war.

52. Long, by contrast, had the "greatest dislike" for the Soviet system. Nonetheless, he concurred that the United States had to assist the Russians against Hitler. See Long, *War Diary*, pp. 206–7.

53. Harris, "The Shifting Winds," p. 295.

54. Cable of Hull to Steinhardt, 28 February 1941, 740.0011 EW 1939/8656, RG 59, NA. Quoted in Harris, "The Shifting Winds," p. 296.

55. Hull, *Memoirs*, Vol. 2, p. 968.

56. Welles, *Time for Decision*, p. 170. When Sam Woods learned of Welles's claim after the war, he was so incensed at this "calculated credit-seeking author" that he told Hull he wanted to come back to the States to disprove Welles's allegation. See Woods's cable to Hull, 15 August 1945 (Folder 176), Hull Papers.

57. Welles, *Time for Decision*, p. 170. This is substantiated by what Hull told Woods. See Woods memorandum, p. 12, Hull Papers.

58. Woods memorandum, p. 12.

59. Vladimir Petrov, *22 June 1941: Soviet Historians and the German Invasion*, 1st ed. (Columbia, S.C.: Univ. of South Carolina Press, 1968), pp. 176–77.

60. Philip Knightley, *The Second Oldest Profession: Spies and Spying in the Twentieth Century* (New York: W. W. Norton, 1986), p. 196.

61. Hinsley, *British Intelligence*, p. 453.

62. Ibid.

63. Knightley, *Second Oldest Profession*, p. 195.

64. According to Whaley, *BARBAROSSA*, at least 80 separate warnings were received.

65. Whaley, *BARBAROSSA*, p. 34. Cf. Knightley, *Second Oldest Profession*, p. 195.

66. Cable of Leland Morris to Hull, 8 June 1941, Section 1, Box 27, Binder No. 4, Dispatches 1939–41, Safe File, FDRL.

67. See Kennan, "Draft Memorandum for Mr. Shaw," 18 August 1942, Box 23, Category 1-D, Kennan Papers, Seeley G. Mudd Manuscript Library, Princeton University.

68. Kennan, *Memoirs*, p. 127.

69. Ibid., p. 130.

70. Interview with Angus M. Thuermer, 28 June 1985.

71. Kahn, *Hitler's Spies*, p. 75.

72. For example, Joseph Harsch passed on to navy captain Paul Pihl photographs of Danube River barges being towed to the Rhine following the fall of France. See Harsch letter to the author, 25 November 1985.

73. Interview with Dana Schmidt, 20 October 1985. See also Oechsner, *Enemy*, p. 267.

74. Cf. Shirer, *Nightmare Years*, pp. 138–39.

75. Interviews with Dana Schmidt, 20 October 1985, and Richard C. Hottelet, 29 July 1985.

76. Cable of Leland Morris to Secretary of State Hull, 15 March 1941, Section 1, 811.91262/185, RG 59, NA.

77. Howard K. Smith, *Last Train from Berlin* (New York: Knopf, 1942), p. 225.

78. In his diary Goebbels recorded that Hottelet's arrest was in retaliation for the arrest of German journalists. See *The Goebbels Diaries, 1939–1941* (New York: Penguin Books, 1984), entry for 14 March 1941, p. 268. But Hottelet, like many foreign journalists, was also involved in black-market currency transactions, and the Nazis may have wanted to make an example of him.

79. Signs were detected by Frederick Oechsner, Howard K. Smith, Louis Lochner, and Alvin Steinkopf. See interview with Oechsner, 4 November 1985; Smith, *Last Train*, p. 69; and letter of Angus M. Thuermer to the author, 8 October 1985.

80. *Time*, 23 June 1941, p. 23. Cf. Laird letter to the author, 19 June 1985.

81. Memorandum of Raymond Geist to Breckenridge Long, 15 May 1941, 761.62/942, Box 1208, RG 165, NRC.

82. Ibid.

83. Letter of Hull to President Roosevelt, 12 May 1941, "Germany" Folder, Box 4, Safe File, FDRL.

84. See "Supplement to the Economic Balance Sheet," undated memorandum, "Germany" Folder, Box 4, Safe File, FDRL.

85. Memorandum 5a, April 1941, pp. 1–2, "Germany" Folder, Box 4, Safe File, FDRL.

86. Ibid., p. 2.

87. Ibid., pp. 6, 7.

88. Memorandum 8, dated "End of April," p. 3, "Germany" Folder, Box 4, Safe File, FDRL.

89. Ibid., pp. 4–5.

90. Liddell Hart, *History of the Second World War*, p. 149.

91. Quoted in Joachim Fest, *Hitler* (New York: Harcourt, Brace & Jovanovich, 1974), p. 648.

92. For these statistics, see Paul Carrell, *Hitler Moves East, 1941–1943* (Boston: Little, Brown, 1964), p. 22.

93. This phrase appears in U.S. Chief of Counsel for the Prosecution of Axis Criminality, *Nazi Conspiracy and Aggression*, Vol. 6 (Washington, D.C.: U.S. Govt. Printing Office, 1946), pp. 847–48.

CHAPTER 6. THE MASTER SPY AT WORK

1. Hull, *Memoirs*, Vol. 2, p. 987.

2. See Woods memorandum, p. 12, Hull Papers.

3. In fact, Hitler, himself a victim of a British gas attack at Ypres, remained opposed to the use of this weapon throughout the war. See Albert Speer, *Inside the Third Reich: Memoirs* (New York: MacMillan, 1970), p. 413.

4. Respondek report of May 1946, p. 3, Stauffer Papers.

5. Speer, *Third Reich*, p. 413, note 2.

6. Respondek report, May 1946, p. 3.

7. MI Report No. 17,806, 12 December 1940, 2314-B–143 31, RG 165, NA.

8. Unsigned letter to U.S. embassy, Berlin, 27 December 1940, 2016–1326–7, RG 165, NA.

9. Quoted in Fleming, *Sea Lion*, p. 293.

10. Interview with Agnes Dreimann, 26 July 1986.

11. Interview with Valeska Hoffmann, 22 March 1986.

12. Respondek report, May 1946, p. 3.

13. MI Report No. 17,806, 12 December 1940, RG 165, NA.

14. Ibid., p. 1.

15. See Respondek's German-language report, 3 January 1941, attached to MI Report No. 17,875, 2016–1326 7, RG 165, NA.

16. Long, Diary, entry for 24 March 1941, p. 40, Box 5, 1941, Long Papers.

17. Hermann Bauermeister, "Die Entwicklung der Magnetminen bis zum Beginn des Zweiten Weltkriegs," *Marine Rundschau*, 55, 1 (1958): 25.

18. For particulars of German development of the magnetic mine, see Bauermeister, "Die Entwicklung," pp. 25–29, 30–31.

19. Cajus Bekker, *Hitler's Naval War* (Garden City, N.Y.: Doubleday, 1974), pp. 59, 72.

20. Quoted in ibid., p. 60.

21. Winston S. Churchill, *The Second World War*, Vol. 1: *The Gathering Storm* (London: Cassell, 1948), p. 505.

22. Bekker, *Hitler's Naval War*, p. 73.

23. "From this moment," Churchill recalled with relief, "the whole position was transformed." Churchill, *Gathering Storm*, p. 506.

24. Robert C. Duncan, *America's Use of Sea Mines* (White Oak, Md.: U.S. Naval Ordnance Laboratory, 1963), pp. 108–9. See also Churchill, *Gathering Storm*, p. 508.

25. Bauermeister, "Die Entwicklung," p. 31.

26. Exchange of naval intelligence between Washington and London did not start until May 1941. See Book 4: "Exchange of Military Information with Great Britain, May 1941," Sherwood Coll., Box 305, Hopkins Papers, FDRL.

27. MI Report No. 18,018, 24 February 1941, p. 4, 2016–1326/10, RG 165, NA.

28. Memorandum of Gen. Sherman Miles to Army Chief of Staff, 24 March 1941, 2657-B–815/2, RG 165, NA.

29. For specifics of U.S. magnetic mine development, see Duncan, *Sea Mines*, p. 87, 90, 119.

30. MI Report No. 18,018, p. 1.

31. Ibid., p. 4.

32. Interview with Arthur Graubart, 9 October 1985. See also Hinsley, *British Intelligence*, p. 309.

33. Hinsley, *British Intelligence*, p. 309.

34. Memorandum of Gen. Miles, G-2, to Army Chief of Staff, 24 March 1941, RG 165, NA.

35. Liddell Hart, *Second World War*, p. 381.

36. Respondek, addendum to compensation claim, 21 May 1970, LVA.

37. Letter of Respondek to the International Committee of the Red Cross, 1 July 1970, LVA. Author's translation.

38. Respondek, addendum to compensation claim, 21 May 1970, LVA.

39. Martin Höllen, *Heinrich Wienken, Der "unpolitische" Kirchenpolitiker: Eine Biographie aus drei Epochen des Katholizismus* (Mainz: Matthias Grünewald, 1981), p. 2.

40. Memorandum 5a, April 1941, p. 3, "Germany" Folder, Box 4, Safe File, FDRL.

41. Milton Dank, *The Glider Gang: An Eyewitness History of World War II Glider Combat*, 1st ed. (Philadelphia: J. B. Lippincott, 1977), pp. 23, 28.

42. Quoted in James E. Mrazek, *The Glider War* (London: Robert Hale, 1975), p. 53.

43. Ibid.

44. Ibid., p. 191.

45. David Mondey, *Concise Guide to Axis Aircraft of World War II* (Feltham, England: Temple Press, 1984), p. 108.

46. MI Report No. 17,875, p. 7.

47. Liddell Hart, *Second World War*, p. 382.

48. MI Report No. 17,875, p. 7.

49. "The German Military and Economic Position," 12 December 1941 (Co-ordinator of Information, Monograph No. 3), p. 18, "Germany" Folder, Safe File, FDRL.

50. MI Report No. 17,875, p. 5. Japanese foreign minister Matsuoka discussed this commission with Hitler in April 1941.

51. See "The Significance of German Artificial Materials," Memorandum of Col. Peyton to Assistant Chief of Staff, 3 March 1941, 2655-B–392/2, RG 165, NA.

52. MI Report No. 18,214, Col. Peyton to Asst. Chief of Staff, 28 April 1941, 2655-B–392/3, RG 165, NA.

53. For a discussion of Japanese attitudes, see Harris, "The Shifting Winds," p. 279.

54. Ibid., p. 280. In January, Matsuoka favored a treaty with the Russians. By June he was arguing for an attack against the Soviet Union.

55. Toshikazu Kase, *Journey to the "Missouri"* (New Haven, Conn.: Yale University Press, 1951), pp. 45–46, says Matsuoka desired a rapprochement in 1941.

56. Interview with Toshikazu Kase, 27 August 1955, Box 10, Series I: "K," John Toland Papers, FDRL (hereafter cited as Toland Papers). Shortly after his return from Europe, the Japanese foreign minister wrote that he had a "fond dream of reaching an understanding with America in the Pacific." Yosuke Matsuoka, "Regarding My Visit to Europe and U.S.–Japanese Negotiations" (English translation), IPS Doc. No. 491, IMT 33 (Reel WT9), Records of the Japanese Ministry of Foreign Affairs, NA.

57. Kase says the Moscow agreement was the main reason for Matsuoka's trip, with any pact with Hitler being regarded as "incidental." Kase interview, Toland Papers.

58. Cf. Hull, *Memoirs*, Vol. 2, pp. 900–1.

59. So claimed Matsuoka. See interview with Matsuoka, Box 13, Series I, Toland Papers.

60. As it turned out, Matsuoka got more than he could have hoped for when Hitler pledged to declare war on the United States if Japan should enter a conflict with the Americans.

61. John Toland, *The Rising Sun: The Decline and Fall of the Japanese Empire, 1936–1945* (New York: Random House, 1970), p. 66.

62. Kase was an attaché in Germany from 1932 to 1934, when he was transferred to the League of Nations. See interview with Kase, 27 August 1966, Box 10, Series I: "K," Toland Papers.

63. See Fumihiko Togo, ed., *The Cause of Japan* (New York: Simon and Schuster, 1956), p. 59.

64. For an extensive discussion of Kase's wartime career, see Kase, *Journey.*

65. Matsuoka had the reputation of speaking loosely. Matsuoka interview, Box 13, Toland Papers.

66. This Respondek claims in his letter to Cordell Hull, 4 April 1948, Brüning Papers. Kase has denied that he ever knew Respondek or met with him during his April sojourn in Berlin. Letter of Reiko (Kase) Nagura to the author, 20 February 1989.

67. In his 4 April 1948 letter to Hull about contact with the Japanese diplomat,

Respondek spells his name "Kahse" and refers to him as "Matsouka[sic]'s traveling companion."

68. Interview with Agnes Dreimann, 26 July 1986.

69. Kase was apparently eager to avoid a war with the United States. He believed that if he could speak personally with President Roosevelt, the two countries' differences could be peacefully resolved. See Kase interview, Toland Papers. This view is substantiated by the late Edwin O. Reischauer, who stated in a letter to the author that "Kase, like many highly placed people in Japan, felt that if the right person could talk with Roosevelt the danger of war could somehow be avoided." Letter of 17 April 1989.

70. Donald Goldstein, coauthor of two books on Pearl Harbor, says that there was some "hearsay" about an attack coming from the U.S. embassy in Berlin. Interview with Goldstein, 21 April 1987.

71. Gordon W. Prange et al., *At Dawn We Slept: The Untold Story of Pearl Harbor* (New York: McGraw-Hill, 1981), p. 31.

72. Respondek told both Douglas Miller and Thomas Stauffer that he had held the important post of whip in the Center Party, but he had not. He also repeatedly stated that two generations of his family had served in the Reichstag, but this claim was also not true. See, for example, his letter to Jacob D. Beam, 16 October 1948, 740.00119 Control (Germany)/10–1648, RG 59, NA.

73. Respondek's daughter, Valeska Hoffmann, remembers his being angry that the Americans had failed to heed his warning. See interview of 18 April 1987. Respondek also expressed this disappointment in another letter to Cordell Hull, in which he claims his information on a Japanese attack was ignored. See his letter to Hull, 4 April 1948, Brüning Papers.

74. Kase himself has been wary about revealing much in his postwar interviews. See letter of John Toland to the author, 13 May 1987, commenting on Kase's inscrutability.

CHAPTER 7. THE SCREW TIGHTENS

1. Oechsner, *Enemy*, p. 220.

2. Marianne Feuersenger, *Mein Kriegstagebuch: Führerhauptquartier und Berliner Wirklichkeit* (Freiburg: Herder Verlag, 1982), pp. 71–72.

3. Smith, *Last Train*, pp. 82ff.

4. Ibid., p. 104.

5. See "triple priority" cable of State Department to Woods, 2 December 1941, No. 2892, Decimal File 123, Woods, Sam E., RG 59, NA, ordering him to return to the States immediately by plane for "consultations."

6. Kennan, *Memoirs*, p. 135.

7. Woods memorandum, p. 10, Hull Papers.

8. Ibid., p. 10. According to Respondek, Woods also offered as an identifying token an antique glass amulet, from Czechoslovakia, that belonged to his wife. See Respondek's May 1946 report, p. 8, Stauffer Papers.

9. Respondek confidential report, May 1946, p. 8, Stauffer Papers.

10. The Bernheimer antique store had among its customers several members of the Nazi leadership, including Goering, Ribbentrop, and Hitler. The business

was confiscated in 1938. See "Zurück zum Barock," *Der Spiegel*, 11, 52 (25 December 1957): 42–50.

11. Letter of Respondek to Thomas B. Stauffer, 2 May 1961, Stauffer Papers.

12. Ibid. Author's translation.

13. Ibid. Author's translation. Respondek was told that Roosevelt had received the statue in mid-1942.

14. This conclusion is based on the author's examination of the auction catalogues of items formerly at the Roosevelt Museum. Interestingly enough, this did include a 17th-century "brass enameled icon of St. George."

15. The St. George carving was not among the items in Sam Woods's possession presented to the University of Southern Mississippi in the 1950s. See letter of Terry S. Latour, Director of Special Collections and University Archivist, to the author, 6 March 1987.

16. Woods told Respondek that Ochsenbein would be his "future contact man" on an equal basis. See letter of Respondek to Jacob D. Beam, 20 January 1949, Stauffer Papers.

17. Letter of Hildegard Ochsenbein to the author, 25 September 1986.

18. Ibid. In his cable to Harrison, 15 March 1943, Box 10, Bern Confidential File, RG 84, NRC, Woods says he was "closely associated" with Ochsenbein.

19. Hildegard Ochsenbein letter to author.

20. Letter of Max König to the author, 29 May 1987. König served in the Swiss embassy in Berlin from May 1939 to May 1945. Ochsenbein's wife says she visited the Woodses often in Switzerland. Letter of Hildegard Ochsenbein to the author, 25 September 1986.

21. Letter of Respondek to Thomas B. Stauffer, 3 February 1961, Stauffer Papers. However, Frölicher's daughter says it would have been "extremely unlikely" for her father to have authorized or approved such a role for Ochsenbein. See letter of Helen Geiser-Frölicher to the author, 28 May 1987.

22. Interview with Agnes Dreimann, 26 July 1986.

23. In referring to his dealings with Ochsenbein, Respondek often simply called him "Mr. O." See, for example, his memorandum to Robert Murphy, 28 March 1946, Folder 10, Box 746, POLAD Files, RG 84, IZG. But he does refer to Ochsenbein by name in his 16 October 1948 letter to Jacob Beam, Stauffer Papers.

24. Sir John Lomax, *The Diplomatic Smuggler* (London: Arthur Barker, 1965), p. 138.

25. Pierre Accoce and Pierre Quet, *A Man Called Lucy, 1939–1945* (New York: Coward-McCann, 1967), p. 52.

26. Accoce and Quet, *Lucy*, p. 182, passim.

27. Ochsenbein was extremely discreet in keeping his work a secret. His wife, Hildegard, married to him for 46 years, never knew anything about his help to Respondek. See letters of Hildegard Ochsenbein to the author, 1 September 1986 and 28 September 1986.

28. Ernest G. Fischer, Diary, entry for 11 December 1941, private collection, New Orleans (hereafter cited as Fischer Papers). See also interview with Frederick Oechsner, 4 November 1985. See also Charles Burdick, *An American Island in Hitler's Reich: The Bad Nauheim Internment* (Menlo Park, Calif.: Markgraf, 1987), pp. 21–24.

29. See Alvin Steinkopf, "The Last Chapter," unpublished manuscript, Steinkopf Papers, SHSW.

30. Lochner, *Always the Unexpected*, p. 275.

31. Leland Morris, "Home Rules," 12 December 1941, Fischer Papers.

32. Interview with Clinton B. Conger, 7 January 1986.

33. Letter of Glen M. Stadler to the author, 1 November 1985.

34. Steinkopf, "The Last Chapter," p. 5, Steinkopf Papers, SHSW.

35. Interview with Mary Bancroft, 25 February 1986.

36. Letter of Edwin A. Shanke to the author, 27 August 1985.

37. Burdick, *American Island*, p. 48.

38. Interview with Milada Woods, 12 February 1987.

39. Letter of Ernest G. Fischer to the author, 3 November 1985.

40. Letter of Angus M. Thuermer to the author, 5 August 1985. Among his fellow Americans Woods had the reputation of serving the finest table in Berlin. Burdick, *American Island*, p. 53.

41. For the details of this incident I am indebted to Agnes Dreimann. Interview of 26 July 1986.

42. Woods memorandum, p. 20, Hull Papers.

43. Respondek report, May 1946, p. 9, Stauffer Papers.

44. Woods, Respondek was told, was on a list of suspects compiled by the Sicherheitsdienst.

45. Respondek report, May 1946, p. 9. Author's translation.

46. Ibid.

47. Valeska Hoffmann recalls her father's seeing his interrogation as a game in which he was confident of being the shrewdest player. Interview of 22 March 1986.

48. Ibid., p. 10. Cf. Woods memorandum, p. 20, Hull Papers.

49. Respondek report, May 1946, p. 10.

50. Woods memorandum, p. 11, Hull Papers.

51. Ibid., pp. 11–13.

52. Ibid., p. 13.

53. Ibid., p. 14.

54. Long, Diary, entry of 28 June 1942, Box 6, 1942, p. 240, Long Papers.

55. Knightley, *Second Oldest Profession*, p. 211.

56. Montgomery Hyde, *Room 3603: The Story of the British Intelligence Center in New York during World War II* (New York: Farrar, Straus, 1963), p. 153.

57. Ibid., p. 156. Cf. Richard H. Smith, *OSS: The Secret History of America's First Central Intelligence Agency* (Berkeley/Los Angeles: Univ. of California Press, 1972), p. 33.

58. See memorandum of Donovan to President Roosevelt, 1941, Goodfellow Papers, Stanford, Calif., quoted in Smith, *OSS*, p. 33.

59. Smith, *OSS*, p. 204.

60. Letter of Breckenridge Long to Leland Harrison, 28 July 1942, "L" Folder, Box 31, Harrison Papers, LC.

61. Walter Laqueur and Richard Breitman, *Breaking the Silence* (New York: Simon and Schuster, 1986), p. 156.

62. Letter of Harrison to Sumner Welles, 11 October 1941, "W" Folder, Box 29, Harrison Papers.

63. Interview with Mary Bancroft, 25 February 1986.

64. Woods has expected Long to write an explanatory letter to Harrison, but the secretary never got around to doing this. (Woods memorandum, pp. 14–15, Hull Papers) Long had simply informed Harrison Woods would "amplify" his duties orally when he passed through Bern. Letter of Long to Harrison, 28 July 1942, "L" Folder, Box 31, Harrison Papers.

65. Harrison letter to Long, 20 August 1942, Box 31, Harrison Papers.

66. Woods memorandum, p. 15, Hull Papers.

67. See Jon Kimche, *Spying for Peace: General Guisan and Swiss Neutrality* (New York: Roy Publishers, 1961), pp. 32, 65.

68. See *Neue Zürcher Zeitung*, 21 August 1942, for offerings in the local cinema.

69. Despite strict official controls, nearly 300,000 persons managed to find asylum in wartime Switzerland.

70. Letter of Milada Woods to Mrs. Joseph T. Robinson, 20 October 1943, Robinson Papers.

71. For these details, see letter of Marjorie Meyerhofer to the author, 24 July 1986.

72. Late in the war President Roosevelt would convey his gratitude for Oprecht's "valiant work" on behalf of the Allied cause. For this information I am indebted to Dr. Heinrich Rumpel, Europa Verlag, Zurich.

73. According to Dr. Oprecht's widow, for security reasons no records were ever made of these meetings. Interview with Dr. H. Rumpel, 1 July 1986.

74. Milada Woods spoke five or more European languages fluently and taught herself Russian during the war.

75. For Woods's reports on these matters, see Zurich Confidential File, 1942–45, RG 84, NRC. See also Boxes 4–5, 9–13, Bern Confidential File, 1942–44, RG 84, NRC.

76. Cables of Woods to Harrison, 13 November 1942, 16 November 1942, 19 November 1942, and 16 December 1942, Box 5, Bern Confidential File, RG 84, NRC.

77. Cable of Woods to Harrison, 24 November, Box 4, 24 November 1942, Bern Confidential File, RG 84, NRC.

78. Cable of Woods to Harrison, 10 March 1943, Box 10, RG 84.

79. After the war Woods confided to a friend that he believed Harrison "disregarded" his intelligence work. The same was true, he said, of Swiss authorities. Cook, *McGowan Place*, p. 278.

80. Cable of Woods to Harrison, 5 December 1942, Box 5, RG 84.

81. Interview with J. Bolard More, 14 January 1986.

82. See interview with Fritz Molden, 21 October 1986.

83. Interview with J. Bolard More, 14 January 1986.

84. Milada Woods says her husband had little to do with the "Bern crowd." Interview of 19 October 1986.

85. Interview with Mary Bancroft, 25 February 1986.

86. Mary Bancroft, *Autobiography of a Spy* (New York: William Morrow, 1983), p. 129.

87. For these anecdotes I am indebted to Mary Bancroft. Interview of 25

February 1986. The latter story is confirmed by Dean R. Rexford, former U.S. military attaché in Switzerland. See his letter to the author, 11 Nov. 1990.

88. "Penetration of O.S.S. by Enemy Agents," Folder 60, Box 120A, Donovan Papers.

89. Ibid.

90. "Enemy Intelligence Sources in Switzerland," 1 October 1944, Folder 60, Box 120A, Donovan Papers, USAWC.

91. Bancroft interview.

92. See letter of Hildegard Ochsenbein to the author, 28 September 1986. This vacation was in July 1942.

93. Letter of Respondek to Jacob D. Beam, 16 October 1948, Stauffer Papers.

94. Respondek letter to Beam, 16 October 1948.

95. This is Mary Bancroft's surmise.

96. Logically, this would have been Respondek's idea. Ochsenbein himself was an Episcopalian and had no ties to Catholic priests in Berlin. See letter of Hildegard Ochsenbein to the author, 28 September 1986.

97. Woods memorandum, pp. 15–16, Hull Papers.

98. Ibid., p. 16.

99. Cable of Woods to State Department, 31 December 1942, No. 288, "800 Germany" Folder, Box 10, Bern Confidential File, RG 84, NRC.

100. So reported his source in the Soviet Union, possibly the recently dismissed Gen. Halder.

101. Cable of 31 December 1942, p. 2. This was, in fact, what Hitler ordered in his decree of 19 March 1945. See Speer, *Memoirs*, pp. 447–48.

102. Cable of 31 December 1942, p. 2.

103. Cable of 31 December 1942, RG 84, NRC.

CHAPTER 8. PURLOINING GERMANY'S ATOMIC SECRETS

1. J. L. Heilbron, *The Dilemmas of an Upright Man: Max Planck as Spokesman for German Science* (Berkeley: Univ. of California Press, 1986), p. 32.

2. Respondek report on the history of the Kaiser Wilhelm Gesellschaft, 12 November 1970, p. 3, Files of the General Administration, MPG.

3. In filing a claim for compensation as a victim of Nazism, Respondek stated that he had lived at the Planck household from 1919 to 1921. See *Anlage*, 1, 21 May 1970, p. 1, LVA. This is confirmed by his marriage certificate, filed 14 December 1920, which lists his address as Wangenheimerstr. 21, Grunewald—the same as Planck's.

4. Planck's first wife, to whom he was married 25 years, died in 1909. Planck then lost his son Karl at Verdun in 1916. His daughter Grete died in childbirth in 1917, and the same fate befell her twin sister two years later.

5. Woods memorandum, p. 16. Hahn, Lise Meitner, and other leading scientists frequented the Planck home.

6. Respondek was aware of Planck's talk at the Harnack House on developments in atomic research. He also discussed with Planck the question of a "new atomic weapon." See Respondek, *Anlage* 1, 21 May 1970, p. 1, LVA.

7. See letter of Dr. Phillip Lenard to the Senate of the Kaiser Wilhelm Society,

25 June 1933, calling for ouster of "the Jesuit Muckermann" from the society; and see responding letter from Max Planck to Lenard, 30 June 1933, indicating Muckermann has taken an indefinite leave of absence at his own request. (I. Abt., Rep. 1A, Nr. 531, B11. 57 and 59, Files of the General Administration, MPG.)

8. Interview with Herta Chojnacki, 23 July 1986.

9. Woods memorandum, p. 17, Hull Papers. Valeska Hoffmann remembers Müller as being called "Rainer."

10. Interview with Valeska Hoffmann, 22 March 1986.

11. Interview with Valeska Hoffmann, 4 April 1987.

12. Letter of Viktoria Rienaecker to the author, 7 March 1987.

13. Müller was also one of the directors of a body set up at the Kaiser Wilhelm Society in 1941 to deal with questions of patents and licenses. His title with the central administration was "*syndikus*," or legal advisor. He held this position from February 1938 to 30 September 1945. Letter of Silva Sandow to the author, 7 August 1986.

14. See "Tätigkeitsbericht der Kaiser Wilhelm Gesellschaft zur Förderung der Wissenschaften für das Geschäftsjahr 1942/43," *Die Naturwissenschaften*, 31, 45/46 (5 November 1943): 547.

15. For a description of Müller's role, see *Allgemeine Zeitung*, 16 September 1945. Agnes Dreimann says Müller assisted those scientists who did not want to help Germany develop the bomb. Interview of 26 July 1986.

16. Woods memorandum, pp. 17–18, Hull Papers.

17. Respondek report on history of Kaiser Wilhelm Gesellschaft, 12 November 1970, p. 7, MPG.

18. "Status and Recent Activity of German Scientific Developments in Recent Months," MI Report No. 18,214 (German original dated 6 March 1941), 2655-B–392/3, RG 165, NA.

19. Joseph Borkin, *The Crime and Punishment of IG Farben* (New York: Free Press, 1978), p. 38. Cf. Richard Sasuly, *IG Farben* (New York: Boni & Gaer, 1947), p. 183.

20. Gerard Colby, *Du Pont Dynasty: Behind the Nylon Curtain* (Secaucus, N.J.: Lyle Stuart, 1984), p. 335.

21. Sasuly, *IG Farben*, p. 184.

22. Interview with C. Brooks Peters, 9 October 1985. Peters accompanied his father on this cruise.

23. Colby, *Du Pont Dynasty*, p. 337.

24. Ibid., p. 338. Cf. Knightley, *Second Oldest Profession*, p. 102. In 1933 Du Pont, IG Farben, and Imperial Chemical Industries (ICI) were also exploring agreements on the exchange of technical information related to ammonia, methanol, and nitrogen products. See, "Memorandum: Exchange of Technical Information between Duponts [sic], IG & ICI," 11 September 1933, File 4 (1), 1929–1934, IG Farben Files, Box 1038, Series II, Part 2, Jasper E. Crane Papers, Hagley Museum and Library, Wilmington, Del.

25. According to Wilhelm Kalle, IG Farben expelled its older executives after 1933 and replaced them with more pro-Nazi individuals. See Respondek's "Note on the I.G. Farbenindustrie," 6 June 1946, p. 2, Folder 3, Ambassador Murphy's Files, Box 459, POLAD Files, RG 84, IZG.

26. Colby, *Du Pont Dynasty*, p. 338.

27. Ibid., p. 305. Cf. Thomas H. Etzhold, "The (F)utility Factor: German Information Gathering in the United States," *Military Affairs* 39, 2 (1975): 78. In 1934 Du Pont was apparently eager to sell off shares it held in IG Farben. See letter of Arthur Murphy, Manager, Du Pont's Foreign Exchange Division, to H. H. Ewing of the firm's London office, 25 May 1934, File 4 (1), "IG Farben Industrie, 1929–1934," Box 1038, Series II, Part 2, Crane Papers.

28. Etzhold, "The (F)utility Factor," p. 79. See also "Memorandum of Meeting with IG Officials," 23 October 1936, File 4 (2), 1935–1941, IG Farben Files, Box 1038, Jasper E. Crane Papers. At this meeting Fritz ter Meer of IG Farben declared his firm was "very anxious" to reach an agreement with Du Pont regarding synthetic rubber, in exchange for first options on IG products in the field of cellulose.

29. In October 1936 Dodd wrote the president about Du Pont's links to the German armaments industry and about Standard Oil's spending half a million dollars a year to help IG Farben develop *ersatz* gasoline "for war purposes." Dodd letter to Roosevelt, 19 October 1936, "Germany: Dodd," Box 45, Safe File, FDRL.

30. Colby, *Du Pont Dynasty*, p. 386.

31. Sasuly, *IG Farben*, p. 185. Cf. Colby, *Du Pont Dynasty*, pp. 386–87. In April 1941 the IG's Fritz ter Meer cabled Jasper E. Crane of Du Pont: "Am writing you today suggesting that in view government restrictions our two companies mutually agree discontinue exchange technical information patent applications, etc., on all existing contracts until present emergency has passed but all other obligations in contract to remain in force." Cable of ter Meer to Crane, 18 April 1941, File 4 (2), Box 1038, Crane Papers. Ter Meer agreed to this proposal in a letter to Crane, 25 June 1941.

32. Hyde, *Room 3603*, p. 198.

33. Colby, *Du Pont Dynasty*, p. 198.

34. Howard W. Ambruster, *Treason's Price: German Dyes and American Dupes* (New York: Beechhurst Press, 1947), pp. 344–48.

35. Respondek report on Kaiser Wilhelm Gesellschaft, 12 November 1970, p. 7, MPG.

36. Ibid.

37. Ibid. Author's translation.

38. Ambruster, *Treason's Price*, pp. 109–10.

39. Respondek report, 12 November 1970, p. 7, MPG.

40. Peter Hayes, *Industry and Ideology: IG Farben in the Nazi Era* (New York: Cambridge Univ. Press, 1987), p. 361.

41. Hans Radant, ed., *Fall 6: Ausgewählte Dokumente und Urteil des IG Farben Prozesses*, (Berlin: Deutsche Verlag der Wissenschaften, 1970), p. 255.

42. Ibid., p. 256.

43. See his section entitled "Bacteriological and Chemical Weapons of Destruction," 12 November 1970 report, p. 6, MPG.

44. Respondek had worked together with Kalle in the Reichstag. They had to break off contact in 1937 because of Respondek's "difficulties with the Gestapo." See Respondek's "Note on the I.G. Farbenindustrie," 6 June 1946, Folder 3, Box 459, POLAD, files RG 84, 12G.

45. Respondek report, 12 November 1970, p. 7–8, MPG.

46. There is no trace of the report dealing with this matter, which Respondek says Robert Murphy forwarded to the State Department, either in the National Archives or at the Institute for Contemporary History, Munich.

47. Respondek report, 12 November 1970, p. 8, MPG. Author's translation.

48. Speer, *Memoirs*, p. 227.

49. Vannevar Bush, *Pieces of the Action* (New York: William Morrow, 1970), p. 57.

50. Heilbron, *Dilemmas*, pp. 163ff. Cf. Speer, *Memoirs*, p. 228.

51. Heilbron, *Dilemmas*, p. 172.

52. For a discussion of Hahn's experiment, see David Irving, *The German Atomic Bomb: The History of Atomic Research in Nazi Germany* (New York: DeCapo Press, 1967), pp. 22–26.

53. See Planck's November 1941 speech at Harnack House, Berlin, described in Heilbron, *Dilemmas*, p. 186.

54. Woods memorandum, p. 16, Hull Papers.

55. See letter of Paul Harteck and Wilhelm Groth to the German War Office, April 1939, discussed in Irving, *German Atomic Bomb*, pp. 36–37.

56. Werner Heisenberg, "Research in Germany on the Technical Applications of Atomic Energy," *Nature*, 160, 409 (16 August 1947): 211. Cf. Elisabeth Heisenberg, *Das unpolitische Leben eines unpolitischen: Erinnerungen an Werner Heisenberg* (Munich: R. Piper, 1980), p. 91.

57. Irving, *German Atomic Bomb*, pp. 41–46.

58. Werner Heisenberg, "Research," p. 212.

59. Irving, *German Atomic Bomb*, pp. 53, 56, 79.

60. See letter of Dr. Erich Bagge to the author, 15 July 1986. Cf. Elisabeth Heisenberg, *Erinnerungen*, pp. 91–92. Cf. Irving, *German Atomic Bomb*, pp. 117–18, 108.

61. See Irving, *German Atomic Bomb*, pp. 106–7, note 1.

62. Speer, *Memoirs*, p. 225.

63. Irving, *German Atomic Bomb*, pp. 115ff.

64. Speer, *Memoirs*, p. 226.

65. Vannevar Bush told President Roosevelt on 17 June 1942 that a bomb could affect the outcome of the war. Irving, *German Atomic Bomb*, p. 135.

66. For a full treatment of this decision, see Mark Walker, *German National Socialism and the Quest for Nuclear Power, 1939–1949* (New York: Cambridge Univ. Press, 1990).

67. Arnold Kramish, *The Griffin: Paul Rosbaud and the Nazi Atomic Bomb That Never Was* (Boston: Houghton-Mifflin, 1986), pp. 127–28.

68. Speer, *Memoirs*, p. 227.

69. Woods memorandum, pp. 16–17, Hull Papers. Cf. Respondek report of May 1946, p. 7, Stauffer Papers.

70. For particulars on Bücher's relationship with Respondek, see Mowrer, *Triumph and Turmoil*, p. 165. See also Respondek's letter to Friedrich Dessauer, 14 June 1932, Dessauer Papers. Here Respondek writes that he has known Bücher well for "more than twelve years, in government as well as private service, during which association I have often worked extremely closely with him in the areas of economic and financial policies." Author's translation.

71. See Henry A. Turner, Jr., *German Big Business and the Rise of Hitler* (New York: Oxford Univ. Press, 1985), p. 467, note 70.

72. Quoted in ibid., p. 328.

73. See cable of Woods to Cordell Hull, No. 109, 13 May 1943, 740.0011 EW/ 29326 1/2, RG 59, NA. Bücher began making contributions of between 30,000 and 50,000 marks to the SS and NSDAP in 1933. See Eberhard Koebel-Tusk, *AEG: Energie, Profit, Verbrechen* (Berlin: Verlag der Wirtschaft, 1958), p. 136. But prior to 1939, Bücher remained hostile to the Nazis' extreme measures, such as their anti-Semitic campaign. He never became a member of the Nazi Party.

74. Hayes, *Industry and Ideology*, p. 323.

75. Speer, *Memoirs*, p. 394, note.

76. Koebel-Tusk, *AEG*, p. 132.

77. Cable of Woods to Hull, No. 109, Part 6, 13 May 1943, 740.0011 EW/ 29326 1/2, RG 59, NA.

78. For biographical data on Dällenbach, see A. Stäger, "Persönliches," *Physikalische Blätter*, 33, 7, (July 1977): 318–20.

79. Ibid., p. 318.

80. Letter of Walter Dällenbach to Paul Scherrer, 30 June 1945, HS 911:59, Dällenbach Papers, ETH.

81. Declaration of Johann J. Sommer, 14 December 1949, Appendix B, HS 911:58, Dällenbach Papers.

82. Dällenbach letter to Hermann Weyl, 18 November 1947, HS 911:53, Dällenbach Papers.

83. Walter Dällenbach, "Ein Auslandsschweizer im Nationalsozialistischen Deutschland," 13 March 1982, HS 911:14, Dällenbach Papers.

84. Dällenbach letter to Paul Scherrer, 30 June 1945, HS 911:59, Dällenbach Papers.

85. Letter of Dällenbach to Hermann Weyl, 26 December 1947, HS 911:54, Dällenbach Papers.

86. Contract between the Firm AEG and Dr. Walter Dällenbach, 19 December 1942, HS 911:17, Dällenbach Papers.

87. Appendix to Dällenbach contract with AEG, p. 2, Dällenbach Papers.

88. See Walter Dällenbach, "Neue Vorschläge für Maschinen zur Beschleunigung elektrische-geladene Teilchen," *Experientia*, 2, 12 (1946): 3, passim.

89. Travel report of Dr. Ernst Telschow, 26 August 1945, p. 10, II Abt., Rep. 1A Gründung, Nr. 2/1–14, MPG.

90. Declaration of Johann J. Sommer, 14 December 1949, p. 1, Dällenbach Papers.

91. Telschow, travel report of 26 August 1945, p. 10, MPG.

92. Letter of Dällenbach to Hermann Weyl, 18 November 1947, Dällenbach Papers.

93. Ibid.

94. Ibid. Samuel Goudsmit, scientific head of the "Alsos" mission, believed that Dällenbach's laboratory was tasked with constructing a "cylotron based on new principles," with the "full support and confidence of the Nazi research council." Samuel A. Goudsmit, *Alsos* (New York: Henry Schuman, 1947), p. 96.

95. Letter of Prof. Karl Wirtz to the author, 20 November 1986. Cf. letter of Elisabeth Heisenberg to the author, 8 January 1986.

CHAPTER 9. A SCARE FOR THE AMERICANS

1. See letter of Walter Dällenbach to Johann Sommer, 18 October 1944, quoted in Dällenbach's letter to Hermann Weyl, 25 Dec. 1947, Dällenbach Papers. Here Dällenbach says that his work was "basic research." Cf. his letters to Paul Scherrer, 30 June 1945, and to the author, 9 September 1986. Whatever the merits of this claim, it should be noted that Dällenbach's view reflects those of German scientists who, after the war, sought to draw a line between their "theoretical" research and work on the bomb.

2. Declaration of Johann J. Sommer, 14 December 1949, Dällenbach Papers.

3. Telschow, travel report of 26 August 1945, MPG. See also Telschow's certificate, 31 July 1959, stating that Dällenbach's laboratory had "not the slightest to do with war or war production." Supplement C, HS 911:58, Dällenbach Papers.

4. But the reliability of most of these sources is dubious. Yet as early as August 1943 Allied intelligence learned from a Swiss contact about Dällenbach's working on a new kind of high explosive.

5. On 23 September 1944, Speer wrote to Himmler about the need to give priority to atomic research projects that "would be of essential importance to our war effort." Added Speer, "the main issue in research is that projects advantageous to the war effort should be given preference, while we hold back those projects that challenge or hinder the concentrated advancement of the important projects." Quoted in Speer, *Infiltration* (New York: MacMillan, 1981), pp. 150–51.

6. This explanation has been advanced by Arnold Kramish. See interview of 12 October 1987.

7. Memorandum of 17 March 1943, SAA 11, Lg 43, Flir Files, Siemens Archives, Deutsches Museum, Munich.

8. Ibid.

9. Letter of Dällenbach to Hermann Weyl, 25 December 1947, Dällenbach Papers.

10. Letter of Rosbaud to Samuel Goudsmit 5 September 1945, Folder 42, Series IV, Goudsmit Papers, AIP.

11. See sheet attached to Rosbaud letter to Goudsmit, 5 September 1945.

12. Letter of Dällenbach to Paul Scherrer, 30 June 1945, Dällenbach Papers.

13. See Boris T. Pash, *The Alsos Mission* (New York: Award House, 1969), pp. 209–11. Pash also said he had not been told to focus on Dällenbach's laboratory. See his letter to the author, 22 January 1987.

14. The physicist argued his entry visa was declared invalid because the Gestapo suspected him of being a U.S. agent. But it appears Dällenbach may have left before Christmas 1944 with no intention of returning to his lab. See Telschow's travel report of 26 August 1945, MPG. Dällenbach also left a sign on the door of his office in Bisingen, stating in English that the contents were under

the protection of the Swiss government. For a copy of this statement I am grateful to Arnold Kramish.

15. Telschow, travel report of 26 August 1945, pp. 10–11. A plaque at the site of Dällenbach's research facility testifies to this. One member of the French team characterized the work at Bisingen as being of "doubtful" interest, since it involved short-wave physics, and not nuclear physics. For this information I am grateful to Prof. Hélène Langevin-Joliot, Frédéric Joliot's daughter. See her letter to the author, 25 April 1989.

16. See letter of Karl Weimer to Ernst Telschow, 29 September 1949, No. 2979, Forschungsstelle D, Main Files, 12 May 1945–24 February 1955, Files of the General Administration, MPG.

17. Note dated "5 October 1946" at bottom of letter of Karl Weimer to Telschow, 29 September 1949, 2979, Forschungsstelle D, MPG.

18. Captured at Heidelberg, Walther Bothe, head of a major cyclotron project, admitted that an accelerator was considered a means of obtaining material to make bombs.

In a letter prepared for his signature by Johann Sommer of the Armaments Ministry, Heisenberg indicated that Dällenbach's proposed cyclotron would have the advantage of saving on materials. A "serious testing" of his device might lead to "an increase in the degree of effectiveness" of existing cyclotrons, which thus far had not been achieved. See letter of Heisenberg to the Kaiser Wilhelm Institut für Physik, 9 December 1942, Heisenberg Papers, Werner-Heisenberg-Institut für Physik, Munich.

19. At the author's request Prof. Peter Brix, a German physicist, reviewed Dällenbach's patent application for his cyclotron, currently on file at the Niels Bohr Library, American Institute of Physics, in New York. See G-209, "Patent Application & General Correspondence with the German Patent Office on a Particle Accelerator by W. Dällenbach, 1943," in *German Reports on Atomic Energy* (Oak Ridge, Tenn.: U.S. Atomic Energy Comm., 1952). Professor Brix noted that this particular kind of accelerator has "nothing directly to do with atomic weapons." But he also pointed out that such accelerators can be used to create streams of high-speed neutrons, which may play a role in the construction of an atomic bomb. See letter of Prof. Peter Brix to Silva Sandow, 14 August 1987. This view is confirmed by Spencer Wearth, Director, Center for the History of Physics, New York. Interview of 5 Feb. 1991.

20. Irving, *German Atomic Bomb*, pp. 18, 67, 132. Hans A. Bethe, the German-born physicist who directed theoretical physics research at Los Alamos from 1943 to 1946, recalls that the U.S. government was first briefed on the need to develop an atomic bomb by a visiting delegation of British scientists in 1941. See Bethe's letter to the author, 4 May 1989.

Thomas Powers has revealed that an important warning about German nuclear research was passed on to "a Washington official" in April 1941. See Powers's review, "How the Bomb Was Kept from Hitler," *Atlantic Monthly*, May 1990, p. 129.

21. For a full discussion of Rosbaud's accomplishment, see Arnold Kramish's *Griffin*.

22. See Respondek's May 1946 report to Cordell Hull, p. 7, Stauffer Papers.

23. Ibid.

24. Ibid.

25. Woods memorandum, p. 18, Hull Papers.

26. Respondek report of May 1946, p. 7, Stauffer Papers.

27. Woods memorandum, p. 16, Hull Papers.

28. Cable of Woods to Hull, 25 January 1943, 740.0011 EW/27457, RG 59, NA.

29. Cable of Woods to Hull, No. 109, Section 1, 10 May 1943, 740.0011 EW/29326 1/2, RG 59, NA. On April 23rd, Speer and Milch presented their demand for 2.1 million new workers "for the entire economy." Speer, *Memoirs*, p. 264.

30. Cable of Woods to Hull, No. 109, Section 2, 11 May 1943, 740.0011 EW/29326, RG 59, NA. This is an English paraphrase of Respondek's original report, which could not be located in the National Archives.

31. Cable No. 109, Section 4, 12 May 1943, RG 59, NA.

32. Cable No. 109, Section 6, 15 May 1943, RG 59, NA. Cf. Harrison cable to the State Department, 14 May 1943, No. 2958, "863.4 Uranium" Folder, Box 14, Bern Confidential File, RG 84, NRC.

33. Cable No. 109, Section 7, 13 May 1943, NA.

34. This same quantity was cited in a 1939 article by Siegfried Flugge, which appeared in the periodical *Naturwissenschaften*.

In his letter to the author, Hans A. Bethe has pointed out that this idea was "crazy": releasing one or two neutrons in uranium oxide will not produce a chain reaction; the neutrons first have to be slowed down. Letter of Bethe to the author, 4 May 1989.

35. The German original, which said the manufacture of parts needed for the cyclotron had been postponed and that the resulting loss of an atomic bomb doomed the Nazis, has not survived in the National Archives. Cf. Woods memorandum, p. 18. Hull Papers.

36. See Berle, Diary, 29 August 1943, p. 352, Box 5, Berle Papers.

37. Long, Diary, entry for 19 May 1943, p. 335, Box 5, Long Papers.

38. Ibid. Long noted that Gen. Strong read the report with "avidity and concern."

39. Gen. Strong felt this was unlikely, however, due to the lack of sufficient uranium for atomic experiments in Germany.

40. Long, Diary, 19 May 1943, pp. 335–36, Long Papers.

41. Bush, *Pieces of the Action*, p. 34.

42. Ibid., p. 88.

43. This is recorded in the Usher's Diary, 24 June 1943, FDRL.

44. Letter of Raymond Geist to Breckenridge Long, 18 May 1943, 740.0011 EW/2936 1/2, RG 59, NA.

45. Interview with Carl Norden.

46. Letter of Geist to Long, 18 May 1943, 740.0011EW 29326 1/2, RG 59, NA.

47. Young's copybooks for this period do not show his having been queried about German atomic research. Nor do his surviving secretaries or family members recall Young's having been contacted about this matter. See letter of Everett Case to the author, 10 January 1986.

48. See cable of Long to Harrison, No. 415, 19 May 1943, "863.4 Uranium" Folder, Box 14, Bern Confidential File, RG 84, NRC.

49. Cable of Harrison to Hull, 29 May 1943. Contents of this message are found in a memorandum of Harrison to Gen. Legge, 29 May 1943, "863.4 Uranium" Folder, Box 14, RG 84, NRC.

50. A plant for this purpose was set up by IG Farben at the Leuna ammonia works in 1940. See Irving, *German Atomic Bomb*, pp. 60–61.

51. See letter of Harrison to Long, 19 May 1943, "863.4 Uranium" Folder, RG 84. The Norsk-Hydro plant had actually been captured intact by the Germans in 1940.

52. Ibid. This remark suggests a possible rationale for Dällenbach's "new type" of cyclotron.

53. Irving, *German Atomic Bomb*, p. 132.

54. Ibid., p. 135.

55. Samuel A. Goudsmit, *Alsos: The Failure in German Science* (London: Sigma Books, 1947), p. 3.

56. Cable of Gen. Strong to Gen. Legge, No. 427, 2 June 1943, "863.4 Uranium" Folder, Box 14, RG 84, NRC.

57. Memorandum of Harrison to Gen. Legge, 7 June 1943, "863.4 Uranium" Folder, RG 84.

58. Cable of Strong to Legge, No. 429, 4 June 1943, "863.4 Uranium" Folder.

59. Letter of Gen. Legge to Harrison, 8 June 1943, "863.4 Uranium" Folder.

60. Irving, *German Atomic Bomb*, p. 224.

61. Cable of Long to Harrison, No. 1954, 14 August 1943, "863.4 Uranium" Folder.

62. On the cable of Hull to Harrison, 14 August 1943, Harrison's aide, Landreth Harrison, wrote: "If SEW [Woods] is in town today, we can ask him. I think he no longer hears from Ralph."

63. Respondek report of 12 August 1943, "800 Germany Folder," Box 10, RG 84, NRC. Speer felt the war would have ended in 1943 if Allied bombers had concentrated on key war-related industries. Speer, *Memoirs*, p. 280.

64. Respondek report of 12 August 1943, p. 4. Author's trans.

65. What came to be known as the Battle of Berlin began on 18 November 1943 and ended in March 1944, with between 1,000 and 2,000 tons of bombs being dropped during each of 24 separate raids.

66. Ibid., p. 6. Cf. Josef Geiss, *Obersalzberg* (Berchtesgaden: Verlag Josef Geiss, 1977), p. 164.

67. Respondek report of 12 August 1943, p. 6. In his postwar report to Hull, Woods claimed Respondek had furnished him with "additional information on the 'buzz bombs,' " Woods memorandum, p. 19, Hull Papers.

68. Liddell Hart, *Second World War*, p. 599.

69. Ibid., p. 602.

70. Cloudy weather and German air defenses kept the raids from doing much damage.

71. Goudsmit, *Alsos*, pp. 10–11. Cf. Irving, *German Atomic Bomb*, pp. 219–20, and OSS report of 23 October 1943, "863.4 Uranium" Folder, Box 14, RG 84, NRC.

72. Letter of Hans Bethe and Edward Teller to Robert Oppenheimer, 21 August 1943, Box 20, Oppenheimer Papers, LC, quoted in Richard Rhodes,

The Making of the Atomic Bomb (New York: Simon and Schuster, 1986), pp. 511–12.

73. Vincent C. Jones, *The United States Army in World War II*. Special Studies: *Manhattan: The Army and the Atomic Bomb* (Washington, D.C.: Center for Military History, 1985), p. 280.

74. See Woods memorandum, pp. 18–19, Hull Papers. A series of foreshocks occurred on 4, 14, and 22 July 1943, at the coordinates 9 degrees east, 48.2 degrees north. This was not in Bavaria, but in the Schwäbische Alb, about 30 miles south of Stuttgart and, by coincidence, very close to where German scientists had relocated from Berlin that summer. The main seismic event in this series of disturbances took place at the same spot on 17 September 1973, at 6:47 A.M., Greenwich time. For this information I am grateful to Dan Byrne at the Lamont-Doherty Geological Observatory, Palisades, N.Y.

CHAPTER 10: THE POPE AND OTHER SECRET WEAPONS

1. See comments of Fr. Robert A. Graham, *Washington Post*, 3 August 1980.

2. Harold C. Deutsch, *The Conspiracy against Hitler in the Twilight War* (Minneapolis: Univ. of Minnesota Press, 1968), p. 121.

3. So maintains, among others, Johannes Schwarte in his *Gustav Gundlach, SJ. Massgeblicher Repräsentant der katholischen Soziallehre während der Pontifikate Pius XI and Pius XII* (Paderborn: F. Schonigh, 1975), p. 114.

4. Anthony E. R. Rhodes, *The Vatican in the Age of the Dictators, 1922–1945* (New York: Holt, Rinehart & Winston, 1973), pp. 219–20.

5. Stewart A. Stehlin, *Weimar and the Vatican, 1919–1933: German–Vatican Relations in the Interwar Years* (Princeton, N.J.: Princeton Univ. Press, 1983), p. 93.

6. Ibid.

7. Ibid., p. 337.

8. Rhodes, *Vatican*, p. 226. Cf. Owen Chadwick, *Britain and the Vatican during the Second World War* (New York: Cambridge Univ. Press, 1987), p. 46.

9. Deutsch, *Conspiracy*, p. 111.

10. Ibid., p. 116.

11. F. Muckermann, *Kampf*, p. 380.

12. Ibid., pp. 226ff, 234.

13. Ibid., p. 451. In 1925 he did urge the Center Party to ally itself with the SPD, however. George May, *Ludwig Kaas: Der Priester, der Politiker, und der Gelehrter aus der Schule von Ulrich Stutz* (Amsterdam: Grüner, 1981), Vol. 1, p. 668.

14. F. Muckermann, *Kampf*, pp. 451–52. This was in March 1933.

15. "News of the Secret State Police," 28 September 1933, III C Nd./8, Friedrich Muckermann File, RW 58, No. 30 119, NRWHSA.

16. F. Muckermann, *Kampf*, p. 564. Cf. Boberach, *Berichte der SD*, p. 42. See Muckermann's article in *Katholische Korrespondez*, 8 February 1934.

17. See report of Staatspolizeistelle, Düsseldorf, 31 August 1934, dealing with Muckermann's activities. RW 58, No. 30 119, Friedrich Muckermann File, Records of the Gestapo, NRWHSA.

18. F. Muckermann, *Kampf*, p. 618.

19. Office of Strategic Services Mission for Germany, "German Government Personnel," 6 August 1945, No. XL 22686, p. 4, RG 226, NA.

20. Friedrich Muckermann died on 2 April 1946.

21. Deutsch, *Conspiracy*, pp. 114–15.

22. May, *Ludwig Kaas*, Vol. 3, p. 433.

23. Muckermann became fearful he might be implicated in Respondek's espionage after 1942 and so avoided contact with the family. Interview with Agnes Dreimann, 26 July 1986.

24. For Gestapo knowledge of Muckermann's activities, see RW 58, 24730, NRWHSA.

25. Interview with Mary Bancroft, 25 February 1986.

26. Interview with Agnes Dreimann, 26 July 1986. She quoted this phrase from Charlotte Respondek's travel diary.

27. Letter of Agnes Dreimann to the author, 26 July 1987. Kaas had met frequently with Muckermann while both men were living in Berlin. See May, *Ludwig Kaas*, Vol. 1, p. 7.

28. This may have been part of a group audience, but Agnes Dreimann insists it was a private meeting.

29. Rhodes, *Vatican*, p. 198.

30. Father Leiber likely helped draft this document. See May, *Ludwig Kaas*, Vol. 3, p. 437.

31. Rhodes, *Vatican*, p. 202.

32. Chadwick, *Britain and the Vatican*, p. 46. Cf. Deutsch, *Conspiracy*, p. 111.

33. Kaas conferred with Osborne in November and December 1939, as well as on 23 February 1940. See Josef Müller, *Biz zur letzten Konsequenz: Ein Leben für Frieden und Freiheit* (Munich: Süddeutscher Verlag, 1975), pp. 103, 122–23.

34. "X" stood for Müller.

35. Hoffmann, *History of the German Resistance*, p. 163, Cf. Müller, *Konsequenz*, p. 131.

36. Hoffmann, *History of the German Resistance*, p. 161.

37. According to Hoffmann, Halder had "neither hope or desire" to win over Brauchitsch to a coup. Both generals were then, in April 1940, immersed in plans for attacking the Lowlands, confident of a German victory. Hoffmann, ibid., pp. 164–65. Cf. Müller, *Konsequenz*, p. 137.

38. Interview with Valeska Hoffmann, 22 March 1986. Cf. interview with Agnes Dreimann, 26 July 1986, and her letter to the author, 26 July 1987.

39. Chadwick, *Britain and the Vatican*, p. 150.

40. Interview with Valeska Hoffmann, 22 March 1986.

41. For evidence of Woods's bankrolling Charlotte Respondek's trip, see his letter to Cordell Hull, 28 June 1945, 740.00119 Control (Germany)/6–2845, RG 59, NA.

42. Interview with Valeska Hoffmann, 4 April 1987.

43. Interview with Agnes Dreimann.

44. Letter of Agnes Dreimann to the author, 2 November 1986.

45. Müller, *Konsequenz*, p. 107.

46. May, *Ludwig Kaas*, Vol. 3, p. 510.

47. Ibid., p. 433.

48. Deutsch, *Conspiracy*, p. 114.

49. Peter Ludlow, "Papst Pius XII, die britische Regierung und die deutsche Opposition im Winter 1939–40," *Vierteljahrshefte für Zeitgeschichte*, 22, 3 (1974): 301.

50. May, *Ludwig Kaas*, Vol. 1, p. 6.

51. Interview with Agnes Dreimann.

52. After the war, Charlotte attempted to reestablish contact with Josef Müller on behalf of her paramour, Herbert Müller (no relation). See letter of Maria Schachtner to the author, 30 November 1986. Nothing came of this, however.

53. Chadwick, *Britain and the Vatican*, p. 178.

54. Long, Diary, entry for 3 September 1943, p. 359, Box 5, Long Papers.

55. Woods memorandum, Hull Papers. Wilhelmina Busch's role was disclosed by Woods in a 27 March 1948 article in the *St. Louis Post-Dispatch*.

56. Ibid., p. 18. This may have been Cardinal Faulhaber of Munich, who was on a "Du" basis with his friend from student days, Josef Müller. See Müller, *Konsequenz*, p. 61.

57. Interview with Valeska Hoffmann, 22 March 1986.

58. Woods memorandum, p. 19, Hull Papers.

59. Ibid.

60. Reginald V. Jones, *The Wizard War: British Scientific Intelligence, 1939–45* (New York: Coward, McCann & Geohegan, 1978), p. 340.

61. Martin Middlebrook and Chris Everitt, *The Bomber Command War Diaries: An Operational Reference Book, 1939–1945* (Harmondsworth, England: Viking, 1985), p. 424.

62. David Irving, *The Mare's Nest* (London: W. Kimber, 1964), p. 178.

63. Ibid., pp. 213–14.

64. Ibid., pp. 214, 219.

65. Ibid., p. 138.

66. Cable of Harrison to Hull, No. 6516, Section 2, 16 October 1943, 740.0011 EW 3/1596, RG 59, NA.

67. Ibid.

68. Koebel-Tusk, *AEG*, p. 128.

69. Cable of Harrison to Hull, No. 6516, 16 October 1943, Section 2, p. 1.

70. These assertions were not accurate.

71. "*Aufzeichnung*," 18 September 1943, p. 5, attached to cable of Woods to Harrison, 13 October 1943, 862.00/4508, RG 59, NA.

72. The Messerschmidt 262 was not made available to the *Luftwaffe* until April 1944. See Mondey, *Axis Aircraft*, pp. 186–87.

73. "*Aufzeichnung*," 18 September 1943, p. 3.

74. After Soviet offensives against their northern flank and the outposts of Orel and Kursk in July, the Germans started a major retreat to a line just to the east of what Respondek had predicted by December 1943.

75. This was, indeed, what the Germans did.

76. "*Aufzeichnung*," 18 September 1943, p. 4.

77. Respondek, note of 18 September 1943, p. 5.

78. Ibid., p. 5.

79. Ibid., pp. 7, 8. Author's translation.

80. Cable of Harrison to Hull, No. 6516, Section 1, 16 October 1943, 740.0011 EW/3 1596, RG 59, NA.

81. Ibid.

82. Cable of Harrison to Hull, No. 6521, Section 2, 17 October 1943, 740.0011 EW/ 3 1623, RG 59, NA.

83. Cable of Harrison to Hull, No. 6516, Section 1, 16 October 1943.

84. Cable of Harrison to Hull, No. 6521, Section 1.

85. These reached Woods in mid-May. See cable of Harrison to Hull, No. 2985, 15 May 1943, "861 Germany" Folder, RG 84, NRC.

86. This manuscript was typed at Respondek's home with help from Agnes Dreimann. See Dreimann interview. See also untitled German manuscript, dated 24 September 1943, attached to cable of Woods to Harrison, 13 October 1943, 862.00/4508, RG 59, NA.

87. Untitled, undated plan for postwar Germany attached to letter of Harrison to Hull, No. 5258, 8 June 1943, "860 Germany" Folder, Box 10, Bern Confidential File, RG 84, NRC.

88. Ibid., pp. 3, 14, 25, 27.

89. John L. Snell, *Wartime Origins of the East–West Dilemma over Germany*, (New Orleans: Hauser Press, 1959), p. 28.

90. Ibid., p. 33.

91. Letter of Harrison to Hull, 8 June 1943, "800 Germany" Folder, Box 10, RG 84.

92. See Long, Diary, entry for 1 January 1944, p. 384, Box 5, Long Papers.

93. Long, Diary, entry for 1 January 1944, p. 384.

94. Ibid.

95. The only blow to atomic research in the city was a raid that scored a direct hit on Otto Hahn's laboratory at the Kaiser Wilhelm Institute for Chemistry. But this raid took place on 15 February 1944. See Irving, *German Atomic Bomb*, p. 225.

96. Gen. Groves successfully pressured Gen. Marshall into directing an Eighth Air Force raid of Flying Fortresses against the Rjukan factory, decimating its heavy-water producing capabilities. But this occurred on 16 November 1943. Irving, *German Atomic Bomb*, pp. 153–70, 194.

97. U.S. Strategic Bombing Survey, "V Weapons [Crossbow] Campaign," *Bomber Command Narrative of Operations*, 1945, pp. 5–6, Historical Research Division, Maxwell Air Force Base, Montgomery, Ala.

98. Woods statement of 5 August 1948, Stauffer Papers. Woods was not certain of this information, but he pointed out that these facilities were destroyed by Allied bombers shortly after Respondek's information reached Washington. He also pointed out that both William Donovan and Allen Dulles knew of Respondek's report about German laboratories working on an atomic bomb.

99. See *Times-Picayune* (New Orleans), 13 January 1949, p. 1. Woods also spoke of a Peenemünde raid to Robert A. Brand, a visa officer in postwar Munich. See interview of 17 April 1991.

100. Woods's biographical profile appears in the *National Cyclopedia of American Biography* (New York: James T. White, 1962), Vol. 45, p. 55.

101. Letter of Mrs. Arnold (Long) Wilcox to the author, 18 February 1987.

102. See memorandum of William Donovan to the Joint Chiefs of Staff,

"Memorandum of Information for the Joint Chiefs of Staff, Subject: OSS Operations in Switzerland, 1942–45," 26 September 1944, "Dulles" Folder, Box 120B: 82, Donovan Papers, USAWC.

103. See letter of Walt Rostow to the author, 17 November 1986; of Charles Hitch to the author, 8 December 1986, of Charles Kindleberger to the author, 17 January 1987, and of Lord Zuckerman to the author, 19 January 1987.

104. Speer, *Memoirs*, p. 346.

105. None of the laboratories in southern Germany involved in atomic research was attacked from the air.

CHAPTER 11. ANOTHER BRUSH WITH THE GESTAPO

1. Liddell Hart, *Second World War*, p. 493.

2. Martin Gilbert, *Winston S. Churchill*, Vol. 7: *Road to Victory, 1941–1945* (Boston: Houghton Mifflin, 1986), p. 438. Cf. Hinsley, *British Intelligence*, p. 750.

3. See Goebbels, *The Goebbels Diaries, 1942–43* (Garden City, N.Y.: Doubleday, 1948), entry for 23 September 1943, pp. 476–77.

4. Fest, *Hitler*, p. 698.

5. Moltke did write to his old friend Alexander Kirk about the possibility of shortening the war, but Kirk informed him on 10 January 1944 the Allies would press ahead with their policy of "unconditional surrender." Hoffman, *History of the German Resistance*, p. 227.

6. Respondek report, May 1946, p. 11, Stauffer Papers.

7. In October 1939 Schacht tried to arrange a U.S. lecture tour to promote peace with the Americans, but the State Department rejected this. See Christopher Sykes, *Tormented Loyalty: The Story of a German Aristocrat Who Defied Hitler* (New York: Harper & Row, 1969), p. 306.

8. Ibid., p. 11. Author's translation.

9. Lejeune-Jung was a Catholic and had studied Catholic theology at the University of Bonn.

10. Respondek, *Anlage*, 2, p. 6, compensation claim of 21 May 1970, LVA.

11. Respondek, *Anlage*, 2, pp. 6–7.

12. Lejeune-Jung had known Goerdeler since having been introduced to him at a National People's Party gathering prior to 1933. See *Spiegelbild einer Verschwörung: Die Kaltenbrunner Berichte an Bormann und Hitler über des Attentats vom 20 Juli 1944* (Stuttgart: Seewald Verlag, 1961), p. 359.

13. Ibid., p. 359.

14. These included the former trade union leaders Wilhelm Leuschner and Jakob Kaiser, Count Fritz Diellof von Schulenburg, the attorney Joseph Wirmer, Ulrich-Wilhelm Count Schwerin von Schwanenfeld, and Eduard Brücklmeier, a Foreign Ministry official.

15. Respondek, *Anlage*, 2, p. 7.

16. Lejeune-Jung wanted to nationalize the mines, for example. See Gerhard Ritter, *The German Resistance: Carl Goerdeler's Struggle against Tyranny* (New York: Praeger, 1959), p. 253.

17. *Spiegelbild*, p. 188.

18. Elisabeth Wiskemann, *Europe of the Dictators, 1919–1945*, 1st ed. (New York: Harper & Row, 1966), p. 27.

19. Hans Rothfels, *German Opposition to Hitler: An Appraisal* (Hinsdale, Ill.: H. Regnery, 1948), p. 151.

20. Respondek, *Anlage*, 2, p. 1.

21. Ibid.

22. Margaret Boveri, *Treason in the Twentieth Century* (London: MacDonald, 1961), p. 234.

23. Quoted in Ulrich von Hassell, *The Hassell Diaries, 1938–1944: The Story of the Forces against Hitler Inside Germany as Recorded by Ambassador Ulrich von Hassell* (London: Hamilton, 1948), p. 28.

24. Hoffmann, *German Resistance*, p. 180, 183.

25. Ibid., p. 149.

26. Hassell, *Diaries*, p. 96.

27. Goebbels, *Diaries*, entry for 10 September 1943, p. 429.

28. Alan Clark, *Barbarossa: The Russian–German Conflict, 1941–1945* (New York: William Morrow, 1965), p. 339.

29. Hoffmann, *German Resistance*, p. 295.

30. Roger Manvell and Heinrich Fraenkel, *The July Plot: The Attempt in 1944 on Hitler's Life and the Men Behind It* (London: Bodley Head, 1964), p. 70. Cf. Clark, *Barbarossa*, p. 347.

31. Quoted in Clark, *Barbarossa*, p. 348.

32. Ibid., p. 350.

33. Hitler came to feel Popitz was his enemy by September 1943. See Goebbels, *Diaries*, entry for 23 September 1943, p. 474.

34. Respondek, *Anlage*, 1, p. 2. This was the forerunner of the Finance Ministry.

35. Ibid., p. 2. When Respondek sought to become a "unity" candidate for the Reichstag in November 1933 he listed Popitz as one of his supporters. Letter of Respondek to Wilhelm Frick, 22 October 1933, NS 46/25, BA.

36. Respondek, *Anlage*, 2, p. 2.

37. Ibid., p. 2.

38. Hoffmann, *German Resistance*, p. 117. Cf. Sykes, *Tormented Loyalty*, p. 187.

39. Rothfels, *German Opposition*, p. 130.

40. The British thought the Gestapo had sent him. Sykes, *German Opposition*, p. 263.

41. Hoffmann, *German Resistance*, p. 117. Cf. Sykes, *German Opposition*, p. 304.

42. *Roosevelt–Frankfurter: Their Correspondence, 1928–1945* (Boston: Little, Brown, 1967), p. 514. J. Edgar Hoover's agents thought Trott might be a "Nazi agent." Rothfels, *German Opposition*, p. 132.

43. Sykes, *Tormented Loyalty*, p. 307.

44. According to Trott's widow, he gained access to Brüning through the latter's secretary, who was also a Rhodes Scholar. Letter of Dr. Claritta von Trott zu Solz to the author, 28 November 1987.

45. Brüning recommended him as a "thoroughly honest man" to Messersmith. Hoffmann, *German Resistance*, p. 116.

46. Brüning, *Briefe*, p. 200.

47. Rothfels, *German Opposition*, p. 132.

48. Sykes, *Tormented Loyalty*, p. 341.

49. Hoffmann, *German Resistance*, p. 232.

50. Papen, *Memoirs*, p. 494.

51. Ibid., pp. 498–99, 504.

52. Respondek, *Anlage*, 1, p. 2.

53. Ibid., pp. 2–3. Author's translation.

54. Ibid., p. 3. Cf. *Anlage*, 2, p. 5.

55. *Anlage*, 2, p. 5.

56. *Anlage*, 1, p. 3.

57. Frau Claritta von Trott zu Solz cannot confirm any attempt of her husband's to contact the president in 1943. See her letter to the author, 28 November 1987.

58. *Anlage*, 1, p. 3. Cf. *Anlage*, 2, p. 8.

59. Muckermann was on good terms with the bishop of Berlin. It was to Muckermann's home in Frohnau that Preysing fled as the Red Army entered the city in 1945. Interview with Herta Chojnacki, 23 July 1986.

60. Goebbels branded him a critic of the German war leadership. See *Diaries*, entry for 21 February 1942, p. 96.

61. Walter Adolf, *Kardinal Preysing und zwei Diktaturen: Sein Widerstand gegen die totalitäre Macht* (Berlin: Morus Verlag, 1971), pp. 183–84.

62. Respondek, *Anlage*, 2, p. 8.

63. Ibid., p. 8.

64. Ibid., pp. 8–9.

65. Gisevius, *To the Bitter End*, p. 510.

66. Quoted in Fest, *Hitler*, p. 710.

67. Gisevius, *To the Bitter End*, pp. 593–94.

68. Fest, *Hitler*, p. 713.

69. Eventually some 7,000 persons would be incarcerated.

70. Himmler speech in Posen, 3 August 1944. Quoted in Fest, *Hitler*, p. 712.

71. For Respondek's concerns about being rounded up as part of "Special Action Z," see his letter to the International Red Cross, 1 July 1970, LVA.

72. Interview with Agnes Dreimann, 26 July 1986.

73. Valeska Hoffmann recalls her father felt that the Gestapo could not pin anything on him. Interview with Valeska Hoffmann, 22 March 1986.

74. Respondek letter to International Red Cross, LVA.

75. Respondek report, May 1946, p. 11, Stauffer Papers.

76. Respondek letter to the International Red Cross, LVA.

77. Charlotte Respondek was on good terms with the director of the Alexanderplatz prison, who unknowingly brought in the bundles of food for her. Interview with Agnes Dreimann.

78. Respondek letter to International Red Cross, LVA.

79. Woods memorandum, pp. 22–23, Hull Papers.

80. Interview with Agnes Dreimann. She also believes Goering's help was enlisted by Lili von Hartmann, a member of Respondek's circle. Goebbels may have been persuaded to speak on Respondek's behalf as well. He knew Respondek from their having participated in Nazi-Center discussions about forming a coalition government in 1931.

81. Respondek report, May 1946, p. 11, Stauffer Papers.

82. Woods memorandum, p. 21, Hull Papers.

83. Ibid.

84. Respondek report of May 1946, p. 12, Stauffer Papers.

85. Papen was also rumored to have been part of a peace bid to the Soviet Union and the Western Allies in 1942. See Goebbels, *Diaries*, entry for 21 March 1942, p. 139.

86. Papen, *Memoirs*, p. 529.

87. Ibid., pp. 531, 534.

88. Ibid., p. 534.

89. Kaltenbrunner testimony of 12 April 1946, *Trial of the Major War Criminals*, Vol. 11, p. 300.

90. Hoffmann, *German Resistance*, p. 522.

91. Planck was finally executed on 23 February 1945, after frantic pleas from his father failed to save him. See Heilbron, *Dilemmas of an Upright Man*, p. 195. Popitz, kept alive by Himmler in his bid to make peace with the Allies, was executed on 2 February 1945, also at the Plötzensee prison.

92. There are no extant reports from Respondek dating after his release. However, it appears, from what he told Cordell Hull after the war, that his information gathering continued. In an April 1948 letter to Hull, Respondek complained that U.S. "experts" had "brushed aside my early informations regarding the possibilities of a breach in the Western front." This was Operation Autumn Mist—what became known as the Battle of the Bulge. See Respondek letter to Hull, 4 April 1948, Brüning Papers.

93. Memorandum of Woods to Harrison, 10 August 1944, Box 14, Bern Confidential File, RG 84, NRC.

94. Anthony Cave Brown, *The Last Hero: Wild Bill Donovan: The Biography and Political Experience of William J. Donovan, Founder of the OSS and "Father" of the C.I.A.* (New York: Times Books, 1985), p. 286.

95. Laqueur and Breitman, *Breaking the Silence*, p. 214.

96. Gisevius, *To the Bitter End*, p. 479. Waetjen assumed this role with the help of Col. Georg Hansen, the anti-Nazi head of the German Abwehr.

97. This is according to Mrs. Irene Waetjen. See her letter to the author, 17 May 1986.

98. Hoffmann, *German Resistance*, p. 233.

99. Gisevius, *To the Bitter End*, p. 492.

100. Dulles, Introduction to Gisevius, *To the Bitter End*, xiv.

101. Memorandum of Woods to Harrison, 10 August 1944, Box 14, RG 84, NRC.

102. For example, Gisevius had briefed Dulles about the July 20th plot at about the same time Woods found out. See Donovan, "OSS Reports to the White House," 12 June 1945, Box 126C, Donovan Papers.

103. See letter of Woods to Harrison, 25 July 1944, Box 13, RG 84, NRC.

104. For particulars, see cable of Woods to Harrison, 6 June 1944, Box 18, Bern Confidential File, RG 84, NRC.

105. Interview with Robert A. Long, 3 February 1988. See also letter of Forrest S. Clark to the author, 1 February 1988.

106. See Max Steiner, *Die Internierung von Armeeangehörigen kriegsführender*

Mächte in neutralen Staaten insbesondere in der Schweiz während des Weltkriegs, 1939/ 45 (Zurich: Ernst Lang, 1947), p. 97.

107. Heinz K. Meier, *Friendship under Stress: U.S.–Swiss Relations, 1900–1950* (Bern: Herbert Lang, 1970), p. 51.

108. See letter of Hull to the U.S. Legation, Bern, 6 December 1943, Box 14, Bern Confidential File, RG 84, NRC.

109. Interview with Robert A. Long. Cf. Memorandum of Gen. Legge to Asst. Chief of Staff, War Department, 27 November 1944, Box 1020, RG 319, NRC. This outraged the U.S. pilots, who felt duty-bound to escape back to their bases in England.

110. Memorandum of William Donovan to Joint Chiefs of Staff, 26 September 1944, Folder 82, Box 120B, Donovan Papers, USAWC.

111. Letter of Forrest S. Clark to the author, 7 January 1988.

112. This is according to Cook, *McGowan Place*, p. 278.

113. Graham H. Stuart, *American Diplomatic and Consular Practice*, 2nd ed. (New York: Appleton, Century & Crofts, 1952), p. 329.

114. Ibid.

115. *Hattiesburg American*, 30 January 1954, p. 8.

116. Interview with Mary Bancroft, 25 February 1986.

117. Stuart says Woods would keep the airmen at his home in Zurich until it was time to make their escape. Stuart, *Diplomatic and Consular Practice*, p. 329.

118. Cook, *McGowan Place*, p. 279.

119. *Columbian-Progress* (Columbia, Miss.), 16 October 1952. Cf. Cook, *McGowan Place*, p. 279.

120. Cook, *McGowan Place*, p. 279.

121. Letter of W. C. Lier to Thomas J. Watson, 15 November 1942, Watson Papers, IBM Archives, Armonk, N.Y.

122. Letter of Price, Waterhouse & Co. to Thomas J. Watson, 7 November 1945, Watson Papers.

123. *Hattiesburg-American*, 30 January 1954.

124. Memorandum of Woods to Gen. Legge, 17 November 1945, Box 7, Zurich Confidential File, RG 84. Other Swiss in Zurich helped as well.

125. Interview with Albert Thompson, 8 March 1988.

126. Interview with Milada Woods, 12 February 1987.

127. The figure 200 is cited in Rep. William Colmer's remarks on Woods, which appeared in the *Congressional Record*, August 1952, p. A4795 (Appendix). Senator John C. Stennis, in his tribute to Woods, says "more than 1,000" escaped as a result of the diplomat's "personal attention." See *Congressional Record—Senate*, 31 July 1953, p. 10631.

128. Quoted in Sen. Stennis remarks, *Congressional Record*, 31 July 1953, p. 10631.

129. Interview with Mrs. Hardin [Woods] McClendon, 6 June 1985.

CHAPTER 12. BITTER FRUITS OF VICTORY

1. Respondek, Supplement, compensation claim, 21 May 1970, LVA.

2. Interview with Valeska Hoffman, 22 March 1986.

3. Ibid.

4. Letter of Respondek to Hull, 4 April 1948, Brüning Papers.

5. Ursula von Kardoff, *Berliner Aufzeichnungen aus den Jahren 1942–1945* (Munich: Deutscher Taschenbuch Verlag, 1981), entry for 8 February 1945, p. 233.

6. Ibid., entry for 27 March 1945, p. 246.

7. Ibid., entry for 1 May 1945, p. 261.

8. For a description of the Russians in Lichterfelde, see Bishop von Preysing, Enclosure 1, 14 July 1945, pp. 2–3, attached to reports of Respondek, 15 July 1945, Folder 18: "801.1 German Government," Box 730, POLAD Files, RG 84, IFZ.

9. Respondek, report on history of the Kaiser Wilhelm Society, 12 November 1970, p. 2, MPG. Author's translation.

10. Ibid.

11. See letter of Valeska Hoffman to Woods, 26 May 1945, Decimal File 740.00119 Control (Germany)/6 2845, RG 59, NA.

12. Statement of Woods, 25 June 1945. For a copy of this document I am indebted to Valeska Hoffmann.

13. Letter of Valeska Hoffmann to the author, 28 December 1987.

14. Details of this story were supplied by Valeska Hoffmann, interview of 22 March 1986.

15. Letter of Jacob D. Beam to his father, Jacob N. Beam, 23 July 1945, Jacob D. Beam Folder, Box 1, Jacob N. Beam Papers, Seeley Mudd Manuscript Library, Princeton, N.J.

16. Letter of Jacob D. Beam to Jacob N. Beam, 23 July 1945, Beam Papers.

17. Letter of Respondek to Hull, 4 April 1948, Brüning Papers.

18. Interview with Jacob D. Beam, 17 April 1987.

19. Interview with Jacob D. Beam, 4 December 1985. But the tone of Respondek's postwar memorandums is clearly anti-Soviet.

20. Letter of Respondek to Beam, 20 January 1949, Stauffer Papers.

21. All Beam agreed to do at that time was to set up further interviews. Letter of Beam to the author, 26 January 1988.

22. After hearing, in 1947, that his daughter Valeska intended to follow her husband to the United States, Respondek stalked out of the room and refused to speak with her again. This estrangement would last for the rest of his life. Interview with Valeska Hoffmann, 22 March 1986.

23. To keep the destitute family alive, Charlotte Respondek set up a small vegetable garden near the Soviet garrison in Potsdam. Letter of Respondek to Brüning, 2 December 1947, Brüning Papers.

24. Statement of Woods to U.S. military and civil authorities in Germany, 19 October 1945, p. 2, Stauffer Papers.

25. Cable of Woods to Hull, 15 August 1945 (F 176, Reel 26), Hull Papers, LC.

26. Letter of Woods to Hull, 28 June 1945, 740.00119 Control (Germany)/6–2845, RG 59, NA.

27. See cable of State Department to Murphy, No. 282, 14 August 1945, cited in letter of Murphy to Sec. of State Byrnes, 24 June 1946, Decimal File 862.00/6–2446, RG 59, NA.

28. Woods cable to Hull, 15 August 1945, F 176, Hull Papers.

29. Letters of Hull to Woods, 24 July 1945 and 7 September 1945, F 177, Hull Papers.

30. Letter of Respondek to Beam, 20 January 1949, Stauffer Papers.

31. Letter of Brüning to Beam, 5 November 1948, Brüning Papers. Brüning says he so advised Beam, who presumably passed this along to Hull. By contrast, Woods maintained that Hull decided not to use Respondek's name in order to protect him. See sworn statement of Woods, 5 August 1948, Stauffer Papers.

32. *New York Times*, 18 February 1948, p. 29.

33. Respondek himself supported this decision. In 1945 he told Donald Heath his activities should "remain closed for Germans." See his letter to Heath, 30 August 1945, Brüning Papers.

34. Letter of Woods to Respondek, 16 February 1946, Brüning Papers.

35. McGehee and Woods were good friends. In June 1946 Woods reminded the congressman of his promise to write Gen. Clay on Respondek's behalf. See letter of Woods to McGehee, 9 June 1946, Brüning Papers.

36. Annex, letter of Respondek to Beam, 16 October 1948, Stauffer Papers.

37. Although Woods never personally met President Roosevelt, it appears he may have been on his way to speak to his "boss" about his wartime activities in the spring of 1945. According to one of his postwar associates, Woods set out for the States with that goal in mind, but his ship docked in New York a few days after Roosevelt's death. Interview with Marbury Councell, Jr., 28 March 1988.

38. Annex, letter of Respondek to Beam, 16 October 1948, Stauffer Papers. See also letter of Respondek to Beam, 20 January 1949, Brüning Papers.

39. He counted particularly on assistance from Rep. Francis H. Case of South Dakota. Letter of Respondek to Beam, 16 October 1948.

40. Letter of Respondek to Beam, 20 January 1949. Stefan, a native of Bohemia and a former radio broadcaster, made a vague offer to help Respondek in July 1948. Woods later told Respondek that Stefan would attempt to arrange a lecture tour for him. This did not work out either. See letter of Woods to Respondek, 11 October 1948, Brüning Papers.

41. Letter of Respondek to Thomas Stauffer, 3 February 1961, Stauffer Papers.

42. Respondek, reports on political situation, food supply, liquidation of major industries, and transfer of scientific and technical institutes to the Soviet Union, 15 July 1945, Folder 18, Box 730, POLAD Files, RG 84, IZG.

43. Robert D. Murphy, *Diplomat among Warriors* (Garden City, N.Y.: Doubleday, 1964), pp. 245, 247–48.

44. Ibid., p. 273.

45. Murphy and his military superior, Gen. Lucius Clay, shared many of Respondek's views on currency reform, economic recovery, and the need for greater economic integration of the occupation zones. See Lucius D. Clay, *Decision in Germany*, 1st ed. (Garden City, N.Y.: Doubleday, 1950), p. 74.

46. Respondek, report on the Kaiser Wilhelm Society, p. 2, MPG.

47. For these various reports, see Folder 10, Box 746; Folders 18–22, Box 730; and Folder 34, Box 792, POLAD Files, RG 84, IZG.

48. So claims Respondek in his 4 April 1948 letter to Hull, Brüning Papers.

Respondek's position on German unification was reflected in Clay's statement at the May 1946 meeting of the Council of Foreign Ministers. See Clay, *Decision in Germany*, pp. 73–74.

49. Letter of Brüning to Otto A. Friedrich, 8 July 1949, private collection, Speyer, Germany, cited in letter of Rudolf Morsey to author, 9 October 1986. For bringing this letter to my attention I am grateful to Professor Morsey.

50. Respondek's analysis of Soviet intentions in their zone was also of help to Murphy and his staff. See letter of Respondek to Brüning, 12 February 1947, Brüning Papers.

51. Letter of Respondek to Woods, 28 April 1947. Respondek learned of Soviet progress in developing a bomb that would "outdistance the atomic bomb," but he was not sure this report was accurate.

52. This was helpful at the March–April 1947 meeting of the foreign ministers in Moscow. Letter of Respondek to Brüning, 12 February 1947, Brüning Papers.

53. Letter of Respondek to Beam, 16 October 1948, Stauffer Papers.

54. Respondek apparently turned down an offer of a post with the U.S. zonal government. See letter of Respondek to Jakob Kaiser, 15 October 1949, NL 18, Kaiser Papers, BA.

55. Long left his post in the State Department in 1944.

56. See, for example, Woods's comments to that effect, sworn statement, 5 August 1948, Folder 34, Box 792, POLAD, IZG.

57. Jacob Beam, for one, did not have a high opinion of Woods. Respondek was also at a disadvantage because of the dominant role of the War Department in occupied Germany. He had no ties here.

58. Letter of Thomas Stauffer to the author, 31 October 1986. However, Respondek's name did not appear on the list put together by Allen Dulles. See Office of Strategic Services Mission for Germany, "German Government Personnel," 6 August 1945, No. XL22686, RG 226, NA.

59. Letter of Stauffer to Hull, 16 March 1948, Stauffer Papers.

60. Letter of Stauffer to the author, 18 January 1987.

61. Respondek also impressed Stauffer with some details of his wartime espionage. See letter of Stauffer to the author, 15 August 1986.

62. Letter of Stauffer to Donald Heath, 25 April 1946, attached to letter of Robert Murphy to James F. Byrnes, 24 June 1946, Decimal File 862.00/6–2446, RG 59, NA.

63. Letter of Stauffer to the author, 15 September 1986. Despite his disclaimers of any political ambitions in a divided Germany, Respondek considered seeking a Center Party seat in the new Bundestag in the election of 1949. See his letter to Jakob Kaiser, 15 October 1949, Kaiser Papers, NL 18, BA.

64. Letter of Stauffer to the author, 15 September 1986.

65. Stauffer letter to Heath, 25 April 1946. Stauffer also told Robert Murphy he considered Respondek's views "reactionary." See "Annual Efficiency Report" of Thomas B. Stauffer, signed by Robert Murphy, 1 August 1947, Stauffer Papers.

66. Letter of Stauffer to Heath, 25 April 1946.

67. Letter of Murphy to Brynes, 24 June 1946.

68. Letter of Stauffer to the author, 28 September 1986.

69. Typical of Respondek's neglect by U.S. military authorities was the fact that he had to borrow an old bicycle to travel the several miles to OMGUS (Office of Military Government for Germany, United States) headquarters. See Respondek letter to Hull, 4 April 1948, Brüning Papers.

70. Letter of Stauffer to author, 28 September 1986.

71. Letter of Woods to Respondek, 21 March 1947, Brüning Papers.

72. Apparently Woods offered to bring Respondek to the United States, but Respondek rejected this idea. Interview with Agnes Dreimann, 26 July 1986.

73. Busch made his fortune out of developing a bottling process that allowed his beer to be sold around the world, in all climates.

74. See obituary in the *New York Times*, 11 October 1913, p. 15.

75. For a description of Hitler's visit, see Ernst Hanfstaengl, *Zwischen weissem und brauen Haus: Memoiren eines politischen Aussenseiters* (Munich: R. Piper Verlag, 1970), p. 66.

76. The fact that Wilhelmina had kept her American citizenship also made her vulnerable to this kind of action.

77. *St. Louis Post-Dispatch*, 23 February 1948. This view is upheld by Woods's Mississippi friend Robert C. Cook, who says Wilhelmina was "very much anti-Hitler." See Cook, *McGowan Place*, p. 280.

78. Frau Gontard had been married to the president of the Mercedes Motor Company. He died in 1941. See *St. Louis Post-Dispatch*, 16 February 1948.

79. Decimal File 840.51, "Frozen Assets," 8397 1/2, RG 59, NA. Berghaus was later placed on a Polish war crimes list.

80. See unsigned memorandum, 14 February 1945, Box 18, Bern Confidential File, RG 84, NRC.

81. *New York Times*, 5 May 1944, p. 8.

82. The official in charge of this was Consul Maurice Altaffer. See letter of Dabney Altaffer to the author, 29 March 1986.

83. According to J. Bolard More, then on the consular staff, Wilhelmina was thought to be generally apolitical. Interview with J. Bolard More, 14 January 1986. But Mrs. Norma Lovell, wife of the former U.S. military attaché in Berlin, states that Mrs. Borchard was "pro Nazi." See interview with Mrs. Lovell, 2 March 1987.

84. 840.51, "Frozen Assets," 8397 1/2, RG 84, NA.

85. Letter of Respondek to Stauffer, 3 February 1961.

86. Willard Bond, a close friend in Mississippi, says Woods met Mrs. Borchard in the Baur au Lac and also claims Woods was separated from his wife Milada during the war. See Willard F. Bond, *I Had a Friend: An Autobiography* (Kansas City, Mo.: E. L. Mendenhall, 1958), p. 232. Mary Bancroft asserts that Milada Woods had an affair with Robert Cowan, and this may have contributed to, or resulted from, the estrangement between Milada and Woods.

87. Later, Woods brought Mrs. Borchard's case to the attention of Karl Stefan, ranking minority member of the House Appropriations Committee. See letter of Stefan to Woods, 30 July 1946, and letter of Woods to Stefan, 7 October 1946, Folder 4 ("Sam Woods"), Box 40, Karl Stefan Papers, NSHS (hereafter cited as Stefan Papers).

88. Letter of Woods to Karl and Ida Stefan, 5 November 1946, Folder 4, Box 40, Stefan Papers.

89. Cook, *McGowan Place*, p. 281.

90. Letter of Stefan to Woods, 16 April 1947, Stefan Papers.

91. See, for example, letter of Dabney Altaffer to the author, 29 March 1986. He says his father got along with Woods until the consul general tried to keep certain individuals off the blacklist. Then the senior Altaffer lost all respect for Woods.

92. Letter of Stefan to Woods, 23 May 1947, Stefan Papers.

93. Ibid.

94. Letter of Respondek to Stauffer, 3 February 1961, Stauffer Papers. Author's translation.

95. Letter of Woods to Karl and Ida Stefan, 22 November 1947, Stefan Papers. Woods was then living in Munich.

96. So assert Mary Bancroft and J. Bolard More. Letter of Mary Bancroft to the author, 12 February 1986. Interview with More, 14 January 1986.

97. The divorce was the subject of considerable gossip in Washington circles. See, for example, letter of Stefan to Woods, 6 February 1948, Stefan Papers.

98. This was true of Mr. and Mrs. Theodore Hadraba, good friends of Woods's since his days in Prague.

99. Cable of Woods to Stefan, 23 December 1947, Stefan Papers.

100. Wilhelmina had had the chapel brought to Bernried, stone by stone, from Corsica. See *St. Louis Post-Dispatch*, 23 February 1948.

101. Cook, *McGowan Place*, p. 291.

102. *New York Times*, 23 February 1948, p. 28.

103. *New York Times*, 24 November 1953, p. 23.

104. Respondek later said he realized in October 1947 that Woods had made use of Respondek's accomplishments for his own purposes. Letter of Respondek to Brüning, 20 January 1949, Brüning Papers.

105. Letter of Respondek to Stauffer, 3 February 1961, Stauffer Papers.

106. Letter of Respondek to Hull, 4 April 1948, Brüning Papers.

107. Ibid. Respondek also had Stauffer write to Hull about his present activities and unhappy relations with the U.S. military government. Letter of Stauffer to Hull, 16 March 1948, Stauffer Papers.

108. Letter of Respondek to Beam, 12 July 1948, 740.00119 Control (Germany)/7–1248, RG 59, NA.

109. Cable of Beam to James Riddleberger, 10 September 1948, 740.00119 Control (Germany)/7–2248, RG 59, NA. Beam mentioned obtaining Hull's approval in a letter to the author, 26 January 1988.

110. James W. Riddleberger, chargé d'affaires *ad interim* in Berlin, wrote to Secretary of State George C. Marshall on 22 July 1948 indicating that he, Donald Heath, and Sam Woods had "extended assistance of various kinds to him (Respondek) from their personal resources." But Riddleberger noted that it would be impossible to find Respondek a post with the U.S. military government "at his age." Letter of Riddleberger to Marshall, 22 July 1948, No. 1097, Folder 3, Box 459, POLAD Files, IZG.

111. Letter of Beam to Respondek, 3 November 1948, 740.00119 Control (Germany)/10–1648, NA. All Beam could suggest was that Respondek approach Heinrich Brüning for help. He further had Sam Woods issue a statement saying he had "received far too much credit" for deeds actually performed by Re-

spondek. See Woods's sworn statement, 5 August 1948, Folder 34, Box 792, POLAD Files, IZG.

112. Letter of Beam to Riddleberger, 15 November 1948, Folder 34, Box 792, POLAD Files, RG 84, IZG.

113. In 1949 Beam was named consul general in Djakarta and lost touch with Respondek. Interview with Beam, 17 April 1987.

114. Respondek said his letter to Hull was the "ostensible" reason for Woods's not doing anything more for him after 1948. See his letter to Brüning, 28 February 1950, Brüning Papers.

115. Letter of Respondek to Brüning, 28 February 1950. Author's translation.

116. Letter of Respondek to Brüning, 20 January 1949, Brüning Papers. See also undated manuscript of Respondek's, Brüning Papers.

117. Adenauer and Respondek knew each other from prewar Center Party circles. In 1940 Adenauer visited Berlin and spent a few hours walking between the Reichstag and Unter den Linden, talking to Respondek. Respondek letter to Brüning, 28 February 1950, Brüning Papers.

118. Interview with Claire Nix, 12 February 1987.

119. So he told his daughter, Valeska. Interview of 18 April 1947.

120. Letter of Respondek to Stauffer, 2 May 1961, Stauffer Papers.

121. Adenauer was not on particularly good terms with Brüning and hence not eager to heed his advice. Interview with Claire Nix.

122. These included Hermann Pünder, Erwin Planck's predecessor as state secretary in the Reich chancellery, as well as a cofounder of the Christian Democratic Union (CDU); and Adenauer's economics minister, Ludwig Erhard.

123. Letter of Brüning to Otto A. Friedrich, 8 July 1949, quoted in letter of Rudolf Morsey to the author, 9 October 1986.

124. Letter of Respondek to Brüning, 28 February 1950, Brüning Papers. Respondek complained that the *"Postenjägerei"* ("hunting for positions") had swept him aside.

125. Interview with Valeska Hoffmann, 22 March 1986.

126. See letter of Respondek to Jakob Kaiser, 15 October 1949, Kaiser Papers.

127. Letter of Respondek to Stauffer, 3 February 1961, Stauffer Papers.

128. After working on the constitution for the revived Center Party, Respondek withdrew his backing after the party sought to merge with the CDU.

129. So say Valeska Hoffmann, Hertz Chojnacki, and Agnes Dreimann.

130. So says his second wife, Elsbeth (Respondek) Schukat. See her letter to the author, 22 November 1986.

131. Letter of Respondek to Beam, 12 July 1948, 740.00119 Control (Germany)/7–1248, NA.

132. Ibid.

133. For an account of Dorothea Respondek's final illness, see letter of Respondek to Brüning, 28 February 1950, Brüning Papers.

134. This may have occurred in 1951. See letter of Erika and Horst Teller to the author, 21 November 1986. The Tellers were Respondek's neighbors in Berlin at that time.

135. In a January 1961 summary of his postwar work for the American government, Respondek states that the "reimbursement of aryanized Jewish prop-

erty" was worked out on the basis of his memorandum on this subject. See untitled manuscript, dated "mid-January 1961," Stauffer Papers.

136. According to Respondek, his memorandum, "New Organization the German Currency and Reichs Bank," 30 July 1947, formed the basis for discussions leading to creation of the West German Bundesbank. See his memorandum of mid-January 1961.

137. In his mid-January 1961 statement Respondek says that he informed Ambassador Murphy in March 1948 that the Soviets were preparing a blockade of Berlin.

138. Letter of Karl F. Mautner to the author, 20 October 1986.

139. Letter of Respondek to Stauffer, 6 December 1960, Stauffer Papers.

140. See letter of Hildegard Wieser-Hofmann to the author, 29 May 1986. Mrs. Hofmann lived in Munich after the war.

141. One Christmas Woods procured oranges for the children of employees of the Bavarian state chancellery. See letter of Hans von Herwarth to the author, 31 May 1985.

142. See letter of Kenneth J. MacCormac to the author, 5 March 1986.

143. Bond, *I Had a Friend*, p. 227. This compares with remarks on Woods's popularity in Washington, made by Rep. William Colmer of Mississippi on the occasion of Woods's retirement: "I doubt if there has ever been a man connected with our Foreign Service who was as universally beloved during his career as was Sam Woods." Extension of remarks, Sat. 5 July 1952, *Congressional Record*, Appendix, August 1952, A4795.

144. These Woods had collected during his years of State Department service in Europe. See letter of Kenneth MacCormac to the author, 5 March 1986.

145. Clayton Rand, "Spinal Column," *The Dixie Guide*, September 1949, Rand Papers, Mississippi State University, Mississippi State, Miss.

146. For specifics on the Höhenried estate see *St. Louis Post-Dispatch*, 31 August 1955 and 23 February 1948.

147. Letter of Kenneth MacCormac to the author.

148. This information comes from Patrick Nieburg, interview of 6 December 1985.

149. Cf. Cook, *McGowan Place*, pp. 285–86. Cf. Bond, *I Had a Friend*, p. 228.

150. Letter of Woods to Mrs. Joseph Robinson, 23 May 1950, Robinson Papers.

151. See letters of Woods to Stefan, 16 June 1947, and 3 December 1947, Stefan Papers.

152. *New York Times*, 23 January 1953, p. 21. Another $10 million had already been set aside in a trust fund, to be shared among Busch family members. See *St. Louis Post-Dispatch*, 16 September 1954.

153. Letter of Kenneth MacCormac to the author.

154. Cook, *McGowan Place*, p. 294.

155. *Jackson Daily News*, 5 April 1959. Cf. *Hattiesburg-American*, 21 December 1980.

156. Cook, *McGowan Place*, p. 295.

157. So he intimated in a letter to Robert Cook, cited in Cook, *McGowan Place*, p. 295.

158. In his will, drafted after Minnie's death, Woods left 30 percent of his

estate, valued at $5 million, to Milada, with another 30 percent going to his daughter, Katie Rose McClendon, and the remainder to be divided among other relatives. See Last Will and Testament, Sam E. Woods, 7 December 1952. Milada also received a life income from her $2 million portion of his estate. See article in *St. Louis Post-Dispatch*, 13 June 1953.

159. She came from a family of wrought-iron workers. Letter of Elsbeth Schukat to the author, 15 January 1987.

160. Letter of Respondek to Stauffer, 3 February 1961, Staffer Papers.

161. Letter of Stauffer to Leon Stoltz, 8 July 1961, Stauffer Papers.

162. See Respondek, "Soviet Russian Berlin Note," dated "early January 1959," Stauffer Papers.

163. Letter of Stauffer to Dana Schmidt, 28 January 1961, Stauffer Papers.

164. Respondek had not received a government pension for his Weimar-era service.

165. For evidence of Stauffer's efforts to sell articles of Respondek's to American publications, see his letters, Stauffer Papers.

166. Stauffer's efforts to interest several congressmen and senators in Respondek's views were somewhat more successful but brought Respondek no income.

167. Letter of Respondek to Stauffer, 28 July 1961, Stauffer Papers.

168. A settlement of 5,000 Swiss francs was made against the firm of Kurd Wenkel AG, but no money was ever paid: the company was bankrupt. Letter of Henriette Respondek to the author, 16 February 1987.

169. Letter of Respondek to Stauffer, 7 March 1962, Stauffer Papers.

170. See Respondek's compensation claim, LVA.

171. Letter of Respondek to Stauffer, 4 August 1970, Stauffer Papers. Author's translation. All he could recall with pride was the gratitude of Cordell Hull, conveyed to him by Brüning.

172. Letter of Respondek to Stauffer, 4 August 1970, Stauffer Papers.

REFERENCES

PUBLISHED SOURCES

Accoce, Pierre, and Pierre Quet. *A Man Called Lucy, 1939–1945*. Translated by A. M. Sheridan Smith. New York: Coward-McCann, 1967.

Adlon, Hedda. *Hotel Adlon*. München: Wilhelm Heyne Verlag, 1980.

Adolf, Walter. *Hirtenamt und Hitler-Diktatur*. Berlin: Morus Verlag, 1965.

———. *Kardinal Preysing und zwei Diktaturen: Sein Widerstand gegen die totalitäre Macht*. Berlin: Morus Verlag, 1971.

———. *Verfälschte Geschichte: Antwort an Rolf Hochhuth*. 2d ed. Berlin: Morus Verlag, 1963.

Ambruster, Howard W. *Treason's Peace: German Dyes and American Dupes*. New York: Beechhurst Press, 1947.

An der Stechbahn: Erlebnisse und Berichte in den Jahren der Verfolgung mit dreiundzwanzig Grusswörten von Probst D. Grüber am 24. Juni 1951. Berlin: Evangelische Verlagsanstalt, 1951.

The Army Air Forces in World War II. Vol. 3: *Europe—Argument to VE Day*. Edited by Wesley F. Craven and J. L. Cate. Washington, D.C.: Office of the Air Force History, 1983.

Balzar, Karl. *Verschwörung gegen Deutschland: So verloren wir den Krieg*. Preussisch Oldendorf: R. W. Schutz, 1978.

Bancroft, Mary. *Autobiography of a Spy*. New York: William Morrow, 1983.

Bar-Zohar, Michel. *The Hunt for German Scientists*. Translated by Len Ortzen. New York: Hawthorn Books, 1967.

Bauermeister, Hermann. "Die Entwicklung der Magnetminen bis zum Beginn des zweiten Weltkriegs." *Marine Rundschau*, 55, 1 (1958): 25–31.

Baxter, James P. *Scientists against Time*. Boston: Little, Brown, 1946.

Becker, Josef. "Zentrum und Ermächtigungsgesetz 1933." *Historische Vierteljahrschrift*, 9 (1961): 195–210.

Bekker, Cajus. *Hitler's Naval War*. Translated and edited by Frank Ziegler. Garden City, N.Y.: Doubleday, 1974.

Berle, Adolf A. *Navigating the Rapids*. Edited by Beatrice Bishop Berle and Travis Beal Jacobs. 1st ed. New York: Harcourt, Brace & Jovanovich, 1973.

The Berlin Diaries, May 30, 1932–January 30, 1933. Edited by Helmut Klotz. New York: William Morrow, 1934.

Beyerchen, Alan D. *Scientists under Hitler: Politics and the Physics Community in the Third Reich*. New Haven, Conn.: Yale University Press, 1977.

Binder, Gerhart. *Irrtum und Widerstand: Die deutsche Katholiker in der Auseinandersetzung mit dem Nationalsozialismus*. München: Pfeiffer, 1968.

Boberach, Heinz, ed. *Berichte der SD und der Gestapo über Kirchen und Kirchenvolk in Deutschland, 1934–1944*. Mainz: Matthias-Grünewald Verlag, 1971.

Böckenförde, Ernst Wolfgang. "Der deutsche Katholizismus im Jahre 1933." *Vom Weimar zu Hitler, 1930–1933*, edited by Gotthard Jasper, pp. 317–43. Köln/Berlin: Kiepenheuer & Witsch, 1968.

Bohlen, Charles. *Witness to History, 1929–1969*. 1st ed. New York: W. W. Norton, 1973.

Bond, Willard F. *I Had a Friend: An Autobiography*. Kansas City: E. L. Mendenhall, 1958.

Bonjour, Edgar. *Geschichte der schweizerischen Neutralität: Drei Jahrhunderte eidgenössische Aussenpolitik*. Basel: Helbing & Lichtenbahn, 1946.

Bor, Peter. *Gespräche mit Halder*. Wiesbaden: Limes Verlag, 1950.

Borkin, Joseph. *The Crime and Punishment of IG Farben*. New York: Free Press, 1978.

Boveri, Margret. *Treason in the Twentieth Century*. Translated by Jonathan Steinberg. London: MacDonald, 1961.

Boyd, Carl. "The Significance of MAGIC and the Japanese Ambassador to Berlin: (I) The Formative Months before Pearl Harbor." *Intelligence and National Security*, 2, 1, (Jan. 1987): 150–69.

Boyle, Andrew. *Montagu Norman: A Biography*. London: Cassell & Co., 1967.

Brooks, Lester. *Behind Japan's Surrender: The Great Struggle That Ended an Empire*. New York: McGraw-Hill, 1967.

Brüning, Heinrich. *Briefe, 1946–1960*. Edited by Claire Nix. Stuttgart: Deutsche Verlags-Anstalt, 1974.

———. *Briefe und Gespräche, 1934–1945*. Edited by Claire Nix. Translated from the English and French by Brigitte Weitbrecht. Stuttgart: Deutsche Verlags-Anstalt, 1974.

———. *Memoiren 1918–1934*. Stuttgart: Deutsche Verlags-Anstalt, 1970.

Bührer, Werner. "Auftakt im Paris: Der Marschall Plan und die deutsche Rückkehr auf die internationale Bühne 1948/49." *Vierteljahrshefte für Zeitgeschichte*, 36, 3 (July 1988): pp. 529–56.

Burdick, Charles B. *An American Island in Hitler's Reich: The Bad Nauheim Internment*. Menlo Park, Calif.: Markgraf Publications Group, 1987.

Bush, Vannevar. *Pieces of the Action*. New York: William Morrow, 1970.

Carrell, Paul. *Hitler Moves East, 1941–1943*. Translated by Ewald Osers. Boston: Little, Brown, 1964.

Cave Brown, Anthony. *'C': The Rise and Fall of Sir Stewart Graham Menzies, Spymaster to Winston Churchill*. New York: MacMillan, 1987.

————. *On a Field of Red: The Communist International and the Coming of World War II*. New York: Putnam, 1981.

————. *The Last Hero—Wild Bill Donovan: The Biography and Political Experience of William J. Donovan, Founder of the O.S.S. and "Father" of the C.I.A.* New York: Times Books, 1985.

Cecil, Robert. *Hitler's Decision to Invade Russia*. New York: D. McKay, 1976.

Chadwick, Owen. *Britain and the Vatican during the Second World War*. New York: Cambridge University Press, 1987.

Chronicles of Smith County, Texas, 23 1 (Summer 1984).

Churchill, Winston S. *The Gathering Storm*. Vol. 1: *The Second World War*. London: Cassell, 1948.

Clark, Alan. *Barbarossa: The Russian–German Conflict, 1941–1945*. New York: William Morrow, 1965.

Clay, Lucius D. *Decision in Germany*. 1st ed. Garden City, N.Y.: Doubleday, 1950.

————. *The Papers of General Lucius D. Clay, 1945–1949*. Vol. 1. Edited by Jean Edward Smith. Bloomington: Indiana University Press, 1974.

Colby, Gerard. *Dupont Dynasty: Behind the Nylon Curtain*. Secaucus, N.J.: Lyle Stuart, 1984.

Colvin, Ian G. *Chief of Intelligence*. London: Gollancz, 1951.

Command and Commanders in Modern Warfare. The Proceedings of the Second Military History Symposium, U.S. Air Force Academy, 2–3 May 1968. Edited by William Geffen, Lt. Col., United States Air Force. Office of Air Force History, Headquarters, U.S. Air Force, and U.S. Air Force Academy, 1971.

Compton, Arthur H. *Atomic Quest: A Personal Narrative*. New York: Oxford University Press, 1956.

Cook, Robert Cecil. *McGowan Place and Other Memoirs*. Hattiesburg, Miss.: Educators' Biographical Press, 1973.

Curtius, Julius. *Sechs Jahre Minister der deutschen Republik*. Heidelberg: C. Winter, 1948.

Dank, Milton. *The Glider Gang: An Eyewitness History of World War II Glider Combat*. 1st ed. Philadelphia: J. B. Lippincott, 1977.

Delmer, Sefton. *Trail Sinister: An Autobiography*. Vol. 1. London: Secker & Warburg, 1961.

D'Este, Carlo. *Decision in Normandy: The Unwritten Story of Montgomery and the Allied Campaign*. London: Collins, 1983.

Deuel, Wallace R. *People under Hitler*. New York: Harcourt, Brace & Co., 1942.

Deutsch, Harold C. *The Conspiracy against Hitler in the Twilight War*. Minneapolis: University of Minnesota Press, 1968.

————. *Hitler and His Generals: The Hidden Crisis—January–June 1938*. Minneapolis: University of Minnesota Press, 1974.

Dodd, Martha. *Through Embassy Eyes*. New York: Harcourt, Brace & World, 1939.

Dodd, William E. *Ambassador Dodd's Diary*. Edited by William E. Dodd, Jr., and Martha Dodd. New York: Harcourt, Brace & World, 1941.

Domarus, Max. *Hitlers Reden und Proklamationen, 1932–1945*. Vol. 2. Neustadt a.d. Aisch: Auslieferung Verlagsdruckerei, 1963.

Drexler, Anton. *Mein politisches Erwachen*. 2d ed. München: Deutschervolksverlag, 1920.

Dugan, James, and Carroll Stewart. *Ploesti: The Great Ground-Air Battle of 1 August 1943*. New York: Random House, 1962.

Dulles, Allen W. *Germany's Underground*. New York: MacMillan, 1947.

Duncan, Robert C. *America's Use of Sea Mines*. White Oak, Md.: U.S. Naval Ordnance Laboratory, 1963.

Ebert, Hans. "Hermann Muckermann: Profil eines Theologen, Widerstandskämpfers und Hochschullehrers der Technischen Hochschule Berlin." *Humanismus und Technik*. 20, 1 (30 April 1976): 29–40.

Eppler, John W. *Geheimagent im Zweiten Weltkrieg: Zwischen Berlin, Kabul und Kairo*. 1st ed. Preussisch Oldendorf: K. W. Schutz, 1974.

Etzhold, Thomas H. "The (F)utility Factor: German Information Gathering in the United States, 1933–1941." *Military Affairs*, 39, 2 (1975): 77–82.

Fall Barbarossa: Dokumente zur Vorbereitung der faschistischen Wehrmacht auf die Aggression gegen die UdSSR. Berlin: Deutscher Militärverlag, 1970.

Fall 6: Ausgewählte Dokumente und Urteil des IG Farben Prozesses. Edited by Hans Radant. Berlin: Deutsche Verlag der Wissenschaften, 1970.

Farago, Ladislas. *The Broken Seal: The Story of "Operation Magic" and the Pearl Harbor Disaster*. New York: Random House, 1967.

———. *The Game of the Foxes: The Untold Story of German Espionage in the United States and Great Britain during World War II*. New York: D. McKay, 1972.

Fertl, Anton, ed. *Erinnerungen an Stiftsprobst Albert Graf von Preysing*. Landshut: Owal-Druck, 1948.

Fest, Joachim C. *Hitler*. Translated by Richard and Clara Winston. New York: Harcourt, Brace & Jovanovich, 1974.

Feuersenger, Marianne. *Mein Kriegstagebuch: Führerhauptquartier und Berliner Wirklichkeit*. Freiburg: Herder Verlag, 1982.

Flannery, Harry W. *Assignment to Berlin*. New York: Knopf, 1942.

Fleming, Peter. *Operation Sea Lion*. New York: Simon and Schuster, 1957.

Forman, James. *Codename Valkyrie: Count von Stauffenberg and the Plot to Kill Hitler*. New York: S. G. Phillips, 1973.

Friedrich, Otto. *Before the Deluge: A Portrait of Berlin in the 1920's*. New York: Fromm International Publishing Corp., 1986.

Fugate, Bryan. *Operation Barbarossa: Strategy and Tactics on the Eastern Front, 1941*. Novato, Calif.: Presidio Press, 1984.

Garlinski, Jozef. *Hitler's Last Weapons: The Underground War against the V1 and V2*. New York: Times Books, 1978.

Gilbert, Martin. *Winston S. Churchill: The Prophet of Truth, 1929–1939*. Boston: Houghton-Mifflin, 1977.

———. *Winston S. Churchill: Road to Victory, 1941–1945*. Boston: Houghton Mifflin, 1986.

Gisevius, Hans Bernd. *To the Bitter End*. Translated by Richard and Clara Winston. Boston: Houghton Mifflin, 1947.

Glaus, Beat. *Die nationale Front: Ein schweizer faschistische Bewegung, 1930–1940*. Zürich: Benziger Verlag, 1969.

Glick, David. "Some Were Rescued: Memoirs of a Private Mission." *Harvard Law School Bulletin*, 12, 2 (Dec. 1960): 6–10.

Glum, Friedrich. *Zwischen Wissenschaft, Wirtschaft und Politik: Erlebtes und Erdachtes in vier Reichen*. Bonn: H. Bouvier & Co., 1964.

Goebbels, Joseph. *The Goebbels Diaries, 1942–1943*. Edited and translated by Louis P. Lochner. Garden City, N.Y.: Doubleday, 1948.

———. *The Goebbels Diaries, 1939–1941*. Edited and translated by Fred Taylor. Harmondsworth, England: Penguin Books, 1984.

Goldston, Robert. *Sinister Touches: The Secret War against Hitler*. New York: Dial Press, 1982.

Goudsmit, Samuel A. *Alsos: The Failure in German Science*. London: Sigma Books, 1947.

Graham, Robert A., SJ. *Il Vaticano e il nazismo*. Roma: Cinque lune, 1975.

Groscurth, Helmuth. *Tagebücher eines Abwehroffiziers, 1938–40*. Edited by Helmuth Krausnick and Harold C. Deutsch. Stuttgart: Deutsche Verlags-Anstalt, 1970.

Groueff, Stephane. *Manhattan Project: The Untold Story of the Making of the Atomic Bomb*. New York: Bantam, 1968.

Groves, Leslie R. *Now It Can Be Told: The Story of the Manhattan Project*. New York: Harper, 1962.

Grüber, Probst Heinrich. *Erinnerungen aus sieben Jahrzehnten*. Köln/Berlin: Kiepenheuer & Witsch, 1968.

Halder, Franz. *The Halder Diaries: The Private War Journals of Colonel General Franz Halder*. Boulder, Colo.: Westview, 1976.

Hanfstaengl, Ernst. *Zwischen weissem und brauen Haus: Memoiren eines politischen Aussenseiters*. München: R. Piper, 1970.

Harsch, Joseph C. *Pattern of Conquest*. Garden City, N.Y.: Doubleday, 1941.

Hassell, Ulrich von. *The Von Hassell Diaries, 1938–1944: The Story of the Forces against Hitler Inside Germany as Recorded by Ambassador Ulrich von Hassell*. London: H. Hamilton, 1948.

———. *Vom andern Deutschland: Aus den nachgelassenen Tagebüchern, 1938–1944*. Zürich: Atlantis Verlag, 1946.

Hassett, William D. *Off the Record with F.D.R., 1942–1945*. New Brunswick, N.J.: Rutgers University Press, 1958.

Hastings, Max. *Bomber Command*. New York: Dial Press, 1979.

Hayes, Peter. *Industry and Ideology: IG Farben in the Nazi Era*. New York: Cambridge University Press, 1987.

Heeresadjutant bei Hitler, 1938–1943: Aufzeichnungen des Majors Engel. Edited by Hildegard von Kotze. Stuttgart: Deutsche Verlags-Anstalt, 1974.

Hehl, Ulrich von, ed. *Priester unter Hitlers Terror: Eine biographische und statistische Erhebung*. Veröffentlichungen der Kommission für Zeitgeschichte. Band 37. Mainz: M. Grünewald Verlag, 1984.

Heilbron, J. L. *The Dilemmas of an Upright Man. Max Planck as Spokesman for German Science*. Berkeley/Los Angeles/London: University of California Press, 1986.

Heisenberg, Elisabeth. *Das politisches Leben eines unpolitischen: Erinnerungen an Werner Heisenberg*. München/Zürich: R. Piper & Co. Verlag, 1980.

Heisenberg, Werner. *Physics and Beyond: Encounters and Conversations*. Translated by Arnold J. Pomerans. New York: Harper & Row, 1971.

———. "Research in Germany on the Technical Applications of Atomic Energy." *Nature*, 160, 409 (Aug. 16, 1947): 211–15.

Henderson, Sir Nevile. *Failure of a Mission: Berlin, 1937–1939.* New York: G. P. Putnam's Sons, 1940.

Herber, Helmut. *Hitlers Lagebesprechungen: die Protokollfragmente seiner militärischen Konferenzen, 1942–1945.* Stuttgart: Deutsche Verlags-Anstalt, 1962.

Herbermann, Nanda. *Friedrich Muckermann: Ein Apostel unserer Zeit.* Paderborn: F. Schoningh, 1953.

Herman, Stewart W. *It's Your Souls We Want.* New York/London: Harper & Bros., 1943.

Hernon, Peter, and Terry Ganey. *Under the Influence: The Unauthorized Story of the Anheuser-Busch Dynasty.* New York: Simon & Schuster, 1991.

Hertzman, Lewis. *DNVP: Right-Wing Opposition in the Weimar Republic, 1918–1924.* Lincoln: University of Nebraska Press, 1963.

Herwarth von Bittenfeld, Hans. *Against Two Evils.* New York: Rawson, Wade, 1981.

Higgins, Trumbull. *Hitler and Russia: The Third Reich in a Two-Front War, 1937–1943.* New York: MacMillan, 1966.

Hildebrand, Klaus. *Das dritte Reich.* München/Wien: Oldenbourg, 1979.

Hillgruber, Andreas. *Hitlers Strategie: Politik und Kriegsführung, 1940–1941.* Frankfurt am Main: Bernard & Grafe, 1965.

Hinsley, F. H. *British Intelligence in the Second World War: Its Influence on Strategy and Operations.* Vol. 1. London: Her Majesty's Stationery Office, 1979.

Hitler, Adolf. *Mein Kampf.* Translated by Abbots Langley. 1981 ed. London/New York: Hurst Blackett, 1981.

———. *Table Talk, 1941–1944.* Translated by Norman Cameron and R. H. Stevens. London: Weidenfeld & Nicolson, 1953.

Höhne, Heinz. *Canaris.* Translated by J. Maxwell Brownjohn. Garden City, N.Y.: Doubleday, 1979.

Höllen, Martin. *Heinrich Wienken, der "unpolitische" Kirchenpolitiker: Eine Biographie aus drei Epochen des Katholizismus.* Mainz: Matthias-Grünewald Verlag, 1981.

Hoffmann, Klaus. *Otto Hahn: Stationen aus dem Leben eines Atomforschers: Biographie.* Berlin: Verlag Neues Leben, 1978.

Hoffmann, Peter. *The History of the German Resistance, 1933–1945.* Translated by Richard Barry. Boston: MIT Press, 1977.

Holdermann, Karl. *Im Banne der Chemie: Carl Bosch, Üben und Werk.* Düsseldorf: Econ-Verlag, 1953.

Hull, Cordell. *The Memoirs of Cordell Hull.* Vol. 2. New York: MacMillan, 1948.

Huss, Pierre J. *The Foe We Face.* Garden City, N.J.: Doubleday, 1942.

Hyde, Montgomery. *Room 3603: The Story of the British Intelligence Center in New York during World War II.* New York: Farrar, Straus & Co., 1963. 3rd printing.

Ickes, Harold L. *The Secret Diary of Harold L. Ickes: The Lowering Clouds, 1939–1941.* New York: Simon and Schuster, 1954.

Irving, David. *The German Atomic Bomb: The History of Atomic Research in Nazi Germany.* New York: DeCapo Press, 1967.

———. *Hitler's War.* New York: Viking Press, 1977.

———. *The Mare's Nest.* London: W. Kimber, 1964.

———. *The War Path. Hitler's Germany, 1933–1939.* New York: Viking, 1978.

Jackson, Robert. *Storm from the Skies: The Strategic Bombing Offensive, 1943–1945.* London: Arthur Barker, 1974.

Jahrbuch der Max Planck Gesellschaft. 1961. Part 2. Göttingen: Max Planck Gesellschaft, 1962.

Janssen, Gregor. *Das Ministerium Speer: Deutschlands Rüstung im Krieg.* Berlin: Ullstein, 1968.

Jones, Reginald V. *Most Secret War.* London: Hamilton, 1978.

———. *The Wizard War: British Scientific Intelligence, 1939–1945.* New York: Coward, McCann & Geohegan, 1978.

Jones, Vincent C. *The United States Army in World War II.* Special Studies: *Manhattan: The Army and the Bomb.* Washington, D.C.: Center for Military History, U.S. Army, 1985.

Kahn, David. *Hitler's Spies: German Military Intelligence in World War II.* New York: MacMillan, 1978.

Kaiser Wilhelm Institut für ausländisches und internationales Privatrecht: Jahresbericht, 1940/41. Berlin: Kaiser Wilhelm Gesellschaft, 1941.

Kase, Toshikazu. *Journey to the "Missouri."* New Haven, Conn.: Yale University Press, 1951.

Kennan, George F. *Memoirs: 1925–1950.* Boston: Little, Brown, 1967.

Kimche, Jon. *Spying for Peace: General Guisan and Swiss Neutrality.* New York: Roy Publishers, 1961.

Kirchner, F. "Hochspannungsanlagen (elektrostatische Generatoren)." *Naturforschung und Medizin im Deutschland, 1939–1946.* Band 14. *Kernphysik und kosmische Strahlungen.* Teil 2. Weinheim: Verlag Chemie, 1953: 24–28.

Knightley, Philip. *The Second Oldest Profession: Spies and Spying in the Twentieth Century.* New York: W. W. Norton, 1986.

Koch, Diether. *Heinemann und die Deutschlandfrage.* München: Chr. Kaiser Verlag, 1972.

Koebel-Tusk, Eberhard. *AEG: Energie, Profit, Verbrechen. Manuskript von Eberhard Koebel-Tusk.* Edited by Peter Hess. Berlin: Verlag der Wirtschaft, 1958.

Kordt, Erich. *Nicht aus den Akten: Die Wilhelmstrasse im Frieden und Krieg.* Stuttgart: Union Deutsche Verlagsgesellschaft, 1950.

Kramarz, Joachim. *Claus Graf von Stauffenberg: 15 Nov. 1907–20 Juli 1944. Das Leben eines Offiziers.* Frankfurt am Main: Bernard & Grafe, 1965.

Kramish, Arnold. *The Griffin: Paul Rosbaud and the Nazi Atomic Bomb That Never Was.* Boston: Houghton-Mifflin, 1986.

Kugelmeier, P. H., SJ. "Priester und Wissenschaftler: Hermann Muckermann, 1877–1962." *Unio Apostolica,* 26, 4 (1985): 8–15.

Kurowski, Franz. *Der Luftkrieg über Deutschland.* Düsseldorf: Econ Verlag, 1977.

Kurz, Hans Rudolf. *Nachrichtenzentrum Schweiz: Die Schweiz im Nachrichtendienst des Zweiten Weltkriegs.* Frauenfeld: Huber, 1972.

Langer, William L., and S. Everett Gleason. *The Undeclared War, 1940–41.* New York: Harper, 1953.

Laqueur, Walter. *The Terrible Secret: An Investigation into the Suppression of Information about Hitler's "Final Solution."* London: Weidenfeld-Nicolson, 1980.

Laqueur, Walter, and Richard Breitman. *Breaking the Silence.* New York: Simon and Schuster, 1986.

Leach, Barry A. *German Strategy against Russia, 1939–1941.* Oxford: Clarendon Press, 1973.

Leverkuhn, Paul. *German Military Intelligence.* Translated by R. H. Stevens and Constantine FitzGibbon. New York: Praeger, 1954.

Lewy, Günther. *The Catholic Church and Nazi Germany.* New York: McGraw-Hill, 1965.

Liddel Hart, Basil H. *History of the Second World War.* New York: G. P. Putnam's Sons, 1970.

———. *The Other Side of the Hill: German Generals: Their Rise and Fall, with Their Own Account of Military Events, 1939–1945.* London: Cassell, 1951.

Lochner, Louis P. *Always the Unexpected: A Book of Reminiscences.* New York: MacMillan, 1956.

———. *What about Germany?* New York: Dodd, Mead & Co., 1942.

Lomax, Sir John. *The Diplomatic Smuggler.* London: Arthur Barker, 1965.

Long, Breckenridge. *The War Diary of Breckenridge Long: Selections from the Years 1939–1944.* Selected and edited by Fred L. Israel. Lincoln: University of Nebraska Press, 1966.

Ludlow, Peter. "Papst Pius XII, die britische Regierung und die deutsche Opposition im Winter 1939–40." *Vierteljahrshefte für Zeitgeschichte* 22, 3, (July 1974): 299–341.

Luther, Hans. *Vor dem Abgrund, 1930–1933: Reichsbankpräsident im Krisenzeiten.* Berlin: Propylaen Verlag, 1964.

McCain, William D. "The Life and Labor of Dennis Murphree." *Journal of Mississippi History,* 12, 4, (Oct. 1950).

McGovern, James. *Crossbow and Overcast.* New York: William Morrow, 1964.

Mack Smith, Denis. *Mussolini.* New York: Alfred E. Knopf, 1982.

McLachlan, Donald. *Room 39: Naval Intelligence in Action, 1939–1945.* London: Weidenfeld & Nicolson, 1968.

MacMillan, Norman, Cpt. *The Royal Air Force in the World War.* London: G. G. Harrap, 1950.

Malone, H. *Adam von Trott zu Solz: The Road to Conspiracy against Hitler.* Austin: University of Texas Press, 1980.

Manvell, Roger, and Heinrich Fraenkel. *The July Plot: The Attempt in 1944 on Hitler's Life and the Men behind It.* London: Bodley Head, 1964.

Maser, Werner. *Der Sturm auf die Republik: Frühgeschichte der NSDAP.* Revised ed. Stuttgart: Deutsche Verlags-Anstalt, 1973.

Mason, Herbert M., Jr. *The Rise of the Luftwaffe: Forging the Secret German Air Weapon, 1918–1940.* New York: Dial Press, 1973.

Mason, John Brown. *Hitler's First Foes: A Study in Religion and Politics.* Minneapolis: Burgess Publishing Co., 1936.

Matt, Alphons. *Zwischen allen Fronten: Der zweite Weltkrieg aus der Sicht des Büros Ha.* Frauenfeld, Stuttgart: Huber, 1969.

Matthias, Erich, and Rudolf Morsey, eds. *Das Ende der Parteien, 1933.* Düsseldorf: Droste Verlag, 1960.

May, Georg. *Ludwig Kaas: Der Priester, der Politiker, and der Gelehrter aus der Schule von Ulrich Stutz.* 3 vols. Amsterdam: Grüner, 1981.

Mayer, Arno J. *Why Did the Heavens Not Darken? The "Final Solution" in History.* New York: Pantheon, 1988.

Meier, Heinz K. *Friendship under Stress: U.S.–Swiss Relations, 1900–1950.* Bern: Herbert Lang, 1970.

Meyer, Alice. *Anpassung oder Widerstand: Der Schweiz zur Zeit des deutschen Nationalsozialismus.* Frauenfeld: Huber, 1965.

Middlebrook, Martin. *The Bomber Command War Diaries: An Operational Reference Book, 1939–1945.* London: Viking, 1985.

———. *The Peenemünde Raid: The Night of 17–18 August 1943.* London: Allen Lane, 1982.

Military Tribunals: The Judgment in the Farben Case. Offenbach: Karl Dorff, 1948.

Miller, Douglas P. *Via Diplomatic Pouch.* New York: Didier, 1944.

———. *You Can't Do Business with Hitler.* Boston: Little, Brown, 1941.

Molden, Fritz P. *Exploding Star: A Young Austrian against Hitler.* Translated by Peter and Betty Ross. New York: William Morrow, 1979.

Moltke, Count Helmuth James von. *A German of the Resistance: The Last Letters of Count Helmuth James von Moltke.* 2d ed. London: G. Cumberlege, Oxford University Press, 1948.

Mondey, David. *Concise Guide to Axis Aircraft of World War II.* Feltham, Middlesex, England: Temple Press, 1984.

Morrison, Samuel Eliot. *History of United States Naval Operations in World War II.* Vol 1: *The Battle of the Atlantic.* Boston: Little, Brown, 1962.

Morsey, Rudolf. *Die deutsche Zentrumpartei, 1919–1923.* Düsseldorf: Droste Verlag, 1966.

———., ed. *Die Protokolle der Reichstagfraktion und des Fraktionsvorstands der deutschen Zentrumpartei, 1926–1933.* Mainz: Matthias Grünewald Verlag, 1969.

Mosely, Leonard. *Hirohito: Emperor of Japan.* Englewood Cliffs, N.J.: Prentice-Hall, 1966.

Mowrer, Edgar Ansel. *Triumph and Turmoil: A Personal History of Our Time.* New York: Weybright and Talley, 1968.

Mowrer, Lillian. *Journalist's Wife.* New York: William Morrow, 1937.

Mrazek, James E. *The Glider War.* London: Robert Hale & Co., 1975.

Muckermann, Friedrich. *Der Monsch tritt über die Schwelle: Betrachtungen über die Zeit.* Berlin: E. C. Etthofen, 1932.

———. *Im Kampf zwischen zwei Epochen: Lebenserinnerungen.* Edited by Nikolaus Junk. Mainz: Matthias Grünewald Verlag, 1973.

Müller, Hans. *Katholische Kirche und Nationalsozialismus.* München: Nymphenburger Verlagshandlung, 1936.

Müller, Josef. *Dis zur letzten Konsequenz: Ein Leben für Frieden und Freiheit.* München: Süddeutscher Verlag, 1975.

Müller-Hill, Benno. *Tödliche Wissenschaft.* Reinbek: Rowohlt, 1984.

Murphy, Robert D. *Diplomat among Warriors.* Garden City, N.Y.: Doubleday, 1964.

Murray, Williamson. *Luftwaffe.* Baltimore: Nautical & Aviation Publishing Co., 1985.

Nazi-Soviet Relations, 1939–1941. Edited by Raymond J. Sontas and James S. Beddie. Washington, D.C.: Department of State, 1948.

Oechsner, Frederick. *This Is the Enemy.* Boston: Little, Brown, 1942.

O.M.G.U.S.: Ermittelungen gegen die IG Farben, Sept. 1945. Edited by Hans Magnus Enzensberger. Nordlingen: GRENO Verlagsgesellschaft, 1986.

Orlow, Dietrich. *The History of the Nazi Party*. Vol. 1. Pittsburgh: University of Pittsburgh Press, 1969.

Papen, Franz von. *Memoirs*. Translated by Brian Connell. 1st Amer. ed. New York: Dutton, 1953.

Pash, Boris T. *The Alsos Mission*. New York: Award House, 1969.

Patterson, Jefferson. *Diplomatic Duty and Diversion*. Cambridge: Riverside Press, 1956.

Persico, Joseph E. *Piercing the Reich: The Penetration of Nazi Germany by American Secret Agents during World War II*. New York: Viking, 1979.

Petrov, Vladimir. *"June 22 1941": Soviet Historians & the German Invasion*. 1st ed. Columbia: University of South Carolina Press, 1968.

Pool, James, and Suzanne Pool. *Who Financed Hitler? The Secret Funding of Hitler's Rise to Power, 1919–1933*. New York: Dial Press, 1978.

Prange, Gordon W., et al. *At Dawn We Slept: The Untold Story of Pearl Harbor*. New York: McGraw-Hill, 1981.

———. *Pearl Harbor: The Verdict of History*. New York: McGraw-Hill, 1986.

———, and Donald M. Goldstein. *Target Tokyo: The Story of the Sorge Spy Ring*. New York: McGraw-Hill, 1984.

Price, Alfred. *Luftwaffe Handbook, 1939–1945*. New York: Scribner's, 1977.

Prittie, Terence C. *Germans against Hitler*. London: Hutchinson, 1964.

Pünder, Hermann. *Politik in der Reichskanzlei: Aufzeichnungen aus den Jahren 1929–1932*. Edited by Thila Vogelsang. *Schriftenreihe der Vierteljahrshefte für Zeitgeschichte*. No. 3 (1961). Stuttgart: Deutsche Verlags-Anstalt.

———. *Von Preussen nach Europa: Lebenserinnerungen*. Stuttgart: Deutsche Verlags-Anstalt, 1968.

Punter, Otto. *Der Anschluss fand nicht statt: Geheimagent Pakbo erzählt*. Bern, Stuttgart: Hallwag, 1967.

Raeder, Erich. *Struggle for the Sea*. Translated by Edward Fitzgerald. London: William Kimber, 1959.

———. *My Life*. Translated by Henry W. Drexel. Annapolis, Md.: U.S. Naval Institute, 1960.

Reader, William J. *Imperial Chemical Industries: A History*. Vol. 2: *The First Quarter Century, 1926–1952*. London: Oxford University Press, 1975.

Repgen, Konrad. *Hitlers Machtergreifung und der deutsche Katholizismus: Versuch einer Bilanz*. Saarbrücken: Verlag des Saarlandes, 1967.

Rescue Attempts during the Holocaust: Proceedings of the Second Yad Vashem International Historical Symposium. Jerusalem: Yad Vashem, 1977.

Respondek, Erwin. "Die praktische Durchführung der Industrie-Belastungs-Gesetz." *Veröffentlichungen der Reichsverband der deutsche Industrie*, 24 (Jan. 1925): 31–39.

———. "Verlauf und Ergebnis der Internationalen Wirtschaftskonferenz des Völkerbandes zur Genf (vom 4 bis 23 Mai 1927)." *Veröffentlichungen der Reichsverband der deutschen Industrie*, 35 (Sept. 1927). Berlin: Carl Heymanns Verlag, 1927.

Rhodes, Anthony E. R. *The Vatican in the Age of the Dictators, 1922–1945*. New York: Holt, Rinehart & Winston, 1973.

Rhodes, Richard. *The Making of the Atomic Bomb*. New York: Simon and Schuster, 1986.

Ries, Karl. *Deutsche Luftwaffe über der Schweiz, 1939–1945*. Mainz: Dieter Hoffmann Verlag, 1978.

Ritter, Gerhard. *The German Resistance: Carl Goerdeler's Struggle against Tyranny*. Translated by R. T. Clark. New York: Praeger, 1959.

Rosch, Augustin. *Kampf gegen den Nationalsozialismus*. Edited by Roman Bleistein. Frankfurt am Main: Verlag Josef Knecht, 1985.

Roon, Ger van. *Neuordnung im Widerstand: Der Kreisauer Kreis innerhalb der deutschen Widerstandsbewegung*. München: R. Oldenbourg, 1967.

Roosevelt, Franklin D. *The Public Papers and Addresses of Franklin D. Roosevelt*. Vol. 10. New York: Harper, 1950.

——. *Roosevelt and Churchill: Their Secret Wartime Correspondence*. Edited by Francis L. Lowenheim, Harold D. Langley, and Manfred Jones. New York: Saturday Review Press, 1975.

Roosevelt–Frankfurter: Their Correspondence, 1928–1945. Annotated by Max Freedman. Boston: Little, Brown, 1967.

Rossi, A. *The Russo-German Alliance, 1939–1941*. Boston: Beacon Press, 1981.

Rothe, Alfred, SJ. "Pater Georg von Sachsen." *Mitteilungen aus den deutschen Provinzen der Gesellschaft Jesu*, Vol. 17, Issue 1, No. 113 (1954): 200–208.

Rothfels, Hans. *German Opposition to Hitler: An Appraisal*. Hinsdale, Ill.: H. Regnery Co., 1948.

Rowland, Buford, and William Boyd. *U.S. Naval Bureau of Ordnance in World War II*. Washington, D.C.: U.S. Ordnance Bureau, 1953.

Russell, William. *Berlin Embassy*. New York: Dutton, 1941.

Sasuly, Richard. *IG Farben*. New York: Boni & Gaer, 1947.

Schacht, Hjalmar. *Abrechnung mit Hitler*. Berlin, Frankfurt: Michaelis Verlag, 1949.

——. *Confessions of "the Old Wizard": Autobiography*. Translated by Diane Pyke. Boston: Houghton Mifflin, 1956.

Schall-Riaucour, Heidemarie. *Aufstand und Gehorsam. Offiziertum und Generalstab im Umbruch: Leben und Wirken von Generaloberst Franz Halder, Generalstabschef, 1938–1942*. Wiesbaden: Limes Verlag, 1972.

Schellenberg, Walter. *The Labyrinth: Memoirs of Walter Schellenberg*. Translated by Louis Hagen. New York: Harper, 1956.

Schlabrendorff, Fabian von. *The Secret War against Hitler*. Translated by Hilda Simon. New York: Putnam, 1965.

Schonau, Elisabeth. *Vom Thron zum Altar: Georg Kronprinz von Sachsen*. Paderborn: F. Schoningh, 1955.

Schroeder, Paul W. *The Axis Alliance and Japanese–American Relations, 1941*. Ithaca, N.Y.: Cornell University Press, 1958.

Schwarte, Johannes. *Gustav Gundlach, S.J.: Massgeblicher Repräsentant der katholischen Soziallehre während der Pontifikate Pius XI und Pius XII*. München, Paderborn, Wien: F. Schoningh, 1975.

Schwarz, Urs. *The Eye of the Hurricane: Switzerland in World War II*. Boulder, Colo.: Westview Press, 1980.

Sheinmann, Mikhail. *Der Vatikan im zweiten Weltkrieg*. Berlin: Dietz, 1954.

Shepherd, Naomi. *A Refuge from Darkness: Wilfred Israel and the Rescue of the Jews.* New York: Pantheon, 1984.

Sherwood, Robert. *Roosevelt and Hopkins: An Intimate History.* New York: Harper, 1948.

Shirer, William L. *Berlin Diary: The Journal of a Foreign Correspondent, 1934–1941.* New York: Knopf, 1943.

———. *The Rise and Fall of the Third Reich: A History of Nazi Germany.* New York: Simon and Schuster, 1960.

———. *20th Century Journey: The Nightmare Years, 1930–1940.* Boston: Little, Brown, 1984.

Simon, Leslie E. *German Research in World War II: An Analysis of the Conduct of Research.* New York: J. Wiley & Sons, 1947.

———. *Secret Weapons of the Third Reich.* Old Greenwich, Conn.: We, Inc., 1971.

Smith, Bradley F. *Reaching Judgment at Nuremberg.* New York: Basic Books, 1977.

Smith, Howard K. *Last Train from Berlin.* New York: Knopf, 1942.

Smith, Richard Harris. *OSS: The Secret History of America's First Central Intelligence Agency.* Berkeley/Los Angeles: University of California Press, 1972.

Smith, Truman. *Berlin Alert: The Memoirs and Reports of Truman Smith.* Edited by Robert Hessen. Stanford, Calif.: Stanford University Press, 1984.

Snell, John L. *Wartime Origins of the East–West Dilemma over Germany.* New Orleans: Hauser Papers, 1959.

Speer, Albert. *Infiltration: How Heinrich Himmler Schemed to Build an SS Industrial Empire.* Translated by Joachim Neugroschel. New York: McMillan, 1981.

———. *Inside the Third Reich: Memoirs.* Translated by Richard and Clara Winston. New York: MacMillan, 1970.

Spiegelbild einer Verschwörung: Die Kaltenbrunner Berichte an Bormann und Hitler über des Attentats vom 20 Juli 1944. Stuttgart: Seewald Verlag, 1961.

Stahlberger, Peter. *Der Zürcher Verleger Emil Oprecht und die deutsche politische Emigration, 1933–1945.* Zürich: Europa Verlag, 1970.

Stehlin, Stewart A. *Weimar and the Vatican, 1919–1933: German–Vatican Relations in the Interwar Years.* Princeton, N.J.: Princeton University Press, 1983.

Steiner, Max. *Die Internierung von Armeeangehörigen Kriegsführender Mächte in neutralen Staaten insbesondere in der Schweiz während des Weltkriegs, 1939/45.* Zürich: Ernst Lang, 1947.

Stevenson, William. *A Man Called Intrepid: The Secret War.* New York: Harcourt, Brace, Jovanovich, 1976.

Steward, John S. *Sieg des Glaubens: Authentische Gestapoberichte über den kirchlichen Widerstand in Deutschland.* Zürich: Thomas, 1946.

Strong, Maj. Gen. Sir Kenneth. *Intelligence at the Top: The Recollections of an Intelligence Officer.* London: Cassell, 1968.

Stuart, Graham H. *American Diplomatic and Consular Practice.* 2d ed. New York: Appleton, Century & Crofts, 1952.

Suchy, Barbara. "The *Verein zur Abwehr des Antisemitismus.*" *Leo Baeck Yearbook,* 30, (1985): 67–103.

Sykes, Christopher. *Tormented Loyalty: The Story of a German Aristocrat Who Defied Hitler.* New York: Harper & Row, 1969.

Tardini, Domenico. *Memories of Pius XII.* Translated by Rosemary Goldie. Westminister, Md.: Newman Press, 1961.

Taylor, Telford. *Munich: The Price of Peace.* Garden City, N.Y.: Doubleday, 1979.

Thayer, Charles W. *Bears in the Caviar.* Philadelphia: Lippincott, 1951.

Thiesmeyer, Lincoln R., and John E. Burchard. *Combat Scientists.* Boston: Little, Brown, 1947.

Thomas, Georg. *Geschichte der deutschen Wehr- und Rüstungswirtschaft, 1918–1943/45.* Boppard am Rhein: Haroldt Bolat Verlag, 1966.

Togo, Fumihiko, ed. *The Cause of Japan.* New York: Simon and Schuster, 1956.

Toland, John. *The Rising Sun: The Decline and Fall of the Japanese Empire, 1936–1945.* 1st ed. New York: Random House, 1970.

Treviranus, Gottfried. *Dan Ende von Weimar: Heinrich Brüning und seine Zeit.* Düsseldorf: Econ-Verlag, 1968.

Trevor-Roper, H. R., ed. *Hitler's War Directives, 1939–1945.* London: Sidgwick & Jackson, 1964.

Trial of the Major War Criminals before the International Military Tribunal, Nuremberg, 14 Nov. 1945–1 Oct. 1946. Vols. 1–33. Nuremberg: International Military Tribunal, 1947.

Turner, Henry A., Jr. *German Big Business & the Rise of Hitler.* New York: Oxford University Press, 1985.

United States Army Air Force. *Mission Accomplished: Interrogations of Japanese Military, Industrial, and Civilian Leaders of World War II.* Washington, D.C.: U.S. Government Printing Office, 1946.

United States Chief of Counsel for the Prosecution of Axis Criminality. *Nazi Conspiracy and Aggression.* Vols. 1–18. Washington, D.C.: U.S. Government Printing Office, 1946.

United States Eighth Bomber Command Headquarters. *Bomber Command Narrative of Operations.* Maxwell Air Force Base, Ala.: U.S. Air Force, 1945.

Vassiltchikov, Marie. *Berlin Diaries, 1940–1945.* New York: Knopf, 1987.

Vock, Wilhelm. *Memoiren: Die Erinnerungen des früheren Reichsbank Präsidenten.* Stuttgart: Deutsche Verlags-Anstalt, 1973.

Vogelsang, Theo. *Reichswehr, Staat und NSDAP.* Stuttgart: Deutsche Verlags-Anstalt, 1962. (*Quellen und Darstellungen zur Zeitgeschichte,* Band 11.)

Volk, Ludwig, ed. *Akten Kardinal Michael von Faulhabers.* Vol. 2: *1939–1945.* Mainz: Matthias Grünewald Verlag, 1978.

Von Kardoff, Ursula. *Berliner Aufzeichnungen aus den Jahren 1942–1945.* München: Deutscher Taschenbuch Verlag, 1981.

Von Studnitz, Hans-Georg. *Als Berlin brannte: Tagebuch der Jahre 1943–1945.* Bergish-Gladbach: Gustav Lubbe Verlag, 1985.

Von Weimar zu Hitler, 1930–1933. Edited by Gotthard Jasper. Köln/Berlin: Kiepenheuer & Witsch, 1968.

Wandel, Eckhard. *Hans Schäffer: Steuermann im wirtschaftlichen und politischen Krisen.* Stuttgart: Deutsche Verlags-Anstalt, 1974.

Warlimont, Walther. *Inside Hitler's Headquarters, 1939–1945.* Translated by R. H. Barry. London: Weidenfeld & Nicolson, 1964.

Wedemeyer, Albert C. *Wedemeyer Reports!* New York: Holt, 1948.

Welles, Sumner. *The Time for Decision.* New York, London: Harper Bros., 1944.

Whaley, Barton. *Codeword BARBAROSSA.* Cambridge: MIT Press, 1977.

Wheeler-Bennett, John. *The Nemesis of Power: The German Army in Politics, 1918–1945.* 2d ed. New York: St. Martin's Press, 1964.

Whitaker, John T. *We Cannot Escape History*. New York: MacMillan, 1943.

Wideröe, R. "Some Memories and Dreams from the Childhood of Particle Accelerators." *Europhysics News*, 15, 2 (Feb. 1984): 9–11.

Winterbottam, Frederick W. *The Ultra Secret*. New York: Harper & Row, 1974.

Wiskemann, Elisabeth. *Europe of the Dictators, 1919–1945*. 1st ed. New York: Harper & Row, 1966.

Wistrich, Robert. *Who's Who in Nazi Germany*. London: Weidenfeld & Nicolson, 1982.

Wolf, Walter. *Faschismus in der Schweiz: Die Geschichte der Frontenbewegungen in der deutschen Schweiz, 1930–1945*. Zürich: Flamberg Verlag, 1969.

Wyman, David S. *Paper Walls: America and the Refugee Crisis, 1938–1941*. Amherst: University of Massachusetts Press, 1968.

Young. A. P. *The "X" Documents*. Edited by Sidney Astor. London: Andre Deutsch, 1974.

Zeller, Eberhard. *The Flame of Freedom: The German Struggle against Hitler*. Translated by R. P. Heller and R. R. Masters. Coral Gables, Fla.: University of Miami Press, 1969.

Zuckerman, Solly. *From Apes to Warlords: The Autobiography (1904–1946) of Solly Zuckerman*. London: Hamilton, 1978.

"Zurück zum Barock." *Der Spiegel*, 11, 52 (25 Dec. 1957): 42–50.

20. Juli: Portraits des Widerstands. Edited by Rudolf Lill and Heinrich Oberreuter. Düsseldorf/London: Econ Verlag 1984.

UNPUBLISHED SOURCES

Archival and Private Papers

American Consulate, Zurich. Confidential file, 1940–1944. Records of the Foreign Service Posts of the Department of State. Record Group 84. Washington National Records Center, Suitland, Md.

American Legation, Bern. Confidential File, 1940–1949. Records of the Foreign Service Posts of the Department of State. Record Group 84. Washington National Records Center, Suitland, Md.

American Legation, Bern. OSS cables, 1942–1945. Records of the Office of Strategic Services. Record Group 226. National Archives, Washington, D.C.

Atom Bomb File. Franklin D. Roosevelt Library, Hyde Park, N.Y.

Beam, Jacob D. Papers. Private collection, Washington, D.C.

Beam, Jacob N. Papers. Seeley G. Mudd Manuscript Library, Princeton, N.J.

Berle, Adolf, A., Jr. Diary. State Department Correspondence. Franklin D. Roosevelt Library, Hyde Park, N.Y.

Brüning, Heinrich. Papers. Private collection, Hartland, Vt.

Bücher, Hermann. File. Archives of the Allgemeine Elektricitäts-Gesellschaft. Frankfurt am Main.

Civilian Rehabilitation Reports. Department of Rehabilitation Services, State of Mississippi, Jackson, Miss.

Confidential File. President's Secretary's File. Franklin D. Roosevelt Library, Hyde Park, N.Y.

Crane, Jasper E. Papers, Hagley Museum and Library, Wilmington, Del.

Cyclotron Files. Deutsches Museum. Munich.

Dällenbach, H. Walter. File. Berlin Document Center, Berlin.

———. File. Records of the General Administration. Bibliothek und Archiv zur Geschichte der Max Planck Gesellschaft, Berlin.

———. Papers. Eidgenössische Technische Hochschule, Zurich.

Department of State. Dispatches, 1939–1941. Safe File, President's Secretary's File. Franklin D. Roosevelt Library, Hyde Park, N.Y.

Departmental Correspondence. Department of State. President's Secretary's File, Franklin D. Roosevelt Library, Hyde Park, N.Y.

Departmental Correspondence. United States Navy, 1941. President's Secretary's File. Franklin D. Roosevelt Library, Hyde Park, N.Y.

Dessauer, Friedrich. Papers. Kommission für Zeitgeschichte, Bonn.

Diplomatic Cables. Decimal file 7400.0011 European War 1939. General Records of the Department of State. Record Group 59. National Archives, Washington, D.C.

Dodd, William E. Papers. Manuscript Division, Library of Congress, Washington, D.C.

Donovan, William. Papers. United States Army Military History Institute. Carlisle Barracks, Pa.

Duisberg, Carl. Papers. Archives, Bayer AG, Leverkusen.

Dulles, Allen W. Papers. Seeley G. Mudd Manuscript Library, Princeton, N.J.

Fischer, Ernest G. Diary. Papers. Private collection, New Orleans.

General Records. Records of the United States Strategic Bombing Survey. Record Group 243. National Archives, Washington, D.C.

Germany Folder. Safe File, President's Secretary's File. Franklin D. Roosevelt Library, Hyde Park, N.Y.

Gisevius, Hans Bernd. Papers. Eidgenössische Technische Hochschule, Zurich.

Georg of Saxony. Files. Archiv der norddeutschen Provinz, Cologne.

Gesamtdeutsche Volkspartei. Files. Diether Koch Papers. Private collection, Bremen.

Goudsmit, Samuel. Papers. Center for the History of Physics, Niels Bohr Library, American Institute of Physics, New York.

Harris, Ruth R. "The Shifting Winds: The American–Soviet Rapprochement from the Fall of France to the Attack on Pearl Harbor." Ph.D. diss., George Washington University, 1975.

Harrison, Leland. Papers. Manuscript Division, Library of Congress, Washington, D.C.

Heisenberg, Werner. Papers. Werner-Heisenberg Institut für Physik, Munich.

Hoffmann, Valeska R. Papers. Private collection, Bel Air, Md.

Hopkins, Harry. General Correspondence. Papers. Franklin D. Roosevelt Library, Hyde Park, N.Y.

Hull, Cordell. Papers. Manuscript Division, Library of Congress, Washington, D.C.

Intelligence Reports of the Naval Attaché, Berlin, 1938–1941. President's Secretary's File, Franklin D. Roosevelt Library, Hyde Park, N.Y.

Internal Political Affairs, Germany. Decimal File 862.00. General Records of the Department of State. Record Group 59. National Archives, Washington, D.C.

Kennan, George F. Papers. Seeley G. Mudd Manuscript Library, Princeton, N.J.

Koch, Diether. Papers. Private collection, Bremen.

Koloian, Richard C. "A Myth of History: The American State Department Warning of Operation Barbarossa." Master's thesis, Defense Intelligence College, Washington, D.C., 1988.

Long, Breckenridge. Diary and Papers. Manuscript Division, Library of Congress, Washington, D.C.

Map Room Files. Franklin C. Roosevelt Library, Hyde Park, N.Y.

Military Intelligence Reports, Berlin, 1939–1941. Records of the Office of the Assistant Chief of Staff, G-2, Intelligence, 1939–1945. Records of the Army Staff. Record Group 319. National Archives, Washington, D.C., and National Records Center, Suitland, Md.

Miller, Douglas P. Alumni Files. University of Denver Library, Denver.

Morgenthau, Henry, Jr. Presidential Diary. Franklin D. Roosevelt Library, Hyde Park, N.Y.

Mowrer, Edgar A., and Lillian Mowrer. Papers. Manuscript Division, Library of Congress, Washington, D.C.

Muckermann, Friedrich. File. RW 58: Gestapo Files. Düsseldorf. Hauptstaatsarchiv, Düsseldorf.

———. Files. Archiv der norddeutschen Provinz, Cologne.

Muckermann, Hermann. Files. Hochschularchiv, Technische Universität, Berlin.

———. File. RW 58. Gestapo Files, Düsseldorf. Hauptstaatsarchiv, Düsseldorf.

———. Papers. Konrad Adenauer Stiftung, Sankt Augustin bei Bonn.

Murphy, Robert. Papers. Hoover Institution on War, Revolution and Peace, Stanford, Calif.

National Socialist Reichstag Faction. Files. Bundesarchiv, Koblenz.

Office of Strategic Services. Germany/Switzerland. Files. Franklin D. Roosevelt Library, Hyde Park, N.Y.

———. Numbered Reports. Franklin D. Roosevelt Library, Hyde Park, N.Y.

Official File. Franklin D. Roosevelt Library, Hyde Park, N.Y.

Oprecht, Emil. Papers. Europa Verlag. Zurich.

"Proceedings of the International Military Tribunal for the Far East." Government Documents Dept., University of California, Berkeley.

Rand, Clayton. Papers. Mitchell Memorial Library, Mississippi State University, Mississippi State, Miss.

Records of the Manhattan Engineers District. Records of the Office of the Chief of Engineers. Record Group 77. National Archives, Washington, D.C.

Records of the Office of the Chief of Counsel for War Crimes, 1933–1949. National Archives Collection of World War II War Crimes Records. Record Group 238. National Archives, Washington, D.C.

Reports of the Commercial Attaché, Berlin, 1937–1941. Records of the Bureau of Foreign & Domestic Commerce. Record Group 151. National Archives, Washington, D.C.

Respondek, Alfred. Gestapo File. Berlin Document Center, Berlin.

Respondek, Erwin. *Abschrift*. Bernhard Schwertfeger Papers, Bundesarchiv, Koblenz.

———. Memoranda. Files of the Political Advisor for Germany (POLAD). Record Group 84. Institut für Zeitgeschichte, Munich.

———. File. Archives of the Deutsche Caritasverband, Freiburg i. Br.

———. File. Entschädigungsbehörde. Landesverwaltungsamt, Berlin.

———. Historical Summary. History of the Max Planck Gesellschaft, Bibliothek und Archiv zur Geschichte der Max Planck Gesellschaft, Berlin.

Robinson, Joseph T. Papers. Private collection of H. Grady Miller, Jr., Little Rock, Ark.

Rothe, Alfred, SJ. "Pater Georg von Sachsen: Kronprinz und Priester." Typescript. Berlin, 1954. Archiv der norddeutschen Provinz, SJ, Cologne.

Schäffer, Hans. Diary. Institut für Zeitgeschichte, Munich.

Siemens AG. File. Deutsches Museum, Munich.

Smith, Katharine A. H. "My Life: Berlin—August 1935–April 1939." Katharine Smith Papers. Hoover Institution on War, Revolution and Peace, Stanford, Calif.

Stauffer, Thomas B. Papers. Private collection, Berkeley, Calif.

Steinkopf, Alvin. Papers. Mass Communications History Center, State Historical Society of Wisconsin, Madison.

Subject File. President's Secretary's File. Franklin D. Roosevelt Library, Hyde Park, N.Y.

Taylor, Myron C. "Reports of Myron C. Taylor to President Franklin D. Roosevelt. " President's Secretary's File, Franklin D. Roosevelt Library, Hyde Park, N.Y.

Toland, John. Papers. Franklin D. Roosevelt Library, Hyde Park, N.Y.

Truman, Harry S. Official File. Harry S. Truman Papers. Harry S. Truman Library, Independence, Mo.

Usher's Diary. Franklin D. Roosevelt Library, Hyde Park, N.Y.

"V Weapons [Crossbow] Campaign." United States Strategic Bombing Survey, Maxwell Air Force Base, Ala.

Walker, Mark. "Uranium Machines, Nuclear Explosives, and National Socialism: The German Quest for Nuclear Power, 1939–1949," Ph.D. diss., Princeton University, 1988.

Watson, Thomas. Papers. IBM Archives. Armonk, N.Y.

War Raw Materials Department. Files. Files of the War Office. Bundesarchiv, Freiburg i. Br.

Wessel, Helene. Papers. Friedrich-Ebert Stiftung, Bonn.

Winant, John. Papers. Franklin D. Roosevelt Library, Hyde Park, N.Y.

Woods, Milada P. Diary. Manuscript Division, Library of Congress, Washington, D.C.

Woods, Sam E. Departmental Correspondence. Records of the Office of the Director, Bureau of Foreign and Domestic Commerce. Record Group 151. National Archives, Washington, D.C.

———. File. Mississippi Department of Archives and History, Jackson, Miss.

———. File. Clayton Rand Papers. Mitchell Memorial Library, Mississippi State University, Mississippi State, Miss.

———. Files. Karl Stefan Papers. Nebraska State Historical Society, Lincoln.

————. File. *Neue Zürcher Zeitung*. Zurich.

————. File. Mitchell Memorial Library, Mississippi State University, Mississippi State, Miss.

————. File. McCain Library & Archives, University of Southern Mississippi Library, Hattiesburg, Miss.

————. File. Valparaiso University, Valparaiso, Ind.

————. Personnel Records. Records of the Foreign Commerce Service Officers. Bureau of Foreign & Domestic Commerce. Record Group 151. National Archives, Washington, D.C.

Young, Owen D. Papers. Everett & Josephine Case Papers. Private collection, Hornesville, N.Y.

Interviews

[*denotes telephone interview]

George Anderson*		19 Mar. 1986
Mary Bancroft*		25 Feb. 1986
Jacob D. Beam	Washington, D.C.	4 June 1985
		4 Dec. 1985
		17 April 1987
Robert A. Brand*		17 April 1991
Mary Briner*		24 Sept. 1986
Anthony Cave Brown*		27 Mar. 1986
Herta Chojnacki	West Berlin	23 July 1986
Clinton B. Conger*		7 Jan. 1986
Marbury L. Councell, Jr.*		28 Mar. 1988
Philip M. Davenport*		11 Feb. 1988
Edmund T. Delaney*		29 Sept. 1986
Alex Dreier		3 Jan. 1985*
		2 Mar. 1986*
	Washington, D.C.	8 June 1987
Agnes Dreimann	West Berlin	26 July 1986
Howard Elting, Jr.*		11 Feb. 1986
Phillip H. Fahrenholz*		16 Sept. 1986
Arthur H. Graubart*		9 Oct. 1985
William E. Griffith*		30 Apr. 1985
		11 Feb. 1987
Stewart Herman	Shelter Island, N.Y.	30 May 1985
Russell Hill*		2 Jan. 1986
Valeska R. Hoffmann		21 Jan. 1986*

	Bel Air, Md.	22 Mar. 1986
		18 April 1987
Richard C. Hottelet	New York	29 July 1985
Dagfin Hoynes*		14 April 1988
George Kidd*		17 June 1985
Percy Knauth*		9 Oct. 1985
Renee Kohler–de Simon	Muri/Bern	28 June 1986
Richard Koloian*		30 Sept. 1986
Arnold Kramish*		12 Oct. 1987
H. Kugelmeier, SJ	Osnabruck	30 July 1986
Walter Laqueur*		27 Nov. 1984
Onnie Lattu*		3 July 1985
Perry Laukhuff*		27 Nov. 1984
		30 Sept. 1986
Robert Long*		1 Mar. 1988
Norma Lovell*		2 Mar. 1987
David Lu*		30 April 1987
James McCargar*		6 May 1985
Mrs. Hardin McClendon*		6 June 1985
John Mapother*		28 Mar. 1991
Fritz Molden	New York	21 Oct. 1986
Brewster Morris*		30 Sept. 1985
Lillian Mowrer*		27 April 1987
Patrick Nieburg	Washington	6 Dec. 1985
J. Bolard More*		14 Jan. 1986
Claire Nix	Hartland, Vt.	12 Feb. 1987
Carl F. Norden*		6 Jan. 1986
Frederick Oechsner*		4 Nov. 1985
Mrs. Jefferson Patterson	Washington	6 Dec. 1985
C. Brooks Peters	New York	7 June 1985
		9 Oct. 1985
		22 Nov. 1985
Sr. Irma Rech	West Berlin	26 July 1986
Amelie Riddleberger	Woodstock, Va.	28 June 1985
Heinrich Rumpel	Zurich	1 July 1986
Dana Schmidt*		20 Oct. 1985
Urs Schwarz	Zurich	27 June 1986
Howard K. Smith*		6 Dec. 1985

Katharine Smith	Fairfield, Conn.	13 Sept. 1986
Joanna Stauffer*		18 April 1988
Lucia Stauffer	New York	31 Mar. 1988
Albert L. Thompson*		5 Mar. 1988
		30 Mar. 1988
Angus M. Thuermer		7 Oct. 1985*
	Middleburg, Va.	28 June 1985
		30 Sept. 1986*
William Tinsman, Jr.*		20 April 1988
Arthur Vanaman*		17 June 1985
Spencer Wearth	New York, N.Y.	5 Feb. 1991
Milada Woods	Scarsdale, N.Y.	19 Oct. 1986
	Elmsford, N.Y.	12 Feb. 1987
Peter Wyden*		22 Feb. 1986
Lloyd Yates	Southwest Harbor, Me.	4 Aug. 1987

INDEX

ABOUT THE AUTHOR

JOHN V. H. DIPPEL is a writer at Jan Krukowski Associates in New York. He received his Ph.D. in English and Comparative Literature from Columbia University. His articles have appeared in *The Atlantic Monthly*, *New Republic*, and *The New Leader*.